Samsun

Trabzon

PONTIC ALPS

Kars●

Ani

ARMENIA

Gümüşhane

●Erzurum

R. Yeşilirmak

R. Kizilirmak

Lake Van

Van

IRAN

Kayseri

Malatya●

R. Tigris

Nemrut Dağı●

Diyarbakir

Anavarza

Issos

●Iskenderun

Karataş

●Antakya

R. Euphrates

SYRIA

IRAQ

| 0 | 100 miles |
| 0 | 100 kilometres |

# ACROSS THE HELLESPONT

*By the same author*

Daphne Into Laurel
English Translators of Classical Poetry
A Literary Companion to Travel in Greece
Land of Lost Gods: The Search for Classical Greece

# ACROSS THE HELLESPONT

## A Literary Guide to Turkey

### RICHARD STONEMAN

**HUTCHINSON**

LONDON   MELBOURNE   AUCKLAND
JOHANNESBURG

This edition first published in 1987 by Hutchinson, an imprint of
Century Hutchinson Ltd, Brookmount House, 62–65 Chandos Place,
London WC2N 4NW

Century Hutchinson Australia Pty Ltd
PO Box 496, 16–22 Church Street, Hawthorn, Victoria 3122, Australia

Century Hutchinson New Zealand Limited
PO Box 40-086, Glenfield, Auckland 10, New Zealand

Century Hutchinson South Africa (Pty) Ltd
PO Box 337, Bergvlei, 2012 South Africa

*British Library Cataloguing in Publication Data*

   Across the Hellespont: a literary guide to Turkey.
   1. Turkey – Literary collections
   I. Stoneman, Richard
   808.8′032561     PN6071.T8/

  ISBN 0-09-168370-X

Photoset by Rowland Phototypesetting Ltd
Bury St Edmunds, Suffolk
Printed in Great Britain by
Redwood Burn Ltd, Trowbridge, Wiltshire
and bound by WBC Bookbinders Ltd
Maesteg, Mid-Glamorgan

# Acknowledgements

Acknowledgement is due to the following for permission to reproduce copyright material:

E. J. Brill for material from A. Cameron and J. Herrin, Constantinople in the eighth century; Jonathan Cape Ltd for 'I am the Life of My Beloved' from *The Way of the Sufi* by Idries Shah; Chatto and Windus Ltd for 'Julian and the Citizens of Antioch' by C. P. Cavafy; J. M. Dent Ltd for a passage from *Armenian Legends and Poems* by Z. C. Boyajian; Faber and Faber Ltd for lines from 'Byzance' by Lawrence Durrell; Grafton Books for a passage from *Trebizond and Beyond* by John Marriner; John Murray Ltd for passages from *Alexander's Path* by Freya Stark; The Octagon Press Ltd for 'The Merchant and the Christian Dervish' from *Tales of the Dervishes* by Idries Shah; John Calmann and Cooper for a passage from *Constantinople* by Philip Sherrard; Mrs Nermin Streater for the poems and extracts by B. R. Eyuboglu, M. A. Ersoy and I. Berk; Valentine Mitchell and Co Ltd for a passage from *A Village in Anatolia* by M. Makal; Penguin Books Ltd for passages from *The Book of Dede Korkut*; from Philostratus, *Life of Apollonius* and from Arrian, *Campaigns of Alexander*; Thames and Hudson Ltd for passages from *Pleasure of Ruins* by Rose Macaulay; Collins Publishers for passages from *The Towers of Trebizond* by Rose Macaulay; Princeton University Press for extracts from *The History of Mehmed the Conqueror* by Critoboulos translated by C. Riggs; Harvard University Press for extracts from *Letters from Sardis* by G. A. Hanfmann; Writers and Readers Press for an extract from *Memed My Hawk* by Y. Kemal.

Every effort has been made to contact copyright holders of

material included in this book; publisher and author would be glad to hear from any copyright holder not here acknowledged.

# Contents

# Introduction

'Travellers in Turkey' is an easy phrase which conceals a problematic theme. The modern country of Turkey is an easily recognisable political, and to some extent geographical, entity; but it is not a country where history and tradition enmesh with geography and population in any obvious way – not as they do, for example, in Greece. Turkey geographically encompasses the verdant alluvial plains of Ionia, daggered with mountains which look more to Greek than to Asian geology; the craggy precipices and alluring islands of Karamania and Cilicia as well as the rainy Pontic Alps and the stormy ports of the Black Sea; and the steaming plateaus of the south-east as well as high plains in the interior which are first cousins to the Steppes of Central Asia. And each of these terrains has bred or harboured peoples of distinct types.

Turkey, it may seem, is one of history's crossroads. The Turks themselves are relative latecomers to the land, and there is not that continuity of tradition which made possible the growth of a phenomenon like Philhellenism in relation to Greece, or even the insular charm that England holds for many foreigners. There is no systematic body of writing about Turkey the geographical entity, and hence to talk of travellers in Turkey is to talk of people who would not perhaps have recognised each other as members of the same breed, who would have had next to nothing in common. Such unity as a collection of their reports possesses may seem to be a purely factitious one.

And yet the land of Turkey, as distinct from the country of

the Turks who have dwelt there for less than a millennium, does seem to have a particular role to play in the consciousness of the West. Not only is it a crossroads of civilizations; it is a bridge between east and west, and it has seen as many civilizations be born and die as any comparable area of 780,000 square kilometres in the world.

For many westerners its primary fascination has been as the scene of many of the great dramas of classical history, the land that saw the serried magnificence of Xerxes of Persia march against the Greeks and lash the Hellespont in fury because it blocked his path, and then saw the equal magnificence of his descendant Darius yield at last to the conquering might of Alexander of Macedon. Turkey, too, was the home of the neighbour kingdoms that alternately troubled and supported the Greeks of the coast and the islands; of the kingdom of Lydia famed from the rich legends of Herodotus; and of the mysterious kingdom of Lycia whose rulers borrowed Greek art and bent it to their own still largely hidden purposes. After the death of Alexander the Great Asia Minor became the home of the great Hellenistic kingdoms with their capitals at Pergamum (Bergama), Antioch (Antakya) and elsewhere.

Another perspective on this land has been the Biblical one. If admirers of St Paul found in the terrain of Turkey a fascinating extension of what they had learnt in Roman history of such cities as Tarsus, Iconium (Konya) and Ephesus, both scholars and missionaries could respond to the millennial echoes of names like Laodicea, Thyateira, Smyrna and Colossae. Even more intriguing has been the light shed only in the last century on the Old Testament by the rediscovery of the Hittites. Formerly known only from their appearances in the Bible as neighbours and enemies of the children of Israel, and assumed to be a fringe people of Semitic stock like so many other of those obscure tribes of Kings and Chronicles, the discoveries of the second half of the nineteenth century proved them to have been instead a mighty Empire, of Indo-European and not Semitic origin, with a capital far to the north of Israel at Boğazkale north-east of Ankara.

For the historian of the Crusades Turkey presented another scene again, a staging-post of the series of excursions against the Arabs that resulted in the founding of the magnificent castle at Silifke as well as the extensive refashioning of those at

Alanya and Anamur. And for the medievalist with Greek interests the land of Turkey was of course that which housed for more than a thousand years the Empire of Byzantium, so different in its punctilious and sensuous intellect from the single-minded warriorship of the Turks and the Crusaders who overthrew it.

Both classical and medieval historians, as well as all those interested in the fortunes of the Christian church, would find particular interest in the fate of the kingdom of Armenia, one of the longest continuous civilizations of the western world. With origins going back to the fabulous Queen Semiramis of Babylon and beyond, and veering sharply into focus in its repeated clashes with the Rome of the late Republic and early Empire, Armenia became Christian when most of the world finally did, and preserved its unique culture (not always to the approbation of nineteenth-century travellers who seem to have preferred the Turks) until it was destroyed by expulsion and systematic massacre in 1922.

The Ottoman Empire is the last avatar of the land of Turkey before modern times: travellers from merchants to diplomats, geologists to archaeologists, tourists to despoilers of monuments, all responded in distinctive ways to the alien fascination of the Ottoman character. With bloody ruthlessness mingled with the ostentatious calm of Islam they plunged from the central Asian Steppes with their war-cries and their war-pride – first their cousins the Seljuk Turks with their capital at Konya, then the Ottomans themselves who achieved the act that more than anything shook Christendom to its foundations – the sack of Constantinople. How could anyone in Europe be indifferent to such a power on its threshold, threatening at any moment to bring East to West and to turn religion on its head?

Such then was the land of Turkey that travellers have found: a land of intellectual grace and of the first philosophers, as well as of the warlords of the south and centre; of luxurious diplomacy and cruellest military force; the home of ancient wonder-workers like Apollonius of Tyana and Alexander of Abonuteichos as well as of megalomaniac kings like Antiochus of Commagene or, perhaps, the nameless kings of Lycia with their mausolea at Xanthus and Gülbahçe; the scene of savage battles from Gallipoli to Issus and of genocidal expulsions from Smyrna to Armenia. And, of course, there was the climate, always harsh except on the sub-tropical Mediterranean coasts, of a country that did nothing by halves, from torture to hospitality. Visitors who experience the latter, for which modern Turkey is much famed, will need an effort of imagination to picture some of the brutalities which fill out the portrait of this unique country.

Who then are the travellers who made one or other aspect of the Turkish scene and tradition the subject of their researches? Though their interests inevitably vary according to the part of the country they are writing about, they respond quite well to a chronological survey as one or another part of this vast country rears into historical prominence and then retires, its scene played through.

The father of all travellers, as of all historians, is of course Herodotus. Most of what we know about the early Persian Empire and the kingdom of Lydia (as well as a good deal of miscellaneous information about Egypt and other places) comes from his *Histories*. At the same time classical legend plays itself out as much in Western Turkey as in Greece proper. The Argonauts pursued the search for the Golden Fleece through the Dardanelles and Bosphorus and along the Black Sea coast to Colchis in what is now the USSR, in what may be a legendary memory of early trading voyages. The Trojan War, which is now reckoned to have a good chance of having been historical, took place on the north-western tip of Asia. The architectural legacy of the ancient world is still conspicuous in more places than are easily mentioned, despite centuries of earthquake and the depredations of builders hungry for dressed stone or even for lime. Many classical legends and personalities have become Islamicised or have otherwise lived on: most notably Plato and Aristotle (as Iflatun and Aristu of Flecker's poem) have become sages and wonder-workers of Islamic saga, and more than one spring or well takes its name from the magician Plato. Alexander the Great became the Dhul-qarnain of the Koran, and the exploits of that hero in the medieval Romance of Alexander – his search for the water of life, his conversations with the Brahmins, the transformation of his sister into a mermaid – play themselves out against a background that is always Asian and Moslem, often Turkish. And anyone who thinks that classical legend has lost its power to enliven a scene need only consider the remarks of two travellers, five centuries apart. Here is the fifteenth-century archaeologist Cyriac of Ancona sailing from the Greek island of Thasos to Enos in Turkish Thrace.

There, cutting the furrow of liquid Neptune, we point out the summit of Thasos, reach the confines of Thrace, and graze the shores of savage Diomede, who, we are told, was accustomed to give his visitors as fodder to his huge horses. To prevent us pious souls from suffering such a fate, or entering on the shore, our very own Mercury filled our sails with wind, and a company of Nereids escorted us on either side. On one side Doris, her blonde companion Doto, and Galatea 'ploughed the watery way', while on the right Panopea, Amphitrite and Parthenia Glauce gently assisted us with their white arms, and the finest of them all, Cymodocea, swam in the deep sea and gently bedewed me from time to time with her kisses.

So you think that's fanciful? Here now is Compton Mackenzie, escaping at last from the horrors of Gallipoli.

The spell of that Aegean summer weather is still potent, and when I look back across the years to that cerulean voyage I surrender anew to the drowsy enchantment of it and would fain dream away the pages of this chapter as I dreamed away the soft sea miles that rippled past like the play of light in a precious stone. Our course was south-west, and the illusion was that we were not making it by steam, but rather, as the arid hills of Lemnos slowly merged with the sky astern, that we were being drawn along by the laughing Oceanides.

*Gallipoli Memories*

The medieval world of Turkey is at once more diverse and more productive of contemporary travel accounts. The fate of the city of Constantinople in the writings of its own historians and of the 'Patriographers', the recorders of legends and those who tried to make sense of the little-understood monuments around them is almost emblematic of the purpose of this whole collection of travellers' tales. At fortunate moments the traveller may be able to feel a sense of the past emerging from objects themselves and from places of historic purport. This is not the same as simply understanding the process of historical events that have occurred in a given place – though that helps – but it arises from a kind of empathy when object, relic, landscape, seem suddenly to speak louder than any words.

The Patriographers of medieval Constantinople, having little solid historical fact to build on, were constrained to explain most of the multitude of monuments around them in terms of the miracle-making of early Emperors and their courtiers, of the enshrining of mysterious prophecies in the stones of the city, and of strange riddles we can hardly now unravel. Rather than expand further here on the topic of medieval Constantinople, I refer the reader to Chapter 1, for Byzantium is a topic all its own and not conveniently to be summarised in a paragraph.

For most travellers the world of Byzantium was no less strange than that of the Ottoman Turk was to seem a couple of centuries later. The Ottoman world was inevitably the focus of most of the travel writing about Turkey of the seventeenth and eighteenth centuries. Travellers would seize on examples of spectacular exoticism or barbarism to try to convey the otherness of the country they were describing. Sir John Mandeville's Travels are full of legends of this kind. Even writers one might expect to be reasonably prosaic like the Catalan soldier Ramon Muntaner (1265–1336), or the mercenary Johan Schiltberger (1381–1440?) found legends every bit as believable as the wondrous details of court etiquette and the elaborate ceremonial of the Byzantine courts of Constantinople or Trebizond. Ruy Gonzalez de Clavijo, the Castilian ambassador to the court of Tamburlaine (d. 1412) found his travels a good prop for an account of things hardly to be matched in familiar Europe.

There is little essential difference in the cast of mind of one of the first and most informative and entertaining travellers in the Ottoman dominions, Evliya Celebi Effendi (1611–84), the son of a goldsmith who entered the service of the Sultan but was called by the prophet, in a dream on his twenty-first birthday, to devote his life to visiting the tombs of the Moslem saints. In the years from 1640 onwards he visited nearly every part of the Turkish heartland of the Ottoman Empire and wrote a description both fascinating and of considerable historical importance of the cities he visited. Yet sober accounts of the trades represented in the bazaar at Constantinople mingle with accounts of the talismans erected by the magicians Apollonius of Tyana and Galen to keep, for example, fleas away from the city; details of the distinctive foodstuffs of

Trebizond rub shoulders with warnings of meeting angels while swimming at Eyup.

Evliya had the advantage of being able to speak properly the language which few western travellers could penetrate sufficiently well to learn curious lore of this kind. Most of them were passing through Turkey on trading missions that would lead them to Georgia or Persia – one thinks of Jean Tavernier, Jean Chardin – or on missions which would combine spying with archaeological discovery like that of Joseph Pitton de Tournefort. Or there were tourists *avant la lettre*, men who went a-travelling for the fun of it like Thomas Coryate or William Lithgow (author of the *Rare and Painefull Peregrinations*) or the Frenchman Jean Thevenot. Such men would look on Turkish culture from the outside, and be duly appalled or mystified by its manifestations. Lithgow, for example, on 'The Turks' Justice':

If a Turk should happen to kill another Turk, his punishment is thus: after he is adjudged to death, he is brought forth to the market-place; and a block being brought hither of four feet high, the malefactor is stripped naked, and laid thereupon with his belly downward: they draw in his middle together so small with running cords, that they strike his body in two with one blow . . . and this is the punishment for manslaughter. But for murder, or treason, he is more cruelly used; for, convicted and condemned, he is brought forth before the people, where, in the street, there is an exceeding high stripad erected, much like to a May-pole; which tree from the root, till it almost come to the top, is all set about full of long sharp iron pikes, and their points upward. The villain being stripped naked, and his hands bound backward, they bind a strong rope about his shoulders and cleaving; and then hoisting him up to the pillow, or top of the tree, they let the rope loose; whence down he falls with a rattle among the iron pikes, hanging either by the buttocks, by the breasts, by the sides, or shoulders; and there sticking fast in the air, he hangeth fast till his very bones rot and fall down, and his body be devoured, being quick, with ravenous eagles, kept to prey upon his carcase for the same purpose.

Almost the same ghoulish fascination could be aroused by accounts of the Sultan's harem, or the female slave-market (see Chapter 1).

An opportunity for a profounder look into Ottoman culture was afforded to the ambassadors and their chaplains. Of the latter, one of the most notable was John Covel, chaplain to the English embassy in the late seventeenth century. Besides collecting Turkish songs and books, and Greek coins, he assiduously visited many classical sites and wrote about them; and also described some of the entertainments of Stamboul, like that of the tumblers.

There was an Arab likewise would lay his bare back upon one, and at the same time a great, lusty man stood on his belly, as likewise he would heave on 2 or 3 vast great stones by the help of a pulley, and yet his back never was hurt. I confesse to read this story in Busbequius made me amazed (as this may you); but when I saw the height of it, I counted it a poor thing; for by his buttocks, and his head, neck, and shoulders, he bore up his belly so as the cimiter lay under the hollow of his back, and a strong man may easily bear a vast weight in that posture. The same man took the Cimiter with his hands at each end, and, laying the edge to his bare belly, moved it very hard from right to left without any harme, onely making a little red line where the edge past. He would fasten a pulley to a gibbet, and through ran a rope, fastend at one end to a ring, to which all his hair was tyed at the crown of his head; the other end was in his hand, by which he would pull himself up a great height. Sometimes he did it with another man at his back; once with an Asse fastend to his shoulder; once with a young camel. I have made some conjectures upon it, but I will not anticipate your mechanicks about this φαινόμενον, onely tell you it seems a pretty one. He took a great pole, about 3 yards long and ½ foot thick, but broader at each end, and setting one end upon the teeth of his lower jaw, he dant with it in this posture upright without touching it, but clapping his hands to his musick, by then he put another frame upon it with 8 or 10 branches (or he could adde more) upon it by a hole that was in the top. Upon every stanza he would set a cup of water; then raysing it, he would dance with all these in like manner without spilling one drop. Then by a stick, which he would put into the same hole, he set a little boy crosse-leg'd upon it, and danct with him in like manner. Lastly, he would set a great pitcher of water up on the upper end, and dance with it; then all of a sudden, with great force, he would strike away the end at his mouth from him, and catch the pitcher in his armes. We saw most of these tricks upon the road acted by him, and all again repeated in the Ring.

Of the ambassadors, we shall meet both Ogier de Busbecq and Sir Edward Montagu (through the intermediacy of his wife Lady Mary) later in these pages. But I cannot forbear to include another item from Ogier here. One might select his account, one of the few based on face to face encounter, of Suleiman the Magnificent, or his paean to the camel; but this passage shows well how far an ambassador could penetrate popular feeling as no tourist could.

While I was at Constantinople, a man who had just returned from the Turkish camp told me a story which I shall be glad to record as illustrating how much the Asiatic peoples dislike the religion and rule of the Ottomans. He said that Soleiman, as he was returning, had enjoyed the hospitality of a certain Asiatic and had spent a night at his house. On the Sultan's departure, his host, considering his house to have been defiled and contaminated by the presence of such a guest, purified it with lustral water, much fumigation, and due ceremonial ritual. When this was reported to Soleiman, he ordered the man to be put to death and his house razed to the ground. Thus the man paid the penalty for his aversion of the Turk and his zeal for the Persians.

Ambassadors, too, could be mixed up in the politics of the Empire, and diplomats like Stratford Canning or Robert Curzon were provided with the opportunity for writing about Turkey by their official pursuits.

But these figures bring us into the nineteenth century which is above all the age of the archaeologist. The archaeological travellers had their precursors, for example Cyriac whom we met above, Covel himself, or Jacob Spon and George Wheler who combed western Asia Minor thoroughly for remnants of antiquity (as well as of the Seven Churches of Asia, which occasioned many melancholy reflections). At least as important were the expeditions of the Society of Dilettanti in the second half of the eighteenth century to the Greek sites of Asia Minor. Their style of ponderous narrative and lavish illustration in enormous folio volumes was extended to other parts of the ancient heritage of Turkey, for example by H. de Laborde who with his brother and two companions embarked on a massive *Voyage de l'Asie Mineure* (1838) covering both Turkey and Syria; its volumes are so vast that the reader must take up an entire table in the British Library and will be lucky if he can persuade one of the reading room assistants to bring them any nearer his desk than the entrance to the book lift. But even the Labordes were in search largely of the picturesque. It was only from the 1840s that the Victorian urge for exploration began to manifest itself in the discovery of remote sites, unvisited buildings and unknown civilizations. The great original of all these travellers was William Martin Leake, though his little book on Asia Minor is a less satisfactory production than the nine fat volumes on the topography of Greece on which his fame rests. Some sentences from his preface give a good sense of the apprehensions with which a traveller whose interests were not focused on the peoples he would meet would enter the alien land of Turkey.

In Asia Minor, among the impediments to a traveller's success may be especially reckoned the deserted state of the country, which often puts the common necessaries and conveniences of travelling out of his reach; the continual disputes and wars among the persons in power; the precarious authority of the government of Constantinople, which rendering its protection ineffectual, makes the traveller's success depend upon the personal character of the governor of each district; and the ignorance and the suspicious temper of the Turks, who have no idea of scientific travelling; who cannot imagine any other motive for our visits to that country, than a preparation for hostile invasion, or a search after treasures among the ruins of antiquity, and whose suspicions of this nature are of course most strong in the provinces which, like Asia Minor, are the least frequented by us. If the traveller's prudence or good fortune should obviate all these difficulties, and should protect him from plague, banditti, and other perils of a semibarbarous state of society, he has still to dread the loss of health, arising from the combined effects of climate, fatigue, and privation; which seldom fails to check his career before he has completed his projected tour.
     Asia Minor is still in that state in which a disguised dress, an assumption of the medical character, great patience and perseverance, the sacrifice of all European comforts, and the concealment of pecuniary means, are necessary to enable the traveller thoroughly to investigate the country, when otherwise qualified for the task by literary and scientific attainments, and by an intimate knowledge of the language and manners of the people.

In the next decades came explorer – archaeologists like Charles T. Newton of the British Museum, A. H. Layard the discoverer of Nineveh, Captain Beaufort the inventor of the Beaufort scale and surveyor of Turkey's southern coast, and Charles Fellows who brought the monuments of Xanthus to London. Few travellers can have enjoyed their travelling so little; but Fellows' *Remarks for the Guidance of Travellers* are a fascinating document of the preparations the explorer found it necessary to make. He might, one feels, as well be heading for the Congo with such paraphernalia. Truly this is a document of that 'Orientalist' mentality that subtly demeans the eastern people on whom the traveller will be dependent for his sustenance and, eventually, his fame.

A tent is the first requisite, the old cities and places of the greatest interest being frequently distant from the modern towns or khans; and a good tent makes the traveller quite independent of the state of health of the town, which I found a very important advantage. It is desirable that the tent should be of a waterproof material. I found great use in an oil-cloth hammock, which was occasionally slung from pole to pole, but was always of service to spread under my mattress when the ground was wet. A carpet may be procured in the country, but a mattress must be taken; also a canteen, containing the usual requisites for cooking and for making tea, and a lantern. Arrow-root is the most portable and convenient material for the traveller's store; it may be prepared in five minutes, and a basin of this will stay the appetite until the dinner can be prepared, which – what with pitching the tent, lighting the fire (often with green wood), and the process of cooking – must be frequently delayed an hour or two after the traveller halts. Rice is necessary, and tea a great treasure.

I have always found the convenience of carrying a gimlet among my travelling stores; it is a substitute for nail, hook, and hammer: inserted into the wall it forms a peg by which my clothes are frequently kept from the dirty or damp floor, or to which I can hang my glass, watch, or thermometer. The traveller will of course be prepared with every requisite for the tailor, and will take a few simple medicines.

For economy in travelling it is well to take only five or six horses; if this number be exceeded, another guide is required, and the pay to the ostlers is increased. The traveller who wishes to pay liberally and be well attended by the post, must calculate that five horses will cost him, with these extra payments, as much as seven; and this sum will cover all expenses on the road to guides, ostlers, etc., amounting to seven piastres per hour, or about four miles. On the ordinary lines of road he may travel three hours in two, being six miles an hour; this saves time, but the expense is the same. However proficient the European traveller may be in the Turkish language, I should recommend his taking a servant who can act as dragoman, as he will be thus enabled far better to understand and fall into the manners and customs of the people.

The most acceptable presents to the inhabitants are not such as are of the greatest intrinsic value, but articles of use which it is difficult for them to procure. The traveller will do well to suppy himself with copper caps for the people in authority who have had percussion guns given to them, but which are rendered useless from the want of these, and also gunpowder for the peasantry: by all classes a sheet of writing-paper is much valued; leads for patent pencil-cases are very acceptable; and a common box-compass will furnish much pleasure, occasionally directing the Mahometan to the point for his prayers. I have been often asked in a delicate manner by the Greeks if I possessed a picture of our Queen or reigning sovereign; a common print of this kind would be highly prized.

The condescension is apparent too in the books of Sir William Ramsay, and of W. J. Hamilton, whose interests were geographical and geological rather than archaeological, though he gave ruins their due. And F. J. Burnaby was another traveller who regarded archaeology as of only secondary importance to political observation; he, be it noted, was impressed by his Turkish hosts, and reserved his venom for the Armenians.

No traveller can be entirely charmed, of course, by the strangers among whom he travels, but female archaeologists like Gertrude Bell and Freya Stark seem to have reached a more even-tempered appraisal of their hosts and helpers – perhaps because of their greater dependence. That dependence does not diminish their importance in their archaeological activities. The partnership of Gertrude Bell and Sir William Ramsay is famous, and resulted in at least one masterpiece, *The Thousand and One Churches of Asia*.

The turning point in the archaeological exploration of Turkey was surely Charles Texier's discovery in 1834 of the ruins of Boğazkale, now known to be the Hittite capital of Hattusas. From there on the classical perspective was skewed, and room had to be made for other ancient races in the Turkish hinterland. But that has not prevented later travellers from doing much valuable work on classical sites; among those represented in this book are William Burkhardt Barker, Louis Robert and George Hanfmann; and besides, no one can travel long in Turkey without making use of those invaluable guide-books, the four volumes by George Bean, as well as the frequently updated compilation by Ekrem Akurgal; these

two books will give the visitor much information on the
contemporary history of archaeology in Turkey.

Last, but by no means least, among our travellers come the
tourists. A. W. Kinglake created a new genre with his *Eothen*
(1844), and his account of that distinctive motion of the soul
which takes place on stepping out of Europe, of Christendom,
into Asia, sets the tone for many responses from those who
travel to see what they may find.

After coming in contact with any creature or thing belonging to the
Ottoman Empire it would be impossible for us to return to the
Austrian territory without undergoing an imprisonment for fourteen days in the Lazaretto. We felt therefore that before we committed ourselves, it was important to take care that none of the
arrangements necessary for the journey had been forgotten; and in
our anxiety to avoid such a misfortune we managed the work of
departure from Semlin with nearly as much solemnity as if we had
been departing this life. Some obliging persons from whom we had
received civilities during our short stay in the place, came down to
say their farewell at the river's side; and now, as we stood with them
at the distance of three or four yards from the 'compromised' officer,
they asked if we were perfectly certain that we had wound up all our
affairs in Christendom, and whether we had no parting requests to
make. We repeated the caution to our servants, and took anxious
thought lest by any possibility we might be cut off from some
cherished object of affection: – were they quite sure that nothing had
been forgotten – that there was no fragrant dressing-case with its
gold-compelling letters of credit from which we might be parting
for ever? – No – every one of our treasures lay safely stowed in the
boat, and we – we were ready to follow. Now, therefore, we shook
hands with our Semlin friends, and they immediately retreated for
three or four paces, so as to leave us in the centre of a space between
them and the 'compromised' officer; the latter then advanced, and
asking once more if we had done with the civilized world, held forth
his hand – I met it with mine, and there was an end to Christendom
for many a day to come.

We soon neared the southern bank of the river, but no sounds
came down from the blank walls above, and there was no living
thing that we could yet see, except one great hovering bird of the
vulture race flying low and intent, and wheeling round and round
over the Pest-accursed city.

But presently there issued from the postern a group of human
beings, – beings with immortal souls, and possibly some reasoning
faculties, but to me the grand point was this, that they had real,
substantial, and incontrovertible turbans.

Now for the first time Ottoman topics become the dominant focus. Travellers like Hobhouse or Chandler at the end of the eighteenth century could devote descriptions to the delights of the baths or the curiosities of the whirling dervishes (and of course Coryate never missed a trick in topics of this kind), but now they are the meat and drink of the travel account. Here one singles out Dickens' friend Albert Smith, Miss F. M. Skene and W. M. Thackeray. Richard Davey wrote one of the most thorough accounts of contemporary Turkey to bring the country alive for the reader who had never been there; and Mark Twain found the travel account a sufficiently established genre to be able to debunk it at every turn, as in his account of a Turkish bath.

When I think how I have been swindled by books of Oriental travel, I want a tourist for breakfast. For years and years I have dreamed of the wonders of the Turkish bath; for years and years I have promised myself that I would yet enjoy one. Many and many a time in fancy I have lain in the marble bath and breathed the slumbrous fragrance of Eastern spices that filled the air; then passed through a weird and complicated system of pulling and hauling, and drenching and scrubbing, by a gang of naked savages who loomed vast and vaguely through the steaming mists like demons; then rested for a while on a divan fit for a king; then passed through another complex ordeal, and one more fearful than the first; and finally, swathed in soft fabrics, been conveyed to a princely saloon and laid on a bed of eiderdown, where eunuchs, gorgeous of costume, fanned me while I drowsed and dreamed or contentedly gazed at the rich hangings of the apartment, the soft carpets, the sumptuous furniture, the pictures, and drank delicious coffee, smoked the soothing narghile, and dropped, at the last, into tranquil repose, lulled by sensuous odors from unseen censers, by the gentle influence of the narghile's Persian tobacco, and by the music of fountains that counterfeited the pattering of summer rain.

That was the picture just as I got it from incendiary books of travel. It was a poor, miserable imposture. The reality is no more like it than the Five Points are like the Garden of Eden. They received me in a great court, paved with marble slabs; around it were broad galleries, one above another, carpeted with seedy matting, railed with unpainted balustrades, and furnished with huge rickety chairs, cushioned with rusty old mattresses, indented with impressions left by the forms of nine successive generations of men who had reposed upon them. The place was vast, naked, dreary; its court a barn, its galleries stalls for human horses. The cadaverous, half-nude varlets that served in the establishment had nothing of poetry in their appearance, nothing of romance, nothing of Oriental splendor. They shed no entrancing odors – just the contrary. Their hungry eyes and their lank forms continually suggested one glaring, unsentimental fact – they wanted what they term in California 'a square meal'.

I went into one of the racks and undressed. An unclean starveling wrapped a gaudy tablecloth about his loins and hung a white rag over my shoulders. If I had had a tub then, it would have come natural to me to take in washing. I was then conducted downstairs into the wet, slippery court, and the first things that attracted my attention were my heels. My fall excited no comment. They expected it, no doubt. It belonged in the list of softening, sensuous influences peculiar to this home of Eastern luxury. It was softening enough, certainly, but its application was not happy. They now gave me a pair of wooden clogs – benches in miniature with leather straps over them to confine my feet (which they would have done, only I do not wear No. 13s). These things dangled uncomfortably by the straps when I lifted up my feet, and came down in awkward and unexpected places when I put them on the floor again, and sometimes turned sideways and wrenched my ankles out of joint. However, it was all Oriental luxury, and I did what I could to enjoy it.

They put me in another part of the barn and laid me on a stuffy sort of pallet, which was not made of cloth of gold or Persian shawls, but was merely the unpretending sort of thing I have seen in the Negro quarters of Arkansas. There was nothing whatever in this dim marble prison but five more of these biers. It was a very solemn place. I expected that the spiced odors of Araby were going to steal over my senses now, but they did not. A copper-colored skeleton, with a rag around him, brought me a glass decanter of water, with a lighted tobacco pipe in the top of it, and a pliant stem a yard long with a brass mouthpiece to it.

It was the famous 'narghile' of the East – the thing the Grand Turk smokes in the pictures. This began to look like luxury. I took one blast at it, and it was sufficient; the smoke went in a great volume down into my stomach, my lungs, even into the uttermost part of my frame. I exploded one mighty cough, and it was as if Vesuvius had let go. For the next five minutes I smoked at every pore, like a frame house that is on fire on the inside. Not any more narghile for me. The smoke had a vile taste, and the taste of a thousand infidel tongues that remained on that brass mouthpiece was viler still. I was getting discouraged. Whenever hereafter I see the cross-legged Grand Turk smoking his narghile, in pretended bliss, on the outside of a paper of Connecticut tobacco, I shall know him for the shameless humbug he is.

This prison was filled with hot air. When I had got warmed up sufficiently to prepare me for a still warmer temperature, they took me where it was – into a marble room, wet, slippery, and steamy, and laid me out on a raised platform in the center. It was very warm. Presently my man sat me down by a tank of hot water, drenched me well, gloved his hand with a coarse mitten, and began to polish me all over with it. I began to smell disagreeably. The more he polished, the worse I smelled. It was alarming. I said to him:

'I perceive that I am pretty far gone. It is plain that I ought to be buried without any unnecessary delay. Perhaps you had better go after my friends at once, because the weather is warm and I cannot "keep" long.'

He went on scrubbing and paid no attention. I soon saw that he was reducing my size. He bore hard on his mitten, and from under it rolled little cylinders, like maccaroni. It could not be dirt, for it was too white. He pared me down in this way for a long time. Finally I said:

'It is a tedious process. It will take hours to trim me to the size you want me; I will wait; go and borrow a jack plane.'

He paid no attention at all.

After a while he brought a basin, some soap, and something that seemed to be the tail of a horse. He made up a prodigious quantity of soapsuds, deluged me with them from head to foot, without warning me to shut my eyes, and then swabbed me viciously with the horsetail. Then he left me there, a snowy statue of lather, and went away. When I got tired of waiting I went and hunted him up. He was propped against the wall, in another room, asleep. I woke him. He was not disconcerted. He took me back and flooded me with hot water, then turbaned my head, swathed me with dry table-cloths, and conducted me to a latticed chicken coop in one of the galleries, and pointed to one of those Arkansas beds. I mounted it and vaguely expected the odors of Araby again. They did not come.

The blank, unornamented coop had nothing about it of that Oriental voluptuousness one reads of so much. It was more sugges-tive of the county hospital than anything else. The skinny servitor brought a narghile, and I got him to take it out again without wasting any time about it. Then he brought the world-renowned Turkish coffee that poets have sung so rapturously for many generations, and I seized upon it as the last hope that was left of my old dreams of Eastern luxury. It was another fraud. Of all the unchristian bever-ages that ever passed my lips, Turkish coffee is the worst. The cup is small, it is smeared with grounds; the coffee is black, thick, unsavory of smell, and execrable in taste. The bottom of the cup has a muddy sediment in it half an inch deep. This goes down your throat, and portions of it lodge by the way and produce a tickling aggravation that keeps you barking and coughing for an hour.

Here endeth my experience of the celebrated Turkish bath, and here also endeth my dream of the bliss the mortal revels in who passes through it. It is a malignant swindle. The man who enjoys it is qualified to enjoy anything that is repulsive to sight or sense, and he that can invest it with a charm of poetry is able to do the same with anything else in the world that is tedious, and wretched, and dismal, and nasty.

But the doyen of writers on Turkey, and especially Constantinople, is surely Pierre Loti. He will reappear several times in this book; but here he can be represented, along with Richard Davey, by two accounts of that distinctive Turkish art form, the puppet play of Karagöz, which has also become naturalised in Greece under the name of Karagiozis.

The adventures and misdeeds of Monsieur Karagheuz have amused an incalculable number of generations of Turks, and nothing indicates that the favour of this personage is on the wane.

Karagheuz offers many analogies with the old French Polichinelle; after beating everyone, including his wife, he is beaten himself by Cheytan – the devil – who finally carries him off, to the spectators' great joy.

Karagheuz is made of wood or cardboard; he is presented to the public as a marionette or as a shadow puppet; in either case, he is equally funny. He discovers intonations and postures which Guignol never suspected; the caresses he offers Mme Karagheuz are irresistibly comic.

Karagheuz may also converse with the spectators and engage in brawls with the public. He is permitted witticisms that are entirely incongruous, and to do in full view of everyone things that would scandalise even a Capuchin. In Turkey, that is accepted; censure says not a word, and one sees every evening good Turks, lantern in hand, leading troops of little children to Karagheuz. In these halls full of babies a spectacle is put on which in England would make a troop of guardsmen blush.

Pierre Loti, *Aziyadé* (1879)

The wooden Karagheuz seems to be no longer current, and one normally sees the puppets made of transparent camel hide, richly coloured, in such performances as Richard Davey describes.

In Ramazān, when the Mohammedans turn day into night and night into day, when, in the exquisite moonlight of the East, the enchantment of olden times reasserts itself, and envelopes Stambul with its magic romance; when the minarets and domes of the illuminated mosques stand out ghostly white, against a deep blue sky, gemmed with myriad stars; when the quaint open shops in the narrow streets sparkle with coloured lamps, and groups of veiled women, guarded by eunuchs, each of whom bears a lantern fixed to a long pole, flit by mysteriously on their way to the mosque of Shah-zadé or of Ahmed of the six minarets – Karagheuz, the Turkish Punch, performs before rapturous audiences, who crowd the *cafés* (almost exclusively patronised by Moslims) behind the beautiful Bāyezīdieh Mosque, the loveliest of all the hundreds Constantinople boasts.

.   .   .   .

My introduction to him was made in Ramazān, 1894, in an outlandish little *café*, established in a ruined Byzantine building, immediately behind the great Bazaar, and close to the Harem or courtyard of the Mosque of Bāyezīd.

.   .   .   .

Suddenly, the lights in the area of the improvised auditorium were extinguished, the sheet that was to serve for a stage shone opaquely transparent, and now the fun began in earnest. The orchestra – two drums, a flute, a viola, and a triangle – struck up those quavering sounds which enchant the Eastern ear, but which nearly drive the European listener mad. For a minute, or two the transparency remained empty. Presently a funny little figure on a camel's back scurried across, speedily followed by a cat running after a mouse. The cat played with the mouse an unconscionable time, and finally swallowed it whole. At this the orchestra emitted the most appalling noises, a sort of quivering shriek, intermingled with a rumbling rattle – possibly intended to illustrate the agonies of the luckless mouse in the torture-chamber of the cat's stomach; then, with a deafening tattoo on the quaint-shaped drum, it gradually settled into silence. Pussy's repast was evidently over. The incident of the cat and the mouse had so delighted the audience that a little wave of admiring whispers rippled through the chamber, to be presently silenced, as the figures of two ladies were projected upon the screen. One was dressed in European and the other in Turkish fashion. They were apparently in earnest conversation, when, suddenly, they were joined by a Turkish 'masher' in 'Stambuline' or frock-coat, with a straight collar, lavender trousers, patent leather boots, etc., *au grand complet*. On his head he wore a fez. A prodigious moustache, curling up under his nose, added a rakishness to his appearance that was irresistibly funny. Presently the masher slipped a piece of paper into Madame's hand, after which he made obvious overtures to elope with the Hanum. For a few minutes everything seemed rose-coloured; but alas! Karagheuz was at hand, keen to make mischief – bringing with him, on this his first appearance, the outraged husband of the lady. Then there was much animation upon the sheet. The husband and the lover fought right valiantly, the husband, I am sorry to say, continually getting the worst of it, much to the delight of the public. His fez flew off, his frock-coat was torn, and reduced at last to a pitiable plight, he was obliged to beat an ignominious retreat. Once more the Turkish lady, she of Europe, and the masher were grouped together, and judging from the manner in which their heads met and the earnest whispered consultation in which they apparently engaged, they were evidently plotting some fresh outrage against the offended husband. Nemesis, however, was at hand, again in the shape of Karagheuz, who shortly returned, in company, this time, with his *alter ego*, Hadji-aïvat, of whom anon. Things now became very mixed indeed, for both these iniquitous little gentlemen having cast a longing glance upon the ladies' charms, determined forthwith to rid themselves of the inconvenient masher. When least that luckless youth expected it, they pounced upon him and literally pulled him in two. Then followed a scene with the fair ladies which I may not describe – not even in Greek, let alone Latin!

Though such performances are regrettably rarer than they were, there is a rich repertoire of plays, many of which have been collected by the German scholar Helmut Ritter; their themes are genre scenes from everyday life, and resemble the plays of the consanguineous Karagiozis in Athens, though the latter have been refined for their young audiences and have incorporated many elements of distinctively Greek folklore.

The last spasm of the literary response to Turkey is of course that of the Turks themselves. There is little of this before the twentieth century, at least not accessible to those to whom the language and script before Atatürk are a closed book. But in the last few decades more than one Turkish writer has tried to represent his country to the western world, and those representatives included here are Mahmut Makal and Irfan Orga, as well as the novelist Yashar Kemal and a handful of the poets. Let these not be an unworthy selection of responses to the variety and beauty that Turkey has to offer. Reader, go forth on your literary voyage to new discoveries of your own!

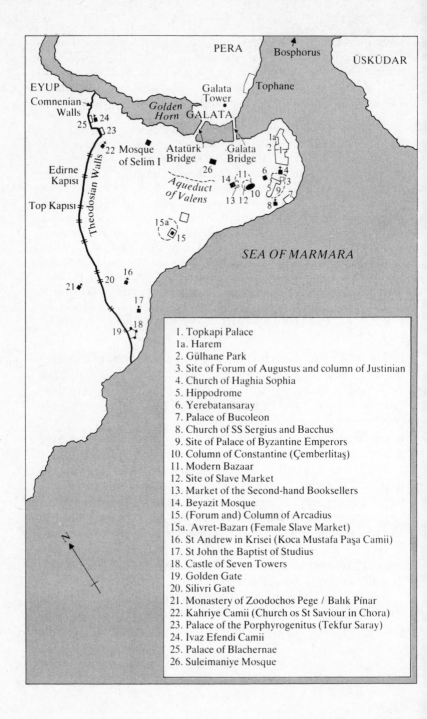

PERA

Bosphorus

ÜSKÜDAR

EYUP

Comnenian Walls

Galata Tower

Tophane

*Golden Horn*

GALATA

25

24

23

22  Mosque of Selim I

Atatürk Bridge

Galata Bridge

Edirne Kapısı

Theodosian Walls

26

1a

2  1

*Aqueduct of Valens*

14  11

6  4

3

5  9

13  12  10

8

Top Kapısı

15a

15

SEA OF MARMARA

16

21  20

17

19  18

1. Topkapi Palace
1a. Harem
2. Gülhane Park
3. Site of Forum of Augustus and column of Justinian
4. Church of Haghia Sophia
5. Hippodrome
6. Yerebatansaray
7. Palace of Bucoleon
8. Church of SS Sergius and Bacchus
9. Site of Palace of Byzantine Emperors
10. Column of Constantine (Çemberlitaş)
11. Modern Bazaar
12. Site of Slave Market
13. Market of the Second-hand Booksellers
14. Beyazit Mosque
15. (Forum and) Column of Arcadius
15a. Avret-Bazarı (Female Slave Market)
16. St Andrew in Krisei (Koca Mustafa Paşa Camii)
17. St John the Baptist of Studius
18. Castle of Seven Towers
19. Golden Gate
20. Silivri Gate
21. Monastery of Zoodochos Pege / Balık Pínar
22. Kahriye Camii (Church os St Saviour in Chora)
23. Palace of the Porphyrogenitus (Tekfur Saray)
24. Ivaz Efendi Camii
25. Palace of Blachernae
26. Suleimaniye Mosque

# CHAPTER ONE

# Istanbul

## 1. Constantinople

> Now sing I of Byzantium; Bosphor's tides,
> Twixt Europe and the Lesser Asia glides,
> Their Hippodrome, adorn'd with triumphs past,
> And blackish sea, the Iadileck more fast:
> The Galata, where Christian merchants stay,
> And five ambassadors for commerce ay:
> The Turkish customs and their manners rude,
> And of their descent from the Scythian blood:
> Their harsh religion, and their sense of hell,
> And Paradise, their laws I shall you tell:
> Then last of Mahomet, their God on earth,
> His end, his life, his parentage and birth.
>
> William Lithgow, *Rare Adventures and Painefull Peregrinations* (1632)

William Lithgow understood something of the complex past of a city that has been four cities in its time: first the Greek city of Byzantium with its legendary founder Byzas; then the new capital of the Roman Empire founded by the Emperor Constantine in AD 330; then the Turkish city of Stamboul or (as it was sometimes called) Islambol, which in modern times has undergone a further metamorphosis into the city of Istanbul. The Greek past is reflected in the modern names which derive from the Greek *eis tin polin*, 'to the city'; but it is impossible to bring to life the original Greek foundation. A few scattered glimpses of the prosperous trading city on its important maritime site are all that can be gained – like that of a merchant in Menander's play *Arrephoros* of the fourth century BC:

Byzantium makes all the merchants drunk. We drank all night, and I
feel quite incapable: in fact when I got up I found I had four heads!

Menander fragment 61 Koeck

It was as the city of Constantinople that the city reached its
long period of glory, more than eleven hundred years. W. B.
Yeats made of the city of Byzantium an image of 'unageing
intellect' and the 'artifice of eternity'; but a more gloomy view
is that of Lawrence Durrell:

> Only the objects of their past estate remain,
> Dispersing now like limbs in different museums.
> The crowns and trumpets tarnish easily,
> The tangles of ribbon rot like heads of hair
> In cupboards where they kept the holy chrism.
> Only the eye in an ikon here or there
> Amends and ponders and reflects neglects:
> Dead monarchs toughened to a stare.

Lawrence Durrell, Byzance

What then can be salvaged of the gold-glittering splendours
of imperial Constantinople, of the excitement of the races in
the Hippodrome and the claustrophobic intrigues of the court;
the splendours of the architecture that housed the largest
collection of antique art in the world, and the inadequate
scholarship that attached the strangest legends to the classical
monuments of the city? So many of the city's treasures have
vanished beyond recall, looted by the Venetians in 1204 or
melted down by the Turks in 1453. It is an exercise of the
imagination to repopulate the city of Istanbul with the buildings and the monuments that were the daily companions of the
Emperors of Rome. Let us visit some of the major sites in turn.

### The Church of Ayia Sophia

This great church was erected by order of the Emperor
Justinian in 532 to replace an earlier one destroyed in the Nika
riots of that year. His official panegyrists alike declared their
inadequacy for the task of describing the splendours of what is
admitted to be one of the finest creations of Byzantine
architecture.

Who could describe the galleries of the portion set apart for women,
or the numerous porticos and cloistered courts with which the

church is surrounded? who could tell of the beauty of the columns and marbles with which the church is adorned? one would think that one had come upon a meadow full of flowers in bloom: who would not admire the purple tints of some and the green of others, the glowing red and glittering white, and those, too, which nature, like a painter, has marked with the strongest contrasts of colour? Whoever enters there to worship perceives at once that it is not by any human strength or skill, but by the favour of God that this work has been perfected; his mind rises sublime to commune with God, feeling that He cannot be far off, but must especially love to dwell in the place which He has chosen; and this takes place not only when a man sees it for the first time, but it always makes the same impression upon him, as though he had never beheld it before. No one ever became weary of this spectacle, but those who are in the Church delight in what they see, and, when they leave it, magnify it in their talk about it; moreover, it is impossible accurately to describe the treasure of gold and silver plate and gems, which the Emperor Justinian has presented to it; but by the description of one of them, I leave the rest to be inferred. That part of the church which is especially sacred, and where the priests alone are allowed to enter, which is called the Sanctuary, contains forty thousand pounds' weight of silver.

Procopius, *The Building of Justinian*; tr. A. Stewart (1886)

The poet Paul the Silentiary was equally enthusiastic.

No word can describe the light at night-time; one might say in truth that some midnight sun illumined the glories of the temple. For the wise forethought of our king has had stretched from the projecting rim of stone, on whose back is firmly planted the temple's air-borne dome, long twisted chains of beaten brass, linked in alternating curves with many windings. And these chains, bending down from every part in a long course, come together as they fall towards the ground. But before they reach the pavement, their path from above is checked, and they finish in unison in a circle. And beneath each chain he has arranged for silver discs to be fitted, hanging circlewise in the air, round the space in the centre of the church. Thus these discs, pendent from their lofty courses, form a coronet above the heads of men. They have been pierced too by the weapon of the skilful workman, in order that they may receive shafts of fire-wrought glass, and hold light on high for men at night.

And not from discs alone does the light shine at night, but in the circles close by a disc you would see the symbol of the mighty cross, pierced with many holes, and in its pierced back shines a vessel of light. Thus hangs the circling chorus of bright lights. Indeed, you might say that you gazed on the bright constellation of the Heavenly

Crown by the Great Bear, and the neighbouring Dragon. Thus through the temple wanders the evening light, brightly shining. In the middle of a larger circle you would find a crown with light-bearing rim; and above in the centre another noble disc spreads its light in the air, so that night is compelled to flee. Near the aisles too, alongside the columns, they have hung in order single lamps apart from one another; and through the whole length of the far-stretching nave is their path. Beneath each they have placed a silver vessel, like a balance pan, and in the centre of this rests a cup of well-burning oil.

Thus through the spaces of the great church come rays of light, expelling clouds of care, and filling the mind with joy. The sacred light cheers all: even the sailor guiding his bark on the waves, leaving behind him the unfriendly billows of the raging Pontus, and winding a sinuous course amidst creeks and rocks, with heart fearful at the dangers of his nightly wanderings – perhaps he has left the Aegean and guides his ship against adverse currents in the Hellespont; awaiting with taut forestay the onslaught of a storm from Africa – does not guide his laden vessel by the light of Cynosure, or the circling Bear, but by the divine light of the church itself. Yet not only does it guide the merchant at night, like the rays from the Pharos on the coast of Africa, but it also shows the way to the living God.

Paul the Silentiary; tr. Philip Sherrard

Besides the visible splendours of the church, it became in the course of centuries the vehicle of legends about the divine protection enjoyed by the whole of the City. The 'Narrative of the Construction of the Church of Ayia Sophia', the latest version of which dates from the tenth century, contains the following story which makes the claim explicit.

One Saturday, the order came from the sovereign to bring the miliaresia (small coins for the workmen's pay) from the Palace; it was the third hour of the day, and Strategios had given permission to the labourers and artisans to go and dine. As he left, Ignatius, the architect and chief engineer, left his son up above, where the third part of the balconies was being built, to watch over the workmen's tools. The child was about fourteen years old. While he was seated there a eunuch appeared to him, dressed in a dazzling robe, of beautiful appearance – one would have taken him for an emissary from the palace – and asked the boy: 'Why do the workmen not haste to complete the work of God and why have they abandoned it to eat?' The child replied, 'Sir, they will be back soon!' The other returned: 'Go and tell them that I am impatient to see the work finished.' The child said that he could not go for fear that the tools would disappear. The eunuch replied: 'Go with all speed and tell them to come quickly; and I will swear an oath to you my son: by the Holy Wisdom, which is to say the Word of God, I shall not leave this place – for it is the place which the Word of God has assigned to me for my service and my watch – before you return.' At these words, the boy ran off, leaving to the angel of God the task of guarding the building site. When the child found his father, the chief architect, with the others, he told him everything. Then the father, taking his son, went to the table of the Emperor; for the Emperor happened to be dining there, at the chapel of St John the Forerunner by the Horologion. Hearing the child's story, the Emperor called together all his eunuchs and showed them to the boy one by one, asking him, 'Is this he?' But the child replied that none of them resembled the eunuch he had seen in the church. Then the Emperor understood that it was an angel of God and that one could rely on his words and his oath. The child added that he was clad in white, that his cheeks sparked fire and that his face was quite changed; the Emperor glorified God aloud in these terms: 'God looks on this work with favour', and 'I was in a great quandary what to call the church'; and thereupon it received the name of the Holy Wisdom, which signifies the Word of God. After reflection, the Emperor said: 'Do not allow the child to return to the building site, for thus the angel will continue his watch, as he has sworn. If the child returns and is found on the site, the angel of the Lord will depart.' The Emperor consulted the most eminent members of the Senate and the priests of the church, who likewise advised him not to send the child back to the church, so that, by virtue of his oath, the angel guards the church on the orders of God until the end of the World.

from G. Dagron, *Constantinople Imaginaire* (1984); tr. R. S.

The Church of Ayia Sofia was the last refuge of the Greeks when the Turkish conquerors burst into the city one April morning in 1453. According to the legend, the priests were celebrating mass at the time; they sank into the walls, and will re-emerge only when the City becomes Greek again.

It was not easy for a giaour to gain admission to the mosque of Ayia Sophia. One who attempted it was the French artist J. P. Grelot, who entered with his drawing equipment with the guidance of a Greek and with the assistance of several bribes. It being Ramadan, he took with him a picnic lunch in the form of a Bologna sausage, a bottle of wine and a loaf. After a good deal of sketching, he had taken a break to eat (while the Turks prayed) when he saw someone approaching him:

I was in a peck of troubles, and knew not what to do in the condition I was: besides that I knew not where to bestow my papers, pencils and bottle, for which I could find no excuse in the world. It was a crime that neither stake nor fire could hardly have expiated, to find a Giaour making figures, eating pork, and drinking wine, in the Turks' Holy of Holies. I must confess I was never in such a panic dread in all my life, and that I never saw the shape and likeness of death so exactly drawn before my eyes in all my days.

However, though I firmly believed myself to be a person no longer of this world, yet that I might not be surprised with my bottle and sausage, I hid them together with my papers under a carpet in a dark corner, with all the speed I could, and so drawing forth my rosary, and a certain book which I had about me, written by Peter Gilius, I returned to my seat, and put myself into a posture of one that had but newly said his prayers. Every step the Turk made towards the upper portico, from whence I had been drawing the bottom of the church, my deadly fears augmented. But in regard he came but slowly on, I had time to recollect my spirits, to put on a good face, and confirm myself in those resolutions I had always undertaken, which were rather to lose my life a thousand times, than my praeputium once.

Thus feigning myself to be at my prayers, I held my book, which I had no great maw to look in at that time, in my left hand, and my rosary in my right hand, with the beads whereof I was fumbling, when the Turk approached me; and instead of a Salamalek, or How d'ye do, cried Bre guidi giaur ne uhlersen bouda: Villain of an infidel! what mak'st thou here? I answered him, after I had looked very seriously in my book, and turned over two or three of my beads according to the Musselmen's manner: Sir, I am at my prayers, stay a little while I beseech ye. – After which, having made a genuflexion, together with the sign of the cross, I rose up to speak to him. Salamalekum Aga, said I, or Good day t'ye, Sir; then going on, You need not wonder, Sir, quoth I, to find a Christian alone in the galleries of St Sophia; adding, he knew it was a church formerly built by the Christians, who had still a great veneration for it, and being one of those, that I had obtained permission to be let in to the end I might spend some few hours in devotion and prayer, and that I expected him who had let me in, to come suddenly and let me out again.

The Turk, who was one of those who had shared my four sequins, having heard me, presently serened his tempestuous countenance, not being able to forbear laughing, to see in what a cold sweat he had put me (for he might easily read my distemper in my looks), and to hear what a fine lie I had got already chewed for him. Thereupon he bid me be of good comfort, and cried Couremas Adam, Fear nothing; I knew, said he, you were here; and so having shewed him some of my draughts which he desired to see, he left me to take off the rest of my bottle to recruit my spirits.

J. P. Grelot, *A Late Voyage to Constantinople*; tr. J. Philips (1683)

## Other Churches

The most exhaustive account of the many churches of Constantinople is the work of Alexander van Millingen, from whom the following tale about the church of St Andrew in Krisei, latterly the mosque of Koca Mustapha Pasha, is taken.

The old church is more definitely identified by the legend of the judicial procedure which clings to the building. In the picturesque courtyard of the mosque, where the colour of the East is still rich and vivid, there stands an old cypress tree around whose bare and withered branches a slender iron chain is entwined like the skeleton of some extinct serpent. As tradition would have it, the chain was once endowed with the gift of judgment, and in cases of dispute could indicate which of the parties concerned told the truth. One day a Jew who had borrowed money from a Turk, on being summoned to pay his debt, replied that he had done so already. To that statement the Turk gave the lie direct, and accordingly, debtor and creditor were brought to the chain for the settlement of the question at issue. Before submitting to the ordeal, however, the Jew placed a cane into the hands of the Turk, and then stood under the cypress confident that his honour for truthfulness and honesty would be vindicated. His expectation proved correct, for the chain touched his head to intimate that he had returned the money he owed. Whereupon taking back his cane he left the scene in triumph. Literally, the verdict accorded with fact; for the cane which the Jew had handed to his creditor was hollow and contained the sum due to the latter. But the verdict displayed such a lack of insight, and involved so gross a miscarriage of justice, that from that day forth the chain lost its reputation and has hung ever since a dishonoured oracle on the dead arms of the cypress, like a criminal on a gibbet.

Alexander van Millingen, *Byzantine Churches in Constantinople* (1912)

Such legends abounded in the later centuries of the Byzantine era, as the original significance of classical and other monuments became forgotten. Straightforward tales of miracles were also plentiful, like this one told of the now ruined Church of St John the Baptist of Studius by Ruy Gonzalez de Clavijo:

In this church there is another great stone tomb, in which another emperor is interred, and this church also contains the other arm of the blessed St. John the Baptist, which was shown to the ambassadors. This was the right arm, and it was fresh and healthy; and, though they say that the whole body of the blessed St. John was destroyed, except one finger of the right arm, with which he pointed when he said 'Ecce Agnus Dei', yet certainly the whole of this arm was fresh and in good preservation, but it wanted the thumb. The reason given by the monks for the thumb being gone was this, – they say that at the time when idolatry prevailed in the city of Antioch, there was a terrible dragon, to which one person was given every year, to be eaten. They drew lots who should be the victim, and the person on whom the lot fell, could not be excused from being eaten by the dragon. Once the lot fell upon the daughter of a good man, and when he saw that his daughter must be given up to the dragon, he was very sad, and gave her to a church of Christian nuns, who were then in that city, saying to the nuns, that he had heard that God had performed many miracles through St. John, and that he wished to believe, and to adore the arm of that saint, which they possessed. He prayed that, in addition to the other miracles which God had performed through him, he would save the girl from being eaten by this ferocious dragon, and deliver her from danger. The nuns, taking compassion on him, showed him the arm, on which he threw himself down to worship it, and bit off its thumb, without letting the nuns see him. When the people were going to give the maiden to the dragon, and the monster opened its mouth to eat her, the good man threw the thumb of the blessed saint into its mouth; upon which the dragon turned round, and fled, which was a great miracle: and that man was converted to the faith of our Lord Jesus Christ.

Ruy Gonzalez de Clavijo, *Narrative of the Embassy . . . to the Court of Timur at Samarkand 1403–6* (tr. 1859)

It was in this church that the Emperor Michael VIII Palaeologus was first received when the Greeks triumphantly re-entered Constantinople in August 1261.

## The Emperors' Palace

There is little to be seen now of the Palace which Constantine erected near the shore of the Marmara. One wall and a few windows of one of its pavilions, the Bucoleon, are visible from the Marmara boulevard (Kennedy Cd), near the church of Ss Sergius and Bacchus. But enough descriptions survive to give imagination a generous rein:

Surpassing all the palaces of the East in magnificence was that which was famous for nearly a thousand years as the Great Palace, the foundations of which were laid by Constantine, and the glories of which were added to by a score of succeeding Emperors. The Great Palace was not one huge building, like the Royal palaces of the West, but a series of detached halls and apartments, linked together by corridors, cloisters, terraces, and gardens. It sloped gradually seaward to where a winding staircase of the purest marble descended to a landing-place, before which the galleys of the Emperor and Empress, and a fleet of gilded State barges and pleasure boats, were anchored in the blue waters of the Marmara. Near by, on the sea-walls, stood two round hollow towers, which were filled with pipes, so that when the wind blew, they, like gigantic Æolian harps, made solemn harmonies, repeating the wild and fascinating strain from tower to tower, 'so that you would have thought you heard the voices of angels, now plaintively whispering, and now wailing as if in sorrow, or again bursting forth in joyous anthems.'

Richard Davey*

The palace contained a fine library, and Pierre Gilles, who was in Constantinople in the sixteenth century to collect books and manuscripts for Francis I of France and wrote the first thorough account of the antiquities of Constantinople, recorded among its more conventional splendours the following oddity:

Among other curiosities of this place, was the gut of a dragon, a hundred and twenty foot long, on which were inscribed in golden characters the Iliads and Odysses of Homer.

Pierre Gilles, *The Antiquities of Constantinople* (1561); tr. J. Bale (1729)

The vestibule of the palace was known as the Chalke or Brazen House, and functioned as one of the many repositories of classical art in the City.

Another collection of antique art housed within the confines of the Great Palace was in the Baths of Zeuxippus[1]; Gilles is our best informant:

Cedrinus relates, that in this bagnio there was a pleasant variety of prospects of surprising art, both in marble and stonework, in statues of brass, and figures of persons of antiquity, who seemed to want nothing but a soul to animate and enliven them. Among these

---

* Indicates a work fully noted in the Bibliography.

[1] Burnt down in the Nika riots of 532 and rebuilt with even greater magnificence.

celebrated pieces of the most exquisite workmanship, was the statue of old Homer, in a thoughtful posture. . . . This place was also beautified with brazen statues of all those renowned personages who had been famous for wisdom, poetry, oratory or courage, throughout the world, but were all destroyed by fire.

Gilles can best be quoted, too, on the cistern now known as Yerebatansaray:

The Imperial Portico, and the Imperial Cisterna, stood in the same place: the Imperial Portico is not to be seen, though the CISTERNA is still remaining. Through the carelessness and contempt of every thing that is curious in the inhabitants, it was never discovered, but by me, who was a stranger among them, after a long and diligent search. The whole ground was built upon, which made it the less to be suspected that there was a Cisterna upon the spot: the people not having the least suspicion of it; although daily drawing water out of wells which were sunk into it. I entered by chance a house where there was a descent into it, and went aboard a little skiff. The master of the house, after having lighted some torches, rowing me here and there across through the pillars, which lay very deep in water, I thus discovered it. He was very intent upon catching the fish wherewith the cistern abounds, and speared some of them by the light of the torches. There is also a small light which descends from the mouth of the well, and reflects upon the water, whither the fish usually resort for air. This CISTERNA is three hundred and thirty-six feet long, a hundred and eighty-two feet broad, and two hundred and twenty Roman paces in circumference. The roof, and arches, and sides, are all of brickwork, covered with terrace, which is not the least impaired by time. The roof is supported by three hundred and thirty-six marble columns. The space of intercolumniation equals twelve feet. Each column is above forty feet nine inches in height. They stand longitudinally, in twelve ranges; and latitudinally, in twenty-eight. The capitals of these columns are partly wrought after the Corinthian order, and partly left unfinished. Over the abacus of the capital of every column is placed a great stone, which seems like another larger abacus, and supports four arches. There are abundance of wells sunk into this CISTERNA. I have seen, when it was filling, in the winter-time, a large stream of water, falling from a great pipe, with a mighty noise, until the columns up to the middle of their capitals have been covered with water. This CISTERNA stands (versus occidentem æstivum) WESTWARD of the Church of St. Sophia; being distant from it about eighty Roman paces.

Pierre Gilles; tr. E. D. Clarke

## The Forum of Augustus

This was located in the space that now lies between S. Sophia and the Mosque of Sultan Ahmet. It was here that the Emperor Constantine dedicated the statue of the Fortune of the City, as part of the ceremonies for the foundation of the new capital. The ceremony was described in the eighth-century works called *Parastaseis* (see p. 36 below).

The statue (*stele*) in the Forum received many solemn hymns. Here the government and the prefect Olbianus, the spatharii, the cubicularii and also the silentiarii, forming an escort with white candles, all dressed in white garments, brought it raised on a carriage from what is now called the Philadelphion but was then called the Proteichisma, in which there was also formerly a gate, built by Carus. But as Diakrinomenos says, it came from the so-called Magnaura. Whereupon it was set up in the Forum and, as has been said above, received many hymns and was revered as the Tyche of the city by all, including the army. And finally it was raised on a pillar in the presence of the priest and the procession, and everyone crying out the 'Kyrie eleison' a hundred times. Diakrinomenos says that many things were placed on top of the pillar where the statue (*stele*) now stands, among them imperial coinage of Constantine, the so-called sotericius, to the amount of ten thousand pounds. Then the city was acclaimed and called Constantinople, as the priests cried out 'O Lord, set it on a favourable course for boundless ages'. And when they had thus with great pomp celebrated fittingly for forty days, and the emperor had bestowed many gifts of corn on the people, each man went away to his own home. And thus on the next day the birthday of the city took place and a great race in the Hippodrome, and the emperor made many gifts there too, instituting these birthday celebrations as an eternal memorial.

                                                      Parastaseis*

Here too stood another famous pillar.

Zonaras writes, that Justinian, in the seventeenth year of his reign, set up this pillar, in the same place where formerly had stood another pillar of Theodosius the Great, bearing his statue in silver, made at the expense of his son Arcadius, which weighed 7400 pounds. When Justinian had demolished the statue and the pillar, he stripped it of a huge quantity of lead, of which he made pipes for aqueducts, which brought the water into the city.

                                                      Pierre Gilles, *op. cit.*

The statue of Justinian was one of the most notable sights of Constantinople. Procopius described it in detail:

On the summit of the column there stands an enormous horse, with his face turned towards the east – a noble sight. He appears to be walking and proceeding swiftly forwards; he raises his left fore-foot as though to tread upon the earth before him, while the other rests upon the stone beneath it, as though it would make the next step, while he places his hind feet together, so that they may be ready when he bids them move. Upon this horse sits a colossal brass figure of the Emperor, habited as Achilles, for so his costume is called; he wears hunting shoes, and his ankles are not covered by his greaves. He wears a corslet like an ancient hero, his head is covered by a helmet which seems to nod, and a plume glitters upon it. A poet would say that it was that 'star of the dog-days' mentioned by Homer. He looks towards the east, directing his course, I imagine, against the Persians; in his left hand he holds a globe, by which the sculptor signifies that all lands and seas are subject to him. He holds no sword or spear, or any other weapon, but a cross stands upon the globe, through which he has obtained his empire and victory in war; he stretches forward his right hand towards the east, and spreading his fingers out seems to bid the barbarians in that quarter to remain at home and come no further.

Procopius, The Buildings of Justinian; tr. A. Stewart

This strangely oriental structure remained intact after the sack of 1204 by the Crusaders, though the Emperor had lost the apple that had rested in his hand,

and men say there that it is a token that the Emperor hath lost a great part of his lands and lordships. . . . And men would many times put the apple into the image's hand, but it will not hold it. The apple betokeneth the lordship that he had had over all the world that is round. And the other hand he lifteth up against the east in token to menace the misdoers.

Sir John Mandeville, Travels

The column survived the fall of Constantinople but was overturned in about 1520. Pierre Gilles saw the remains broken up to build a fountain house in 1550:

This ill treatment of Theodosius by Justinian was revenged upon him by the barbarians; for they used his pillar in the same manner, and stripped it of the statue, the horse and the brass wherewith it was covered, so that it was only a bare column for some years. About thirty years ago the whole shaft was taken down to the pedestal, and that, about a year since, was demolished down to the basis, from whence I observed a spring to spout up with pipes, into a large cistern. At present there stands in the same place a water-house, and the pipes are enlarged. I lately saw the equestrian statue of Justinian, erected upon the pillar which stood here, and which had been preserved a long time, carried into the melting houses, where they cast their ordnances. Among the fragments were the leg of Justinian, which exceeded my height, and his nose, which was above nine inches long.

## The Hippodrome

The Roman monuments of the Hippodrome have not changed greatly since they were described by Ogier de Busbecq who was ambassador of the Emperor Ferdinand in Constantinople from 1554 to 1562:

In the space occupied by the ancient Hippodrome two serpents of bronze are to be seen, also a fine obelisk. Two remarkable columns are also to be seen in the city. One of them stands in the neighbour-hood of the caravanserai where we lodged, the other in the market which the Turks call Avret-Bazar, that is, the Women's Market. This column is covered with reliefs from top to bottom representing some expedition of Arcadius, who set it up and whose statue long surmounted it. It would be more accurate to describe it as a spiral than as a column, on account of the interior staircase which gives access to the summit. The column, which stands opposite the apartments usually occupied by the imperial representatives, is composed, except for the base and capital, of eight solid blocks of porphyry so fitted together that they appear to form a monolith; and indeed this is the popular belief. Where the blocks fit into one another there are laurel-wreaths surrounding the whole column, so that the joints are hidden from those who look up from below. This column, having been shaken by frequent earthquakes and burnt by a neigh-bouring fire, is splitting in many places, and is bound together by numerous iron rings to prevent it from falling to pieces. It is said to have been crowned by statues, first of Apollo, then of Constantine, and finally of Theodosius the elder, all of which were dislodged by gales or earthquakes.

The following story is told by the Greeks about the obelisk in the Hippodrome, which I have mentioned above. It was torn from its base and for many centuries lay upon the ground, until in the days of the later Emperors an architect was discovered who undertook to re-erect it on its base. When the price had been agreed upon, he set up

an elaborate apparatus consisting chiefly of wheels and ropes, where-
by he raised the immense stone and lifted it into the air, so that it was
only a finger's length from the top of the base on which it had to rest.
The spectators imagined that he had wasted his time and trouble on
such vast preparations and would have to make a fresh start with
great labour and expense. However, he was not in the least discouraged, and, profiting by his knowledge of natural science, ordered an
immense quantity of water to be fetched. With this he drenched
his machine for many hours, with the result that ropes which
held the obelisk in position gradually became soaked and naturally
tightened and contracted, so that they lifted the obelisk higher
and set it upon the base, amid the admiration and applause of the
multitude.

    O. G. de Busbecq, *Turkish Letters*; tr. E. S. Forster (Oxford 1927)

The appearance of the Hippodrome would have been in-
finitely more splendid in the middle ages. It was the sack by the
Crusaders in 1204 that put an end to most of its treasures, as
the historian Nicetas Choniates describes with unconcealed
indignation.

These barbarians, who had no love of what is beautiful, spared not
the images which stood in the *Hippodrome*, and all the other precious
works of art, but coined them into money; exchanging what was
precious for what was vile, and giving for small pieces of money
what had been wrought at an immense expense. First, they doomed
to destruction the mighty statute of HERCULES TRIHESPERUS. The
hero was represented recumbent on an osier-basket, the lion's skin
thrown over him: the fierceness of the animal was visible even in the
*brass*, and seemed to affright the idle multitude around: he was sitting
without his quiver, his bow, or his club:

        .    .    .    .

his chest was ample, his shoulders broad, his hair curled, his buttocks
brawny, his arms sinewy, and his size equal to the idea which
*Lysippus* had conceived of the real *Hercules*: he was indeed the
master-piece in *brass* of that artist.

        .    .    .    .

They next laid their hands upon the statue of the ASS LOADED, AND
THE ASS-DRIVER FOLLOWING; which *Augustus* had erected at *Nicopo-
lis*, near the promontory of *Actium*, from an incident which had
occurred to him the night before the battle of *Actium*. As he was
reconnoitring the camp of *Antony*, a man met him, driving an ass:
upon being questioned by *Cæsar*, who he was, and whither he was
going, he replied, 'My name is *Nicon*, and the ass is called *Nicander*,
and I am going to *Cæsar*'s camp.' Nor did they spare the HYÆNA and

the SHE-WOLF which had suckled *Romulus* and *Remus*; but for the sake of the few *staters* of brass, they destroyed and melted down these memorials of the origin of their race. Also the statue of the MAN WRESTLING WITH THE LION; and the·RIVER HORSE OF THE NILE whose hinder-parts terminate in a tail with prickly scales; and the ELEPHANT shaking his proboscis; and the SPHINXES with the faces of women and the bodies of wild beasts, furnished with wings as well as feet, and able to contend in air with the mightiest birds; and the UNBITTED STEED, with his ears erect, neighing, and proudly pawing the ground. There was a group, also, consisting of SCYLLA with the fierce animals into which half her body had been changed; and near her was the ship of *Ulysses*, into which these animals were leaping, and devouring some of the crew. In the *Hippodrome*, also, was placed the BRAZEN EAGLE, the work of *Apollonius Tyaneus*, and a wonderful monument of his magical power.

.   .   .   .   .

On a square plinth of marble, AN ANIMAL rested, which at first sight might have been taken for an *Ox*, only that its tail was too short, and it wanted a proper depth of throat, and its hoofs were not divided. ANOTHER ANIMAL, whose whole body was covered with rough scales, which even in brass were formidable, had seized upon the former animals with his jaws, and nearly throttled him. There were different opinions concerning these *animals*, which I shall not attempt to reconcile. Some imagined them to represent *The Basilisk and the Asp*: others, *The Crocodile and the River-horse of the Nile*. I shall content myself with describing the extraordinary contest between them; how both were mutually injuring and injured; were destroying and destroyed; were struggling for the victory; were conquering and conquered. The body of one animal was swollen from the head to the feet, and appeared greener than the colour of the frog; the lightning of his eye was quenched, and his vital powers seemed failing fast, so that the beholders might have imagined him already dead, only that his feet still supported and kept his body upright. The other animal, which was held fast in the jaws of its adversary, was moving his tail with difficulty; and, extending his mouth, was in vain struggling to escape from the deadly gripe. Thus each was inflicting death upon the other; the struggle was the same, and the victory terminated in the common destruction of both. These examples of mutual destruction I have been led to mention, not only from the sculptured representation of them, and from their taking place among fierce and savage beasts, but because this mutual carnage is not unfrequent among the nations which have waged war against us *Romans*; – they have massacred and destroyed each other, by the favour of *Christ* towards us, who 'scattereth the people that delight in war;' who has no pleasure in blood; who causes the just

man 'to tread upon the *Basilisk* and the *Asp*,' and to 'trample the lion
and the dragon under his feet.'

Nicetas Choniates, *Ravages committed in Constantinople*;
tr. E. D. Clarke★

### The Statues of Imperial Constantinople

Some of those fantastic accounts of the statues of the Hippodrome seem to come strangely from the pen of a sober historian. But the monuments of Constantinople meant more to
its inhabitants than merely relics of ancient art. Over the
centuries much of the educated understanding of classical art
had been lost, and Nicetas wrote in a tradition of 'Patriography' which aimed to explain those mysterious ornaments
of the city as best it could, usually by reference to their creation
by one or other wonder worker – Galen the physician, the
magician Apollonius of Tyana (*c* AD 50–*c* AD 120), or the
philosopher John attached to the court of the Emperor Septi-
mius Severus (193–211 AD), who had indeed done much to
beautify Constantinople. Some of these explanations were
quite ludicrous, though they survived the Turkish conquest
and attached themselves neatly to the Moslem traditions about
the Greek sages. There was, for example, a bronze mosquito
whose role was to keep mosquitoes away from the city, and an
eagle with a serpent who was responsible for keeping away
serpents.

One passage of the anonymous eighth-century work called
the *Parastaseis* shows Patriography in action, in the story of the
seven philosophers who came to the capital.

The Emperor Theodosius (II, 408–50) drove into the Hippodrome
to satisfy the philosophers. And which of them did not participate?
They were seven in number: Kranos, Karos, Pelops, Apelles, Nerva,
Silvanus, Kyrvos. These men met the emperor in the Hippodrome
to see the Olympians. And the Emperor Theodosius, seeing that the
philosophers were amazed, said to them, 'If you are amazed, philosophers, you have been out-philosophized'. And at once one of
them, Apelles by name, replied, and said '(Do not think) I am
†surprised at the horses (. . .) the rider, for I see clearly that horses
will be the riders of men when the Olympians change, and the
amazement will then fade away'. And Nerva replied, '(I see) a bad
sign (*stoicheion*) for the queen (of cities) – the statue (*stoicheion*) which
is like its meaning (*stoicheia*)'. And Silvanus, looking at the statue

(*zodion*) towards the south, up on high, leaning on its knee like . . . ,
said, 'The artificer (*stoicheiosamenos*) has done well, for in that day
times will be barren'. Kyrvos, looking at (the statue) of the People,
said, 'O People, through whom public executioners are unnecessary'. Pelops, looking at the starting-gates of the horses, said, 'Who
posed the riddle?' And when Theodosius said, 'Constantine', he
said, 'Either the philosopher has got it wrong or the emperor did not
keep to the truth'. For the philosopher was looking at the female
statue (*zodion*) inscribed with zodiacal inscriptions on all four sides,
and he said, 'You of four boundaries, through whom Constantine
. . . will come to nought'. Karos, urged by the philosophers to
speak, said, 'All these things are bad in my opinion; I mean, if these
statues (*stoicheia*) tell the truth when they are put to the test, why does
Constantinople still stand?' And Kranos, who was said to be the
leader of the Athenian philosophers, smiled and hooted with laughter. When the emperor asked 'Why are you doing that?' †(. . . he re)
plied 'Enough', more in laughter than mockery. Narcissus, a *praepo-
situs*, gave the philosopher a slap and said to him, 'You are benighted;
answer the sun like the sun he is'. When Kranos *turned the other cheek*,
Narcissus gave him (another slap). The philosopher said to Narcissus, 'It won't be you who makes me speak; it is because I am
disturbed by the inscriptions'. The riddle of Kranos is as follows: he
asked the emperor if he could inspect the statues (*stoicheia*) in the
Hippodrome, and at the emperor's command, he immediately chose
one. The statue (*agalma*) is shaped like a man, with a helmet on its
head, completely naked but with its private parts covered. The
philosopher asked 'Who set it up?' and a *lector* replied 'Valentinian
put it here'. And the philosopher said 'When did he add the donkey?'
And when the other said 'At the same time', he said 'One day a
donkey will be like a man; what a fate, for a man to follow a donkey!'
May the words of the seer not come to pass! This problem, which
Kranos expounded, was found in the books of Leo the Great,
according to Ligurius the astronomer and consul of the same
Emperor Leo.

These baffling riddles[1] show how little the antiquaries had to
go on in interpreting the monuments. Little wonder that
legends arose like that concerning a bronze bull which had
been brought from Sicily, of which it was said that, when it
bellowed, Constantinople would fall (Gilles 190–6). Collections of oracles were current, some of them attributed to the

---

[1] They are lucidly discussed by Averil Cameron and Judith Herrin in their
edition of the *Parastaseis*★.

Emperor Leo I (457–74), which associated particular monuments with epochs of the city's destruction and eventual
doom. One such concerned the column of the Xerolophos,
which was built by the Emperor Arcadius. The military scenes
carved on it were interpreted as prophecies of the fall of the
city, and accepted as such by Crusaders like Robert of Clari.
The chronicler Villehardouin elaborates:

Towards the centre of Constantinople there stood a marble column
[the column of Arcadius], one of the highest and most finely carved
that ever man's eye has seen. Murzuphlus was to be taken to the top
of that column, and made to leap down in the sight of all the people,
because it was fitting that such a signal act of justice should be seen by
everyone. Murzuphlus was led to the column, and taken to the top,
while all the people in the city flocked to the place to see that amazing
sight. Then he was cast down, and he fell from such a height that
every bone in his body was broken as soon as he reached the ground.

Now let me tell you of a marvellous coincidence. On that column
from which Murzuphlus fell were figures of various kinds, and
among them was one representing an emperor falling headlong.
Now a very long time before it had been prophesied that an emperor
would be cast down from that very column. Thus the prophecy, as
portrayed in the marble figure, came true.

Many such prophecies of the doom of the city, and of its
eventual fall to a white race from the north, were collected by
the twelfth-century classical scholar John Tzetzes. It was said
that when all the prophecies contained in the various monuments had been fulfilled, the City would come to an end.

Its longevity proved remarkable. The fulfilment of some
prophecies by the Crusaders left others open to speculation,
and the white race from the north came to be thought of as that
of Russia. The talismanic properties of the monuments survived apparently undimmed into the seventeenth century,
when Evliya recorded them in a fashion modified by time and
the admixture of Islamic tradition. His first talisman is the
column of Arcadius, again:

First talisman. In the 'Avret-Bázárí (female-slave-market), there is a
lofty column (the pillar of Arcadius) of white marble, inside of which
there is a winding staircase. On the outside of it, figures of the
soldiers of various nations, Hindustánies, Kurdistánies, and Múltá-
nies, whom Yánkó ibn Mádiyán vanquished, were sculptured by his

command; and on the summit of it there was anciently a fairy-cheeked female figure of one of the beauties of the age, which once a year gave a sound, on which many hundred thousand kinds of birds, after flying round and round the image, fell down to the earth, and being caught by the people of Rúm (Romelia), provided them with an abundant meal. Afterwards, in the age of Kostantín, the monks placed bells on the top of it, in order to give an alarm on the approach of an enemy; and subsequently, at the birth of the Prophet, there was a great earthquake, by which the statue and all the bells on the top of the pillar were thrown down topsy-turvy, and the column itself broken in pieces: but, having been formed by talismanic art, it could not be entirely destroyed, and part of it remains an extraordinary spectacle to the present day.

Of the total of seventeen talismans he discussed (plus six relating to the sea, and a further twenty-four on columns around Islambol, as he called it), all are fascinating. These are some of them:

*Third talisman.* At the head of the Serráj-kháneh (saddlers' bazar), on the summit of a column stretching to the skies (the pillar of Marcian), there is a chest of white marble, in which the unlucky-starred daughter of king Puzentín (Byzantius) lies buried; and to preserve her remains from ants and serpents was this column made a talisman.

*Fourth talisman.* At the place called Altí Mermer (the six marbles), there are six columns, every one of which was an observatory, made by some of the ancient sages. On one of them, erected by the Hakím Fílikús (Philip), lord of the castle of Kaválah, was the figure of a black fly, made of brass, which, by its incessant humming, drove all flies away from Islámból.

*Fifth talisman.* On another of the six marble columns, Iflátún (Plato) the divine made the figure of a gnat, and from that time there is no fear of a single gnat's coming into Islámbúl.

*Sixth talisman.* On another of these columns, the Hakím Bokrát (Hippocrates) placed the figure of a stork, and once a year, when it uttered a cry, all the storks which had built their nests in the city died instantly. To this time, not a stork can come and build its nest within the walls of Islámból, though there are plenty of them in the suburbs of Abú Iyyúb Ensárí.

*Seventh talisman.* On the top of another of the six marble columns, Sokrát the Hakím (*i.e.* Socrates the sage) placed a brazen cock, which clapped its wings and crowed once in every twenty-four hours, and on hearing it all the cocks of Islámbúl began to crow. And it is a fact, that to this day the cocks there crow earlier than those of other places, setting up their *kú-kirí-kúd* (*i.e.* crowing) at midnight, and thus warning the sleepy and forgetful of the approach of dawn and the hour of prayer.

*Eighth talisman.* On another of the six columns, Físághórát (Pythagoras the Unitarian), in the days of the prophet Suleïmán (Solomon), placed the figure of a wolf, made of bronze (*túj*), the terror of all other wolves; so that the flocks of the people of Islámból pastured very safely without a shepherd, and walked side by side with untamed wolves very comfortably.

*Ninth talisman.* On another of these columns were the figures in brass of a youth and his mistress in close embrace; and whenever there was any coolness or quarrelling between man and wife, if either of them went and embraced this column, they were sure that very night to have their afflicted hearts restored by the joys of love, through the power of this talisman, which was moved by the spirit of the sage Aristatálís (Aristotle).

Evliya Celebi★

## The Walls of Constantinople

The magnificent land walls of Constantinople, built by the Emperor Theodosius II (408–50), have survived the centuries well, and it is still possible to walk alongside or (largely) along the top of them, through patches of market garden and raucous impromptu bazaars, through quiet shades where men sleep away their lunch hour and bright encampments of dishevelled gipsies, through stinking heaps where dogs scavenge and rank oases where sheep and horses graze, from the ancient Golden gate where it has been incorporated in the Castle of the Seven Towers to the striking and brilliantly positioned remains of the Palace of the Porphyrogenitus. In Richard Davey's time, before lorries and trunk roads broke the peace, the variety of life to be observed was even greater.

In these clear spaces, in and about the walls, too, on a Sunday afternoon in summer, you can sometimes see the Armenians dance. They form a circle consisting of from forty to fifty men and women, holding each other by the hand or round the neck, so close together as to form a compact body, the leader of the dance being the only one who detaches himself from the rest. He holds the person next to him at arm's length. In the centre of the ring squat the musicians, whose instruments consist of a small guitar with wire strings, and a couple of bag-pipes, like those common in Scotland, only not played with the same spirit and with no attempt at harmony. The master of the ceremonies has a muslin handkerchief in his hand, which he lifts up and down, now posing himself on one foot, and then on the other, the rest of the party doing exactly the same thing with more or less clumsiness, hopping and balancing themselves from foot to foot as they slowly work round the circle; and so they dance by the hour without showing the least sign of fatigue, or indeed of any particular pleasure. The non-dancers stand in admiring groups outside the magic circle.

The spaces in front of the walls, too, are much used by professional wrestlers for practice. Wrestling is still a very lucrative profession in Constantinople, and a first-class wrestler – usually a Greek – can make a very handsome living by attending the entertainments of the rich Pashas and Effendis. The wrestlers are generally, when exercising, naked to the waist, and some of them are men of enormous strength, who can throw their opponents in a manner which would bring down the house in certain English sporting clubs. The late Sultan Abd-ul-Aziz was exceedingly fond of witnessing a wrestling match, and it was for this reason that a Greek wrestler was introduced by Abd-ul-Hamid to give evidence that his luckless predecessor had been murdered.

. . . .

I returned to the walls again and again. I saw them at sunset, when they were as crimson as the blood which so often, in bygone times, reddened the waters of their broad moat – at noonday, when the yellow stones of which they are built shimmered in the golden light – and after nightfall, when the weird beauty of the scene was enhanced a hundred-fold by the glory of an Eastern moon. Then the tall cypresses, black in the shade of night, contrasted vividly with the thousands of fantastic Turkish tombstones, white as ghosts, that stretched for miles back into the country, while the towers, gates, walls, and bastions – three rows of them – stood, here, in gloomy grandeur, and there, bathed in the radiance of that exquisite light. A thousand nightingales sang in the laurel bushes that cover the base of the prodigious wall which screens the living city from the city of the dead. How beautiful it all was! How full of memories – how calm – how utter in its peace! How overwhelming in its sadness! A gigantic monument to fallen dynasties, faiths, and peoples.

All the time, as we walked along, on that lovely night in June – meeting no one – with the long stretch of wall on one side, and the great cemetery on the other, certain serene movements in Beethoven's 'Moonlight Sonata' stole into my memory; and whenever, since then, that divine melody falls on my ear, the stately walls and towers of Stambul, and the field of death beyond them, rise vividly before me and haunt me for hours afterwards. And a hundred times a hundred have I recalled, with feelings of delight, not unmingled with sadness, that never-to-be-forgotten moonlight saunter by the walls of Constantinople.

Richard Davey★

Many of the gates in the walls have their own history and legends, like this one attached to Greek shrine of Zoodochos Pege (Spring of life) outside the Silivri Kapısı.

The gate now called Silivri Kapısı is the one by which the Greeks entered when they retook the city from the Latins. Just outside this gate, standing in a grove of trees, is the Holy Well of Balukli. I was sorry not to visit, for it is the scene of the legend of the half-fried fish. The place is rich in springs of water, and was formerly called S. Mary ad Fontem. A monk living here at the time of the taking of Constantinople, was quietly frying fish when the city was stormed. On the news reaching him that the Turks had entered the city, he indignantly denied the possibility of such an event. 'I will credit it,' he said, 'when these fish jump out of the pan into the water,' which they immediately did, and their descendants have light and dark markings, like half-fried fish. The beauty of Balukli was a favourite theme with Byzantine writers.

Mrs Max Müller, *Letters from Constantinople* (1897)

More renowned than this was the Golden Gate, erected by Theodosius I in about 390. It was plated with gold, and adorned with various sculptures, including a group of four elephants. According to Pierre Gilles, some of the reliefs were brought from the Temple of Ares at Athens. The gate was still intact in the sixteenth century, when Sir Thomas Roe and William Petty, under orders to collect marbles for the Earl of Arundel, attempted to have its sculptures removed.

We have searched all this city, and found nothing but upon one gate, called anciently Porta Aurea, built by Constantine, beautified with two mighty pillars, and upon the sides and all over it, twelve tables of fine marbles, cut into histories, some of a very great rilievo, set into the wall, with small pillars, as supporters. . . . They are, in my view, extremely decayed; but Mr Petty doth so praise them, as that he hath not seen much better in the great and costly collections of Italy. . . .

I will endeavour to get them. Promise to obtain them I cannot, because they stand upon the ancient gate, the most conspicuous of the city, though now mured up, being the entrance by the castle called the Seven Towers, and never opened since the Greek Emperors lost it: to offer to steal them, no man dares to deface the chief seat of the Grand Signior: to procure them by favour, is more impossible, such envy they bear unto us. There is only one way left; by corruption of some churchman, to dislike them, as against their law; and under that pretence, to take them to be brought into some private place; from whence, after this matter is cold and unsuspected, they may be conveyed. I have practised this for the four, and am offered to have it done for 600 crowns. To send them home chested, and freight, with some other bribes at the water side, may cost 100 more. This is a great price, and yet I rather despair of obtaining them.

Sir T. Roe, Letters; quoted from A. Michaelis,<br>Ancient Marbles in Britain (1882)

Sir Thomas Roe was right to be pessimistic, for it proved impossible to put the plan into effect. The final defeat came, after three months and the expense of a good deal of money in bribes, when the Grand Treasurer announced that the statues were enchanted, and that to remove them would cause 'some great alteration' in the city. It would have been well if the reliefs could have been obtained, since they are now altogether lost.

At the further end of the Theodosian Walls, where the Comnenian Walls of eight centuries later begin, stand the exiguous remains of the Palace of Blachernae, in the garden of the mosque of Ivaz Efendi Camii where washing flaps and children play.

From the two crumbling towers that survive, traditionally known as the Tower of Isaac Angelus and the Prison of Anemas, it is difficult to imagine the splendours described by Benjamin of Tudela when he visited the city in the last days of Imperial Constantinople.

King Emanuel has built a large palace for his residence on the sea shore . . . called Blacherne. The pillars and walls of this palace are covered with sterling gold. All the wars of the ancients as well as his own wars are represented in pictures. The throne in this palace is of gold and ornamented with precious stones. A golden crown hangs over the throne suspended on a chain of the same material, the length of which exactly admits the emperor to sit under it. This crown is ornamented with precious stones of inestimable value. Such is the lustre of these diamonds that, even without any other light, they illumine the room in which they are kept. Other objects of curiosity are met with here which nobody can adequately describe.

Benjamin of Tudela, Travels 1160-1173; tr. A. Asher (1840)

The reputation of the dungeons has perhaps never recovered from the pen of Sir Walter Scott, who imagined peculiar horrors when he had Count Robert of Paris imprisoned here by the Emperor Alexius I Comnenus. No sooner has the hero despatched a tiger sent into his prison to kill him, than he encounters another of the denizens of the imperial menagerie in the form of an orang-outang that has been trained as a servant. (The orang-outang becomes important in the blood-bath that ends the novel, by strangling the chief of the Greek conspirators). The reader who endures the longueurs of the novel is perhaps poorly repaid by the witty and acerbic portraits of the Emperor, his priggish daughter the historian Anna Comnena, and the pompous and abject chamberlains and courtiers of the Emperor.

In the year 1453 the end came. Sultan Mehmed, the Conqueror, already master of much of Asia Minor, pitched camp outside the walls of Constantinople and began a siege which was not to end until the fall of the City. The story of the siege is marvellously described in Sir Steven Runciman's book, *The Fall of Constantinople* (1969).

Constantine Dragases, the last Emperor, distinguished himself in the battle. The Emperor, already middle-aged, plunged into the thick of the battle and vanished from sight for ever.

Fly, news, unto the Frankish lands, and speed to Venice, tidings!
Constantinople they have seized, they've ta'en the famous City,
And Galata they've taken too, they've taken the Fanari;
And St Sophia is taken too, the splendid monastery,
With its four hundred symandras, its bells full two and sixty;
And every bell and its own priest, and every priest his deacon.
Within it were five hundred nuns, and there were monks a
     thousand.
Thousands of Turks had entered in, by the Romano gateway.
And Constantino Dragases is fighting like to Charon.
He strikes to right, he strikes to left, and naught can stay his ardour;
Like a dark cloud he falls on them, and no man can escape him,
'Twould seem as he'd the Turks destroy, and save Constantinople;
Until a Turk, a stalwart Turk, at last slew Constantino.
O weep, my brothers, weep amain, weep for the orphan'd city!
Our Constantino they have slain, slain him who was our standard.
Haste, brothers, to the Patriarch, and pray that he come hither,
And bring the holy censers too, that we may hold the fun'ral.

An onset fierce the Turks have made, and they, the Janissaries;
And the Emir has given command to massacre the Christians.
Three days long have they slaughtered us, three days and three
nights slaughtered,
And Notaras they've massacred, both him and all his kindred.
Fall'n is the City! fall'n into the claws of Hagar's Children!
'The death of Constantine Dragases' from L M J Garnett, *Greek
Folk Poetry* (1896)

Even Mehmed's official historian, the Greek Kritovoulos,
was shocked by the extent of the destruction.

And the desecrating and plundering and robbing of the churches –
how can one describe it in words? Some things they threw in
dishonor on the ground – ikons and reliquaries and other objects
from the churches. The crowd snatched some of these, and some
were given over to the fire while others were torn to shreds and
scattered at the crossroads. The last resting-places of the blessed men
of old were opened, and their remains were taken out and dis-
gracefully torn to pieces, even to shreds, and made the sport of the
wind while others were thrown on the streets.

Chalices and goblets and vessels to hold the holy sacrifice, some of
them were used for drinking and carousing, and others were broken
up or melted down and sold. Holy vessels and costly robes richly
embroidered with much gold or brilliant with precious stones and
pearls were some of them given to the most wicked men for no good
use,

.   .   .   .

And holy and divine books, and others mainly of profane literature
and philosophy, were either given to the flames or dishonorably
trampled under foot. Many of them were sold for two or three
pieces of money, and sometimes for pennies only, not for gain so
much as in contempt. Holy altars were torn from their foundations and overthrown. The walls of sanctuaries and cloisters were
explored, and the holy places of the shrines were dug into and overthrown in the search for gold. Many other such things they dared to
do.

Those unfortunate Romans who had been assigned to other parts
of the wall and were fighting there, on land and by the sea, supposed
that the City was still safe and had not suffered reverses, and that
their women and children were free – for they had no knowledge at
all of what had happened. They kept on fighting lustily, powerfully
resisting the attackers and brilliantly driving off those who were
trying to scale the walls. But when they saw the enemy in their rear,
attacking them from inside the City, and saw women and children

being led away captives and shamefully treated, some were over-whelmed with hopelessness and threw themselves with their weapons over the wall and were killed, while others in utter despair dropped their weapons from hands already paralyzed, and surrendered to the enemy without a struggle, to be treated as the enemy chose.

> Kritovoulos (Critoboulos), *History of Mehmed the Conqueror*;
> tr. C. T. Riggs (Princeton, 1954)

'Lament for Constantinople'

Sun rise up everywhere and shine throughout the universe,
Extend your rays through all the world;
But shine no more on great Constantinople, once our pride
And now the city of the Turk.
It's wrong your rays should shine and see the crimes of those vile
    dogs:
Making churches into stables, burning icons, tearing up
And trampling on the gilded gospels, and insulting
The crosses, stealing their adornments and their emeralds,
And setting fire to holy relics, and throwing them in the sea,
Taking their gems and all their wealth, and getting drunk from
    chalices.
Kings, sons of kings, great empresses, nobles and gently born,
Wise men and simple, famous ones, both married men and widows
Old ladies, maidens, soldiers
(The wind saw not, the sun saw not, how they sang and prayed in
    the holy monasteries)
Were seized without mercy, abused and insulted!
They take them now to Turkey to sell them into slavery,
They scatter them abroad to the rising and setting sun,
Naked, unransomed, beaten and in starvation,
To share with oxen, sheep, horses and buffalo.

Do not endure it, heaven, and earth embrace them not!
Sun, darken now your light, moon shed yours not on them!

> from L. Politis *Poietike Anthologia* II (Athens 1965); tr. R. S.

## 2. Stamboul/Istanbul

Say Istanbul and a seagull comes to mind
Half silver and half foam, half fish and half bird.
Say Istanbul and a fable comes to mind
The old wives' tale that we have all heard.

Say Istanbul and a mighty steamship comes to mind
Whose songs are sung in the mudbaked huts of Anatolia:
Milk flows from her taps, roses bloom on her masts;
In the dreams of my childhood in Anatolia's mudbaked huts
I'd sail on her to Istanbul and back.

Say Istanbul and mottled grapes come to mind
With three candles burning bright on the basket –
Suddenly along comes a girl so ruthlessly female
So lovely to look at that you gasp,
Her lips ripe with grape honey,
A girl luscious and lustful from top to toe –
Southern wind and willow branch and the dance of joy –
As the song goes, 'Like a ship at sea
My heart is tossed and wrecked again.'

　　　　　　　　・　・　・　・

Say Istanbul and a barge comes to mind
Loaded with onions, painted poison-green on coral-red
Sailing in from the Black Sea ports winter and summer
With one more patch on its filthy sail each time
And the rust of its iron rods on our tongue

Its motors speeding along our pulsebeat into our hearts
A mermaid with huge scale-covered buttocks.

Say Istanbul and barges come to mind
Humble wanderers on the high seas
With names like The Sea Tiger or The Triumphant Sword.

Say Istanbul and Sinan the Great Architect comes to mind
His ten fingers soaring like mighty plane trees
On the skyline
Then row upon row of shacks and shanties
Where smoke filth and blight ruthlessly spread.
Our city suckles dwarfs at her giant's breasts.

　Bedri Rahmi Eyuboğlu, *The Sign of Istanbul*; tr. Talat S. Halman

　　The transformation of Constantinople into a Moslem
city began at once after conquest, with the conversion of
churches to mosques and with the construction of the Sultan's
Palace. The pomp of the new rulers is vividly evoked by
one of the first English visitors to the Turkish city, Tom
Coryate (in 1613), alive to every thrill and sparkle of a foreign
culture.

The eight and twentieth of April, being Wednesday, about five of the
clocke in the morning, my Lord and his Company (whereof my selfe

was one) went into Adrinople street in Constantinople neere to the gate of Adrinople, to see the Grand Signior come into the Citie from Adrinople, whether hee went upon the one and twentieth day of December last, the pompe of it was so gallant that I never saw the like in my life; neither doe I thinke that the like hath beene used amongst any Princes of the world saving these Musulmen, since the time of the triumphs of the Romane Emperours, when they went to the Capitol, after the conquering of some famous Country: the place where hence he came that morning is called Dowt Bashaw, a place standing by it self in the Countrey some three miles from Constantinople, the people that attended upon his person at that time, were said to amount to the number of 15000. First rode the Subbashaw of Constantinople and Galata, with one hundred men on horsebacke, and other servants also they had which went a foot, carrying certaine Muskets in their hands. Next followed French Souldiers, a company of fugitive Rogues, that to get a large pay somewhat more then they have, either in their owne Countrey, or could get in the Low Countries fled to Constantinople to bee entertained by the Grand Signior, of whom the greatest part of them doth receive halfe a Doller a day for their pay: their Collonell rode with some twentie of his principall men, and all the rest to the number of one hundred with Muskets on foot, after them the Officers of the Arsenall a foot, with the chiefe of them a horsebacke, certaine of them carrying a Gallie with a man in it, a verie strange and ridiculous conceit: for indeed everie one laughed heartily at it; after them came Squibsters, but how many in number I could not understand; then came a great multitude of Gemiglandes all on foot, whereof one had a feather sticking in his flesh, even in his face somewhat neere to his right eye: then a Coach covered with cloth of Gold, which served for the Grand Signiors riding, wherein himselfe and his Sultana did use to ride: then a Delee, that is a foole with a Bears skinne upon his backe, then Chauses on horsebacke, with Brasse and Iron Maces in their hands, which they carried upon their right shoulders, these were in number 200. and their servants a foot sixe hundred, and after them seven Coaches, then came Janizaries on foot foure thousand with Muskets; some of these weare Beares skinnes; and after them other Janizaries on horsebacke, everie one having a Speare in his hand, with a little Flag in the same; after them againe other kind of Janizaries that weare leather Cappes, on the top of which were great white Ostriches feathers: then came certaine Horses driven by men of purpose, that carried water in Leather Bottles for men to drinke in: then certaine Turkish Saints with verie long haire and ragged clothes. Next followed a black Elephant, after them Ladies, hundred & twelve on horsebacke, with three hundred men attending on them, and the Muftie: then head Visiers, being eight or nine of the most principall of Turkie, with one hundred Chauses their attendants; then squeaking Musicke both Vocall and Instrumentall. The Darvises a foot using a ridiculous shooting and elevation of their voyce. Then some one hundred Pikemen a foot, who besides their Pikes carried also Bowes and Arrowes. Then Mahomets kinsmen a horsebacke, with greene Halberts. Then Vice Cadies on horsebacke, then Ladies againe; then nine goodly Horses of the Kings led by Chiauses, verie richly adorned with Saddles and Horse clothes of great price, a mervellous rich Target, being hanged at the Pomell of the Saddle of each Horse made of massie beaten Gold, and garnished with varietie of precious Stones, each of these Horses is saide to be worth two hundred pound sterling. Next the Kings Grey-hounds, being ledde and clothed with coverings of Cloth of Gold: of these there were at the least one hundred. Then came Chiauses on horsebacke, namely, twentie to attend the Kings person, and had fiftie servants more attending upon them: then rode one with a Streamer of greene Taffata, wherein was an Arabian Inscription in very great Letters; this is said to have beene used by Mahomet himselfe their Prophet, in his warres with Cosoroes King of Persia and others also. Neere unto this Ensigne, was carried another Ensigne (which is the common Standard that they use in their warres, as heeretofore the Romanes used the Eagle) that is the taile of the Horse fastened upon the toppe of a long Staffe. Next went his Archers, called Solackes, with Bowes and Arrowes attired in fine linnen shirts that reached to the calfe of their legges and long sleeves curiously wrought with delicate seames of Needle Worke. Also they had coverings for their head (Hattes I cannot fitly call them) which consisted of Silver fairely guilt, with long feathers, &c.

> Thomas Coryate, Travels, in *Purchas his Pilgrimes* (1625)

But William Lithgow was in his habitual dyspeptic mood when he described the city in 1610.

Truely I may say of Constantinople, as I said once of the world, in the Lamentado of my second Pilgrimage;

> A painted Whoore, the maske of deadly sin,
> Sweet faire without, and stinking foule within.

For indeed outwardly it hath the fairest show, and inwardly in the streets being narrow, and most part covered, the filthiest & deformed buildings in the world; the reason of its beauty, is, because being situate on moderate prospective heights, the universall tectures, a farre off, yeeld a delectable show, the covertures being erected like the backe of a Coach after the Italian fashion with gutterd tyle. But being entred within, there is nothing but a stinking deformity, and a loathsome contrived place; without either internall domesticke furniture, or externall decorements of fabricks palatiatly extended. Notwithstanding that for its situation, the delicious wines, & fruits, the temperate climat, the fertile circumjacent fields, and for the Sea Hellespont, and pleasant Asia on the other side: it may truely be called the Paradice of the earth.

William Lithgow*

Ottoman Constantinople had none the less its own splendours, however they might differ from the rich and brittle brilliance of Byzantium. Over the ruins of the Imperial Palaces and the abandoned churches of the Greeks arose a new imperial city, dedicated to the Peace of Islam that still reigns in the many beautiful mosques in their green courts, in the glowing gardens of Topkapi Palace and the Kiosks of the Sultans. But life was gaudy as well as calm: the mystical brilliance of Byzantine mosaic was displaced by the lustrous and intricate harmony of Iznik tiles, the embroidered robes and tall crowns of the Byzantine emperors and their guards by the no less elaborate brocades, the no less fantastic headgear of the Sultans and their janissaries. If justice or its absence was as bloody as before (see introduction), and the position of women more secluded than ever among the Greeks, the commercial life that is no shame to the Moslem (as it often is to the Christian) added new variety to the Byzantine scene. The panorama of Istanbuli commerce was brilliantly exhibited in the procession of the 1001 guilds that passed before the Sultan's kiosk opposite the Sublime Porte.

All these guilds pass on wagons or on foot, with the instruments of their handicraft, and are busy with great noise at their work. The carpenters prepare wooden houses, the builders raise walls, the wood-cutters pass with loads of trees, the sawyers pass sawing them, the masons whiten their shops, the chalk-makers crunch chalk and whiten their faces, playing a thousand tricks. . . . The toy-makers of Eyüp exhibit on wagons a thousand trifles and toys for children to play with. In their train you see bearded fellows and men of thirty years of age, some dressed as children with hoods and bibs, some as nurses who care for them, while the bearded babies cry after playthings or amuse themselves with spinning tops or sounding little trumpets. . . . The Greek fur-makers of the market-place of Mahmut Paşa form a separate procession, with caps of bear-skin and breeches of fur. Some are dressed from head to foot in lion's, leopard's and wolves' skin, with kalpaks of sable on their heads.

Some dress again in skins, as wild men and savages, so that those who see them are afraid, each one being held by strong chains and led by six or seven people, while others are dressed as strange creatures with their feet apparently turned to the sky, while they walk with their real feet upon the ground. . . . The Bakers pass working at their trade, some baking and throwing small loaves among the crowd. They also make for this occasion immense loaves, the size of the cupola of a hamam, covered with sesame and fennel; these loaves are carried on wagons which are dragged along by seventy to eighty pairs of oxen. No oven being capable of holding loaves of so large a size, they bake them in pits made for that purpose, where the loaf is covered from above with cinders, and from the four sides baked slowly by the fire. It is worth while to see it. . . . These guilds pass before the Alay Köşkü with a thousand tricks and fits, which it is impossible to describe, and behind them walk their Sheikhs followed by their pages playing the eight-fold Turkish music.

. . . .

The Emperor decided that the sugar-bakers should go first, to the great annoyance of the Fish-Cooks, who appealed to their patron Jonah and blamed the Helvacıs, who reproached the Fish-Cooks, saying fish was very unwholesome and infatuating food. In proof they adduced what happened when the famous Yazici-zadeh Mohammed Efendi, the author of the Mohammedieh, sent his work in the year 847 (1443) to Balkh and Bukhara. When the doctors of those two towns were told that the author had written it on the seashore shut up in a cave, they decided that he could never have eaten a fish, because a man who eats much fish loses his intellect and never could have compiled so valuable a work. The disciples of the author averred the fact that neither he, his father, nor his grandfather had ever eaten fish. To this reproach the Helvacıs added the praise of the Helva contained in the Kur'an, and quoted the Prophet, who once said: 'The faithful are sweet, the wicked sour.' Having put forth their claims in this way in the Emperor's presence, they carried the votes of the whole assembly that the precedence was due to them rather than to the Fish-Cooks, and accordingly obtained the imperial diploma.

Evliya Celebi*

There is a marvellous recreation of this procession in John Freely's *Stamboul Sketches*, the best evocation of the atmosphere of Istanbul that I have read.

Let us again make a peripatetic tour of the city, alive to the echoes of the past, and starting naturally from the Sultans' Palace.

## Topkapi Palace

Richard Davey quotes an interesting letter from the Genoese archives, written in 1542, which he translates for our benefit.

'When you go to the Seraglio,' says the writer, who evidently quotes his wife's account of her visit,[1] 'you have to enter by a gate which is very richly gilded, and is called the "Gate of Perpetual Delight."[2] Sometimes you will see over it, stuck upon the point of a pole, the head of a Grand Vizir, or of some other personage, who has been decapitated early in the morning, at the caprice of the Grand Signor. Then you enter the first courtyard, which is surrounded by arches, like the cloister of a Franciscan monastery. This is where the white eunuchs live, and you will generally see a number of them walking about, dressed in their extraordinary costumes, with their pointed turbans and flowing robes of striped silk. They look for all the world like mummified old women, and are, for the most part, very thin and shrivelled. Their duty is to attend upon the Grand Signor when he goes out in State, and also to keep order among the white pages, mostly Christian lads, stolen from their parents, to the number of about 300 to 400 each year; some of these boys are very good-looking and wear magnificent dresses. Their cheeks are plump, and their eyebrows (painted) meet, and they wear very rich garments. Very strange things are told of them, but these things are common hereabouts, and nobody thinks much about them.

'Next you pass into another courtyard, where dwells the Kizlar Aghasi, or chief of the Black Eunuchs, a very great personage indeed, who holds the same rank as the Grand Vizir. There are several hundred black eunuchs. These, in contradistinction to the white (who, as I have said, are very thin), are monstrously fat. They are the veriest savages, and rarely acquire the knowledge of how to read or write. They are deputed to keep watch and ward over the Kadinés, or wives and favourites of the Sultan, who has innumerable female slaves, who dwell in a series of small but very beautiful palaces, each under the management of a great lady of the Court. No one knows the number of these ladies; there must be hundreds of them, and they are of all nationalities. When they go out into the city (which they do very rarely) they are so closely veiled that you cannot distinguish their features, but only their eyes.

Richard Davey*

[1] Why? Only the Harem was closed to men.
[2] Bab-i-Humayun.

The Sultan's women were housed in the harem, one of the
largest buildings in the courts of the Palace.

Lady Mary Wortley Montagu, the wife of the ambassador
from 1716 to 1718, was able to visit the harem with a lady's eye
for the decor and the costumes.

I went to see the Sultana Hafitén, favourite of the late Emperor
Mustapha, who, you know (or perhaps you don't know) was deposed by his brother, the reigning Sultan Achmet, and died a few
weeks after, being poisoned, as it was generally believed. . . . She
has no black eunuchs for her guard, her husband being obliged to
respect her as a queen, and not inquire at all into what is done in her
apartment, where I was led into a large room, with a sofa the whole
length of it, adorned with white marble pillars like a *ruelle*, covered
with pale blue figured velvet on a silver ground, with cushions of the
same, where I was desired to repose till the Sultana appeared, who
had contrived this manner of reception to avoid rising up at my
entrance, though she made me an inclination of her head, when I rose
up to her. I was very glad to observe a lady that had been distinguished by the favour of an emperor, to whom beauties were every
day presented from all parts of the world. But she did not seem to me
to have ever been half so beautiful as the fair Fatima I saw at
Adrianople; though she had the remains of a fine face, more decayed
by sorrow than time. But her dress was something so surprisingly
rich, I cannot forbear describing it to you. She wore a vest called
*donalma*, and which differs from a *caftán* by longer sleeves, and
folding over at the bottom. It was of purple cloth, straight to her
shape, and thick set, on each side, down to her feet, and round the
sleeves, with pearls of the best water, of the same size as their buttons
commonly are. You must not suppose I mean as large as those of my
Lord —, but about the bigness of a pea; and to these buttons large
loops of diamonds, in the form of those gold loops so common upon
birthday coats. This habit was tied, at the waist, with two large
tassels of smaller pearl, and round the arms embroidered with large
diamonds: her shift fastened at the bottom with a great diamond,
shaped like a lozenge; her girdle as broad as the broadest English
ribbon, entirely covered with diamonds. Round her neck she wore
three chains, which reached to her knees: one of large pearl, at the
bottom of which hung a fine coloured emerald, as big as a turkey-
egg; another, consisting of two hundred emeralds, close joined
together, of the most lively green, perfectly matched, every one as
large as a half-crown piece, and as thick as three crown pieces; and
another of small emeralds, perfectly round. But her earrings eclipsed
all the rest. They were two diamonds, shaped exactly like pears, as
large as a big hazel-nut. Round her talpoche she had four strings of

pearl, the whitest and most perfect in the world, at least enough to
make four necklaces, every one as large as the Duchess of Marl-
borough's, and of the same size, fastened with two roses, consisting
of a large ruby for the middle stone, and round them twenty drops of
clean diamonds to each. Besides this, her head-dress was covered
with bodkins of emeralds and diamonds. She wore large diamond
bracelets, and had five rings on her fingers, all single diamonds,
(except Mr. Pitt's) the largest I ever saw in my life. It is for jewellers
to compute the value of these things; but, according to the common
estimation of jewels in our part of the world, her whole dress must be
worth above a hundred thousand pounds sterling. This I am very
sure of, that no European queen has half the quantity; and the
empress's jewels, though very fine, would look very mean near hers.

Lady Mary Wortley Montagu, *Letters*

Edward Daniel Clarke managed to create a nice adventure
from his visit to the harem in 1801.

The *German* gardener, who had daily access to different parts of the
*Seraglio*, offered to conduct us not only over the gardens, but
promised, if we would come singly, during the season of the
*Ramadan*, (when the guards, being up all night, would be stupefied
during the day with sleep and intoxication,) to undertake the greater
risk of shewing to us the interior of the *Charem*, or the apartments of
the women.

A small staircase leads from these apartments, to two chambers
below, paved with marble, and as cold as any cellar. Here a more
numerous assemblage of women are buried, as it were, during the
heat of summer. The first is a sort of antechamber to the other; by the
door of which, in a nook of the wall, are placed the *Sultan's* slippers,
of common yellow morocco, and coarse workmanship. Having
entered the marble chamber immediately below the *kiosk*, a marble
bason presents itself, with a fountain in the centre, containing water
to the depth of about three inches, and a few very small fishes.
Answering to the platform mentioned in the description of the *kiosk*,
is another, exactly of a similar nature, closely latticed, where the
ladies sit during the season of their residence in this place. We were
pleased with observing a few things they had carelessly left upon the
sofas, and which characterized their mode of life. Among these was
an *English* writing-box, of black varnished wood, with a sliding
cover, and drawers; the drawers containing coloured writing paper,
reed pens, perfumed wax, and little bags made of embroidered satin,
in which their *billets-doux* are sent, by negro slaves, who are both
mutes and eunuchs. That *liqueurs* are drunk in these secluded chambers is evident; for we found labels for bottles, neatly cut out with

scissars, bearing *Turkish* inscriptions, with the words '*Rosoglio*', '*Golden Water*', and '*Water of Life*'. These we carried off as trophies of our visit to the place, and distributed them among our friends.

E. D. Clarke★

Some fifty years later, when reform and tourism had made the palace rather easier of access, it was inevitable that Thackeray would enthuse only over the less likely parts of the spectacle.

The kitchens are the most sublime part of the seraglio. There are nine of these great halls, for all ranks, from his highness downwards; where many hecatombs are roasted daily, according to the accounts; and where cooking goes on with a savage Homeric grandeur. Chimneys are despised in these primitive halls; so that the roofs are black with the smoke of hundreds of furnaces, which escapes through apertures in the domes above. These, too, give the chief light in the rooms, which streams downwards, and thickens and mingles with the smoke, and so murkily lights up hundreds of swarthy figures busy about the spits and the cauldrons. Close to the door by which we entered, they were making pastry for the sultanas; and the chief pastrycook, who knew my guide, invited us courteously to see the process, and partake of the delicacies prepared for those charming lips. How those sweet lips must shine after eating these puffs! First, huge sheets of dough are rolled out till the paste is about as thin as silver paper: then an artist forms the dough-muslin into a sort of drapery, curling it round and round in many fanciful and pretty shapes, until it is all got into the circumference of a round metal tray in which it is baked. Then the cake is drenched in grease most profusely; and, finally, a quantity of syrup is poured over it, when the delectable mixture is complete. The moon-faced ones are said to devour immense quantities of this wholesome food; and, in fact, are eating grease and sweetmeats from morning till night. I don't like to think what the consequences may be, or allude to the agonies which the delicate creatures must inevitably suffer.

The good-natured chief pastrycook filled a copper basin with greasy puffs; and, dipping a dubious ladle into a large cauldron, containing several gallons of syrup, poured a liberal portion over the cakes, and invited us to eat. One of the tarts was quite enough for me: and I excused myself on the plea of ill health from imbibing any more grease and sugar. But my companion, the dragoman, finished some forty puffs in a twinkling. They slipped down his opened jaws as the sausages do down Clown's throats in a pantomime. His moustachios shone with grease, and it dripped down his beard and fingers. We thanked the smiling chief pastrycook, and rewarded him hand-

somely for the tarts. It is something to have eaten of the dainties
prepared for the ladies of the harem; but I think Mr. Cockle ought to
get the names of the chief sultanas among the exalted patrons of his
Antibilious Pills.

From the kitchens we passed into the second court of the seraglio,
beyond which is death.

W. M. Thackeray, *Notes of a Journey from Cornhill
to Grand Cairo* (1846)

Near the Palace stood a Byzantine church which the early
Sultans brought into unusual re-use as a menagerie. This
seems, according to the researches of Cyril Mango, to have
been the church of St John the Evangelist, though the site was
changed some time in the seventeenth century. (There is still a
small zoo in the Gülhane Gardens below the Palace). It was the
first church which was described by Thomas Gainsford in
1618.

The banquetting-houses, wherein his concubines and boyes are
aparted from the court hurliburly, exposes divers manner of structures and seeme indeed severall palaces, among whom there is one
called a Caska without the wall of the seraglio, close to the sea-side,
where hee accustometh to take his gally of the delicatest and richest
presence that ever I beheld: for it is a quadrant of seven arches on a
side cloister wise, like the Rialto walke in Venice; in the midst riseth a
core of three or foure roomes with chimnies, whose mantell trees are
of silver, the windows curiously glazed and besides protected with
an iron grate all guilt over most gloriously: the whole frame so set
with opals, rubies, emeralds, burnisht with golde, painted with
flowers, and graced with inlayed worke of porphery, marble, jet,
jasper, and delicate stones, that I am perswaded there is not such a
bird cage in the world. Under the walls are stables for sea horses
called Hippopatami, which is a monstrous beast taken in Nilus,
Elephants, Tigres, and Dolphines: sometimes they have Crocadiles
and Rhinoceros: within are Roebuckes, white Partridges, and
Turtles, the bird of Arabia, and many beasts and fowles of Affrica
and India. The walkes are shaded with Cipres, Cedar, Turpentine,
and trees which wee only know by their names, amongst which,
such as affoord sustenance, are called figs, almonds, olives, pomegranets, limons, orenges, and such like: but it should seeme they are
here as it were enforced and kept in order with extraordinary
diligence: for the sunne kisseth them not with that fervency, as may
make them large, or ripen in their proper kindes.

Thomas Gainsford, *The Glory of England* (1618)

## The Slave Market

Naturally enough one of the sights which most fascinated and horrified visitors to Stamboul was the slave market, which was near the Column of Arcadius.

I have seene men and women as usually sold here in Markets, as Horses and other beasts are with us: The most part of which are Hungarians, Transilvanians, Carindians, Istrians, and Dalmatian Captives, and of other places besides, which they can overcome. Whom, if no compassionable Christian will buy, or relieve; then must they either turne Turke, or be addicted to perpetuall slavery. Here I remember of a charitable deede, done for a sinful end, and thus it was; A Ship of Marseilles, called the great Dolphin, lying here forty dayes at the Galata, the Maister Gunner, named Monsieur Nerack, and I falling in familiar acquaintance, upon a time he told me secretly that he would gladly for Conscience and Merits sake, redeeme some poore Christian slave from Turkish Captivity. To the which, I applauded his advice, and told him the next Friday following I would assist him to so worthy an action: Friday comes, and he and I went for Constantinople, where the Market of the slaves being ready, we spent two houres in viewing, and reviewing five hundredth Males and Females. At last I pointed him to have brought an old man or woman, but his minde was contrary set, shewing me that he would buy some virgin, or young widdow, to save their bodies undefloured with Infidels. The price of a virgin was too deare for him, being a hundred Duckets, and widdows were farre under, and at an easier rate: When we did visite and search them that we were mindfull to buy, they were strip'd starke naked before our eyes, where the sweetest face, the youngest age, and whitest skin was in greatest value and request: The Jewes sold them, for they had bought them from the Turkes: At last we fell upon a Dalmatian widdow, whose pittifull lookes, and sprinkling teares, stroke my soule almost to the death for compassion: whereupon I grew earnest for her reliefe, and he yeelding to my advice, she is bought and delivered unto him, the man being 60 years of age, and her price 36 Duckets. We leave the market and came over againe to Galata, where he and I tooke a Chamber for her, and leaving them there, the next morning I returned earely, suspecting greatly the dissembling devotion of the Gunner to be nought but luxurious lust, and so it proved: I knocked at the Chamber doore, that he had newly locked, and taken the key with him to the ship, for he had tarried with her all that night; and she answering me with teares, told me all the manner of his usage, wishing her selfe to be againe in her former captivity: whereupon I went a shipboord to him, & in my griefe I swore, that if he abused her any more after that manner, and not returned to her distresse, her Christian liberty; I would first make it knowne to his Maister the Captaine of the ship, and then to the French Ambassadour: for he was mindfull also, his lust being satisfied to have sold her over againe to some other: At which threatning the old Pallyard became so fearefull, that he entred in a reasonable condition with me, and the ship departing thence six dayes thereafter, he freely resigned to me her life, her liberty and freedome: which being done, and he gone, under my hand before divers Greekes, I subscribed her libertie, and hyr'd her in the same Taverne for a yeare, taking nothing from her, for as little had she to give me, except many blessings and thankefull prayers: This French Gunner was a Papist, and heare you may behold the dregs of his devotion, and what seven nights leachery cost him, you may cast up the reckoning of 36 Duckets.

William Lithgow*

## The Book Bazaar

At the other end of the modern bazaar, near the Beyazidiye, is the market of the second-hand booksellers. Few unsuspected treasures lurk here now in the welter of ancient retinted postcards, antediluvian textbooks of chemistry in English, French and German, unsaleable works of history and a few choice illuminated Arabic books. In the seventeeth century Jacob Spon found richer store.

We knew that there is at Constantinople a bazaar where are sold manuscript books on the various sciences, in Turkish, Arabic and Persian, and that it is dangerous for Christians to go there, because that their books will be profaned by being sold to us. I discovered this for myself, when passing at Prusa a stall where there were Arabic books for sale; I wished to offer for them, but was repulsed shamefully with the insulting word Giaour which they generally apply to Christians. I withdrew hastily without replying, fearful of receiving some injury. Monsieur Vatz [a Scotsman resident in Constantinople, presumably called Watts], told us that the Turks held annual registers of all that happened throughout their Empire, and of their wars with their neighbours. That one could obtain a copy of these Annals in 5 or 6 large volumes for 200 ecus. That there are historians and writers in the Seraglio who are paid to write these. That one might find another fine book on the government of the Ottoman Empire. That he had himself bought a goodly quantity of Turkish and Arabic books, among which were several very curious ones. . . . An Arabic-Turkish dictionary. A book of Turkish songs, including many ancient ones such as those of Avicenna son of Albuquerque. Alphabets in all languages.

A book of all the revolutions of the kingdom of Egypt, made by an old sheikh or doctor of Cairo who understood astrology. . . . On other visits he showed us a history of Tamburlaine in Arabic. . . . Two books of talismans. . . . He assured us that he had seen a very old book of astronomy, which supposed the use of the magnetic needle, although in truth it was not applied for navigation but for other astronomical purposes. He also showed us a general history of Grand Cairo, and a description of the churches of Constantinople at the time it was taken by the Ottomans, both written in Arabic. And he assured us that there were public professors at Constantinople and at Cairo to teach astrology, astronomy, geometry, arithmetic, poetry, Arabic and Persian.

Jacob Spon, *Voyage* (1679); tr. R. S.

## Yedi Kule

If a visitor could feel a frisson even in the book bazaar, how much more when he beheld the grim dungeons of the Seven Towers, the last resting place of many an enemy of the Sultan. This massive fortress was built around the Golden Gate of Byzantium, and every room is linked with tales of murder – many now indicated by brief placards. Here was the well of blood where the heads of the condemned were thrown; here may still be seen battered instruments of torture as well as the painstakingly carved inscriptions, in Latin, French and Hungarian of those condemned to pass years in its confines. One prisoner who was lucky enough to get out again to describe it was the French officer François Pouqueville, who was arrested in Greece and brought here in the course of the Greek War of Independence.

Since the death of this monarch (Osman), the Seven Towers have been the theatre of the most sanguinary executions, of which each step gives a melancholy proof. On one side is the tomb of a vizier, who, for his services in conquering the isle of Candia, was put to death. On the walls are numerous dull sentences, written and signed by Turks and Greek princes who were murdered at different times; while the towers are filled with chains, ancient arms, tombs, and ruins: the 'Well of Blood', frightful dungeons, and damp vaults, in which are many passages from the koran, and other inscriptions, added to the dismal croakings of vultures and ravens, and the beating of the waves, fill up the melancholy picture.

I shall now give some account of the external form, extent, and signs of the antiquity of this castle, which no other traveller has described.

Besides what I have above related, the Seven Towers are particularly known in Europe as the prison in which the Turks shut up the ambassadors and ministers of the powers with whom they are at war. At the time of which I am speaking, the place contained the French legation and a number of officers, amongst whom I was comprised. The persons detained in this prison are distinguished from all other prisoners of war by having a taïm, or boarding table, allowed them by the sultan, as well as by the name of hostages, of which the Turks are accustomed to speak very high; according to them it is a special favour to be the moussafirs or hostages of the sultan; and indeed, though they are closely guarded, their detention may be considered as a favour, when compared with the situation of the other prisoners of war, whom the barbarians condemn to public labours in the Bagne, or prison for slaves.

. . . .

This [second] tower is in no manner like the first, as it contains nothing but damp and horrible dungeons, in which thousands of prisoners devoted to death have made their lamentations: the principal of these caves is known by the name of the 'Dungeon of Blood', and deserves a particular description. The first door which leads to it, is of wood, and opens into a corridor twelve feet long by four wide; at the end of which, is an ascent of two steps, by which you reach another door of wrought iron, that opens into a semi-circular gallery, which is likewise terminated by a wrought-iron door. At length, ten feet farther you arrive at a door composed of enormous beams, which opens into the dungeon, and into which I think no one can enter without being seized with an involuntary shuddering. Into this place of misery, the light of heaven never penetrates, nor was the voice of a friend ever heard in it, to console the victim whom despotism had condemned to death.

The sombre glare of flambeaux cast a deadly light round this dungeon, so much was the air deprived of its vivifying particles; by its reflections, however, we were able to read a few inscriptions, that had been cut on the humid marble; but the eye could not reach to the roof of this noisome vault, which was buried in darkness. In the middle of this sarcophagus is a well on a level with the ground, which is half-closed by two flag-stones that have been conveyed to its mouth: the Turks give it the name of the 'Well of Blood,' because they used to throw into it the heads of those who were decapitated in the dungeon, from which circumstance it acquired its name. Thus are buried in oblivion the names of many of the greatest men in the empire, whom a mere look of the Sultan can cause to be destroyed at his pleasure.

In the tower which contains the Cavern of Blood, there is a flight of steps leading to several other cells, the height of which being greater than that of the ramparts, admits of the prisoners seeing Constantinople through narrow loop holes. Here the persons detained as hostages were formerly shut; but they are now allowed to hire a lodging, as I shall speedily explain. The same flight of stairs leads to the platform of this tower, and to the triumphal arch, as well as to the second tower; but the entrance to the latter is closed at top by a portcullis, covered with shrubs and ruins, which proves that this spot has been unfrequented for many years.

. . . .

The hopes of our liberty were as distant as ever; we had even lost them entirely, when we learned, that Lord Elgin was closely connected with the Russian Ambassador; for though this minister had never acted against us, yet we dreaded lest any alliance should prolong our captivity. Things, however, took a fortunate turn; and firmans were issued for recalling the prisoners who had been transported to the fortresses of the Black Sea and Asia Minor. We were less watched over, and at length, after a seclusion of twenty-five months, the dawn of liberty seemed to break upon us; the gates of the Seven Towers were opened; and though my firman was only an order for removing me to the house of correction at Pera, I knew that I should soon be liberated.

F. Pouqueville, *Travels in Greece and Turkey* (1820)

Second only to the secular attractions of Ottoman Stamboul and the remains of Imperial Constantinople will surely be the numerous and beautiful mosques of the early Ottoman Empire. Here is Evliya on two of the best-known.

## *The Mosque of Sultan Beyazid II*

The superintendent (Názir) of this mosque is the Sheïkhu-l Islám (*i.e.* the Muftí); he also gives the public lectures in this college. He delivers his lectures once a week, and the students receive a monthly stipened, besides an allowance for meat and wax-lights: this is a very well-endowed foundation. This mosque has altogether 2,040 servants; and none has a better salary than the Muvakkit, or Regulator of Time; because all the seamen and mariners in the empire of Islám depend, for the regulation of time, on the Muvakkit of Sultán Báyazíd Khán; and as the mihráb of this mosque was miraculously placed in the true position of Kiblah: all sea-captains regulate their compasses by it; and all the infidel astronomers in Firengistán, as is universally known, correct their watches and compasses by the mosque of Sultán Báyazíd.

## The Suleimaniye Mosque

There never has been to this day, nor ever will be, any writing which can compare with that of Ahmed Karah Hisárí, outside and inside of this mosque. In the centre of the dome there is this text of the Korán (xxiv. 35): 'God is the light of heaven and earth; the similitude of his light is as a niche in a wall wherein a lamp is placed, and the lamp enclosed in a case of glass:' a text justly called the Text of Light, which has been here rendered more luminous by the brilliant hand which inscribed it. The inscription over the semi-dome, above the Mihráb, has been already given. On the opposite side, above the southern gate, there is this text (vi. 79): 'I direct my face unto him who hath created the heavens and the earth: I am orthodox.' On the four piers are written, 'Allah, Mohammed, Abú Bekr, 'Omar, 'Osmán, 'Alí, Hasan, and Hoseïn. Over the window to the right of the Minber: 'Verily, places of worship belong to God; therefore, invoke not any one together with God.' Besides this, over the upper windows, all the excellent names (of God) are written. These are in the Shikáfí hand; but the large writing in the cupola is in the Guzáfí hand, of which the Láms, Elifs, and Káfs, each measure ten ells; so that they can be read distinctly by those who are below. This mosque has five doors. On the right, the Imám's (Imám kapú-sí); on the left the Vezír's (Vezír kapú-sí), beneath the imperial gallery, and two side doors. Over that on the left is written (Kor. xiii. 24), 'Peace be upon you, because ye have endured with patience! How excellent a reward is Paradise!' Over the opposite gate this text: 'Peace be upon you! Ye are righteous; enter in and dwell in it for ever!' Beneath this inscription, on the left hand, is added, 'This was written by the Fakír Karah Hisárí.'

·   ·   ·   ·

Of the two lofty minarets which have three galleries, that on the left is called the Jewel Minaret, for the following reason: Sultán Suleïmán, when building this mosque, in order to allow the foundations to settle, desisted, as has been already observed, for a whole year, during which the workmen were employed on other pious works. Sháh Tahmás Khán, King of 'Ajem (Persia), having heard of this, immediately sent a great Ambassador to Suleïmán, with a mule laden with valuable jewels, through friendship, as he said, for the

Sultán, who, from want of money, had not been able to complete this pious work. The Ambassador presented the Sháh's letter to the Sultán while surrounded with the innumerable builders and workmen employed about the mosque; and the latter, incensed on hearing the contents of the letter, immediately, in the Ambassador's presence, distributed the jewels which he had brought to all the Jews in Islámból, saying, 'Each Ráfizí, at the awful day of doom changed to an ass, some Jew to hell shall bear! To them, therefore, I give this treasure, that they may have pity on you on that day, and be sparing in the use of their spurs and whips.' Then giving another mule laden with jewels to Sinán, the architect, he said, still in the Ambassador's presence, 'These jewels, which were sent as being so valuable, have no worth in comparison with the stones of my mosque; yet, take them and mingle them with the rest.' Sinán, in obedience to the Sultán's command, used them in building the six-sided basis of this mínaret, which derives its name from thence. Some of the stones still sparkle when the sun's rays fall upon them; but others have lost their brilliance from exposure to excessive heat, snow, and rain.

Evliya Celebi*

## Pera

The modern visitor is more than likely to make his residence in one of the hotels of Pera or Galata, across the Golden Horn. It is to be hoped that he finds the accommodation more pleasant than did E. D. Clarke in 1801.

There can scarcely be found a spot upon earth more detestable than *Péra*, particularly in the most crowded part of it. We might be said to live in *cœmeteries*; the only water used for drinking, passing through sepulchres to the feverish lips of the inhabitants, filled with all sorts of revolting impurities, and even with living *animalculæ*. The owner of the hotel where we resided, wishing to make some repairs in his dwelling, dug near the foundation, and found that his house stood upon graves, yet containing the mouldering relics of the dead. This may perhaps account for the swarm of *rats*; not only in the buildings, but in the streets; whither they resort in such numbers at night, that a person passing through them finds these animals running against his legs. The prodigious multitude, however, of the *rats* is not owing to any want of *cats*; for the latter constitute the greater nuisance of the two. They enter through the crazy roofs, which consist only of a few thin planks, and render the smell of the bedchambers much more offensive than that of a dunghill.

E. D. Clarke*

Lady Mary Wortley Montagu was more susceptible to the charm of its setting.

> Here from my Window I at once survey
> The crouded City, and Resounding Sea,
> In Distant views see Asian Mountains rise
> And lose their Snowy Summits in the Skies.
> Above those Mountains high Olympus tow'rs
> (The Parliamental seat of heavenly Pow'rs).
> New to the sight, my ravish'd Eyes admire
> Each gilded Crescent and each antique Spire,
> The Marble Mosques beneath whose ample Domes
> Fierce Warlike Sultans sleep in peacefull Tombs.
> Those lofty Structures, once the Christian boast,
> Their Names, their Glorys, and their Beautys lost,
> Those Altars bright with Gold, with Sculpture grac'd,
> By Barbarous Zeal of Savage Foes defac'd:
> Sophia alone her Ancient Sound retains
> Thô unbelieving Vows her shrine prophanes.
> Where Holy Saints have dy'd, in Sacred Cells
> Where Monarchs pray'd, the Frantic Derviche dwells.
> How art thou falln, Imperial City, low!
> Where are thy Hopes of Roman Glory now?
> Where are thy Palaces by Prelates rais'd;
> Where priestly Pomp in Purple Lustre blaz'd?
> Where Grecian Artists all their Skill display'd
> Before the Happy Sciences decay'd,
> So vast, that youthfull Kings might there reside,
> So splendid, to content a Patriarch's pride,
> Convents where Emperours profess'd of Old,
> The Labour'd Pillars that their Triumphs told
> (Vain Monuments of Men that once were great!)
> Sunk undistinguish'd in one common Fate!

Lady Mary Wortley Montagu

## The Bosphorus

This is the canal which was cut by Iskender Zulkarnin (Alexander the Great) to unite the Black and White Seas. The traces of this work are even now to be seen on the rocks.

Evliya Celebi*

This further part of the European shore, a little beyond my windows, was at one time one of the most respected and adorable parts
of the Bosphorus. It is there that the high and vast citadel stands
which is known as Roumeli Hisar – the Castle of Europe. I have
known a time when, around its bristling crenellated ramparts, its
fantastic dungeons, placed there four centuries ago to halt the
invasions of the men of the north, there was no more than this
Turkish village, with its old sombre and tranquil dwellings, and this
wood of giant cypresses which falls from the summit of the hill right
to the sea, with the tombs with which it is peopled: green stelae, blue
stelae, all striped with inscriptions in gold, stelae descending, descending far below, doubtless to share the company of the water
which is always at this spot clear, rapid and bubbling.

Is it possible? Today there seem to be fewer of those stelae. In any
case, the cypresses are certainly absent; a barbarous and imbecile axe
has been put to that wood of shadows. And up there, crowning with
derision the hill which should have remained sacred, what new
horrors have arisen in my absence? Hideous blackish edifices, barracks apparently, and the great pipes of some electrical factory.
Yes, I had indeed been warned of this profanation, but the moon
yesterday evening did not want to show it to me. These are the
enlargements to Robert College, an American school, which had
long since begun to dishonour this place, and which stretches like a
leper, plotting craftily to grow and grow until it suppresses
altogether the funereal wood and dislodges the ashes of the companions of Mehmed II; – for it is here that they sleep, those legendary
warriors who came in the train of the Conqueror; they had chosen
such places by the side of the water, doubtless to hear for ever the
sweet music of the currents of the Bosphorus.

> Pierre Loti, *Suprêmes Visions d'Orient* (1921); tr. R. S.

Which perhaps goes to show that one should not revisit in old
age a city known and loved in youth.

The building of the castle by Mehmed II is the subject of one of
Evliya Celebi's lively accounts.

He begged leave of the Emperor to build on the spot where the castle
now stands a hunting house, and consulted with a monk, who in
secret was a Mussulman, and enjoyed his intimacy. Envoys came
from Constantinople with the answer, that the Emperor would
allow as much ground as a bull's hide would cover, but no more.
Sultán Mohammed now traced out in the Envoy's presence the
foundation of a tower no larger than a bull's hide. At the same time
he commanded from Constantinople many thousand workmen and

miners, who brought from the harbour of Borgház on the Black Sea in one night from forty to fifty guns, placed them along the seashore and covered them with bushes. He then began to build the castle, concealing in the same way the foundations by bushes; after which he cut the hide by the monk's advice into small strips, by which he marked out the circumference of the castle on the lime rocks. The monk said, 'Gracious Emperor, your name being Mohammed, the same as the prophet, let this castle be built in the shape of the characters that form the name. It is now forty-one years since I received the destination to superintend this building, being a perfect architect, but I kept it secret from the world.' Thus saying, he called his workmen together, and built the castle of Rúmelí in the form of the word Mohammed, as written in Cufic characters, which is to be read perfectly from the mountains of Anatoli. The tower on the top of the hill, seven stories high, represents the *mím* (m), the gate of the Dizdár the letter *ha* (h), the great tower on the sea-shore, the second *mím*, and the square on the side of the convent of Dúrmish Dedeh the *dál* (d). The letters which form the name of Mohammed, if taken in their arithmetic value give the number 92, which is also that of the bulwarks of this fortress. The arithmetic value of the letters, which compose the word khán being 651, there is the same number of battlements. The castle being built in six months, they burned the bushes, which hid it from the sight; the troops entered it rejoicing, with the necessary artillery and ammunition, and the architect throwing away the mask of a monk, declared himself publicly to be a faithful Moslim. He begged to be made Dizdár, or commanding officer of the castle, which was granted him. The Greek Emperor receiving this news sent an ambassador to complain, that a castle had been built contrary to the peace. Sultán Mohamm'ed in answer sent the hide of the bull cut into small pieces, and said that he would plead guilty of the breach of the peace, if the castle exceeded in the least this granted measure. The Infidels now wished to make a new treaty of peace, but Mahommed would not grant it, and built two other castles at the Dardanelles, by which means he intercepted from both seas the conveyance of provisions, so that he nearly reduced Constantinople by famine.

Evliya Celebi*

## Eyup

Eyup is a favourite excursion destination from Istanbul, conveniently reached by water-bus from the Galata Bridge. It is the site of the largest and most remarkable cemetery in Turkey, excepting the one at Üsküdar. Up the hill from the banks of the Golden Horn cluster millions of turbaned slabs and pillars, now tilting at crazy angles and interspersed with tombs of the most recent date. Its popularity as a burial place results from its being one of the most holy places of Islam (some say third only to Mecca and Jerusalem), for it is the shrine of the Moslem saint Eyup (Job).

On most days it will be found thronged with pilgrims who have arrived on foot or in coaches to pay homage at the shrine, queuing for hours to enter and leaving backwards, arms lifted in prayer until they have again reached the threshold. Until very recently the non-Moslem could see none of this, so that for Richard Davey the spot presented nothing but a scene of picnickers. Now the foreigner may be admitted even to the innermost shrine, if he is prepared to wait or can find a guide; there is no need of the subterfuge engaged in by Pierre Loti (who is supposed to have favoured the café that crowns the hill):

I took my son to Eyoub. Since his first visit to Turkey six years ago, it had been his dream to see the silent courtyards of the mosque of Eyoub, the most sacred place in Constantinople, the only one which was jealously forbidden to strangers. Until now, I had always refused to take my son there, because I was a little afraid.

To give ourselves the air of people of the country, I judged it prudent to arrive at Eyoub via the great cemeteries and to approach the perimeter of the mosque from the side facing the Golden Horn.

Clothed in fezzes and our beads in our hands like good Turks, we opened the little gate which closes the sacred courts and found ourselves in the midst of a green night of tall cypresses and broad planes whose age no one knows. There, below the venerable stelae with their stone turbans, sleep the companions of Mehmed II in this vast enclosure of silence, whose walls are adorned with old ceramic work with blue flowers. Some pious old men were crouched in prayer, while the pigeons and the swans walked familiarly around them on the flagstones. We pass quietly, without attracting attention, into this place whose peace is so profound as to be oppressive and arrive before the kiosk where the Saint Eyoub sleeps. We halt to admire the tomb through the bronze grill of one of the windows. The interior of this kiosk, which is situated slightly below the level of the court, is occupied almost entirely by the great catafalque covered with silk shot with gold and surmounted by an enormous turban. All around, the walls glitter in their covering of ancient faience, with designs in the most beautiful red, that ruby red whose secret has been lost for three centuries. Shut in close to the catafalque, with his back to us, an ancient hoca, seated on his haunches, reads the Koran in a precious manuscript of parchment illuminated with gold. Perhaps we stay too long looking at these things, for the old hoca, as if he had scented infidels, turns sharply towards us and regards us with a mistrustful air which suddenly frightens us; we suddenly have the uncomfortable sensation of being intruders, profaning a sacred place. Nonetheless, it will not do to appear disturbed, which would immediately rouse the alarm, and we depart without hurrying, telling our beads.

Pierre Loti, Suprêmes Visions d'Orient (1921); tr. R. S.

Near Eyup were in Evliya's time plentiful pleasant walks and an unusual bathing place.

The river flows from the vallies near the Levendchiftlik on the shores of the Bosphorus. The washermen here wash shirts and other linen without soap, nevertheless they become extremely white after having been twice washed. Indian merchants also bring their bales to this place to immerse them once in the flood. On both sides the river is adorned with many thousand plane and cypress trees, maples and willows; the meadows yield luxuriantly all kinds of grass and trefoil. The herb Egreh is found here in greater perfection than at Asov, or in the marshes of Canistra. Here also grows good Aloe (Eger-gokí). On days of recreation many thousand lovers with their beloved repair hither in boats, and swim in the water to enjoy the sight of their loves without hindrance. There being many nets laid on both sides of the river, it happens that some of the swimmers entangle their feet in them and are drowned, fancying that they are caught by an angel of the sea. Great precaution is, therefore, necessary, though there is not the least probability of sea-angels sporting here.

Evliya Celebi*

## 3. Appreciations

### W. M. Thackeray

The view of Constantinople resembles the ne plus ultra of a Stanfield diorama, with a glorious accompaniment of music, spangled houris, warriors, and winding processions, feasting the eyes and the soul with light, splendour, and harmony. If you were never in this way during your youth ravished at the play-house, of course the whole comparison is useless: and you have no idea, from this description, of the effect which Constantinople produces on the mind. But if you were never affected by a theatre, no words can work upon your fancy, and typographical attempts to move it are of no use. For, suppose we combine mosque, minaret, gold, cypress, water, blue, caïques, seventy-four, Galata, Tophana, Ramazan, Backallum, and so forth, together, in ever so many ways, your imagination will never be able to depict a city out of them. Or, suppose I say the Mosque of St. Sophia is four hundred and seventy-three feet in height, measuring from the middle nail of the gilt crescent, surmounting the dome, to the ring in the centre stone; the circle of the dome is one hundred and twenty-three feet in diameter, the windows ninety-seven in number – and all this may be true, for anything I know to the contrary; yet who is to get an idea of St. Sophia's from dates, proper names, and calculations with a measuring line? It can't be done by giving the age and measurement of all the buildings along the river, the names of all the boatmen who ply on it. Has your fancy, which pooh poohs a simile, faith enough to build a city with a foot-rule? Enough said about descriptions and similes (though whenever I am uncertain of one, I am naturally most anxious to fight for it): it is a scene not perhaps sublime, but charming, magnificent, and cheerful beyond any I have ever seen – the most superb combination of city and gardens, domes and shipping, hills and water, with the healthiest breeze blowing over it, and above it the brightest and most cheerful sky.

*Notes of A Journey from Cornhill to Grand Cairo* (1846)

## Pierre Loti

Who can ever return to me my Oriental life, my life free in the open air, my long aimless walks, and the uproar of Stamboul.

To leave in the morning from the Atmeidan, to end up at night at Eyoub; to tour the mosques, beads in hand; to stop at all the cafes, turbehs, mausolea, at the baths and in the squares; to drink Turkish coffee in microscopic blue cups with copper bases; to sit in the sun and stupefy sweetly in the smoke of a narghile; to talk with dervishes and passers by; to be oneself a part of this tableau so full of movement and light; to be free, carefree and unknown; and to think that the bed of your beloved awaits you at evening.

.  .  .  .  .

The tableau becomes a little more sombre when one becomes enmeshed in old Stamboul, when one approaches the holy quarter of Eyoub and the great cemeteries. Still some glimpses of the blue surface of the Marmara, the isles and the mountains of Asia, but the passers by are scarce and the houses sad – a seal of antiquity and mystery – and external objects tell the savage tales of old Turkey.

It is nightfall, most often, when we arrive at Eyoub, after having dined no matter where, in one of those little Turkish shops where Ahmet himself tests the cleanliness of the ingredients and oversees their preparation.

We light our lanterns to return to the room – that room so out of the way and peaceful, whose very distance is one of its charms.

*Aziyadé* (1879)

## Rose Macaulay

The deserted Seraglio, the sumptuous great mosques, the ruinous mosques that were Greek churches, vanished Byzantium below Islam, the spacious gardens, the storks, the whole crumbling magnificence standing above those shining seas – in spite of the encroaching vulgarity and modernity of the occidental city, there is still nothing like it. The ancient imperial pomp, remote, ceremonious, Byzantine and strange, whispers like a proud, undefeated ghost among the mosques; the old pomp of Islam, as extravagant, luxurious, fastuous and fantastic, rises like a garden of tulips before our dazzled eyes, among the verdure, terraces and streams of that abandoned, cypress-grown quarter where the Sultans reigned among their viziers, janissaries, harems and pleasure gardens for four sumptuous centuries, before they deserted it for their modern palace on the Bosphorus. Once the capital of imperial Rome; later the greatest city of Christendom, the richest city in the world, the spiritual head of the eastern Church, the treasure house of culture and art; then the opulent capital of Islam; this sprawl of mosques, domes, minarets, ruined palaces, and crumbling walls, rising so superbly above three seas, looking towards Europe, Asia, and ocean, oriental, occidental, brooding on past magnificence, ancient rivalries and feuds, modern cultures and the spoils of the modern world, Constantinople has ruin in her soul, the ruin of a deep division; to look on her shining domes and teeming streets is to see a glittering, ruinous façade, girdled by great, broken, expugnable walls.

*Pleasure of Ruins* (1953)

## Richard Davey

One last look – as I stand on deck, and the great ship bears me away across the Marmara – on the enchanting outline of the city of the Sultans, fast fading into the mists of eventide. A feeling of deepest melancholy steals over me, a regret closely akin to that which stirs us as we bid reluctant farewell to some old familiar friend, whom we know stricken with deadly disease – whose face we shall never see again on this side of the grave. Modern Constantinople, indeed, may still endure; but Stambul! Stambul of the Moslim warrior, Stambul of the Moslim priest, is fast hurrying to its inevitable doom.

# CHAPTER TWO

# Bithynia and the Troad

## Bursa

It is an easy excursion southwards from Istanbul, by ferry and road, to Bursa, the ancient Prusa. For centuries it has been a popular outing for both Turk and foreign visitor. In antiquity famous as the home of the orator Dio called the Golden-Mouthed and, before the transfer to Edirne in the fifteenth century, capital of the Ottoman Empire, it now exhibits, in its impressive setting below Ulu Dağ, all the distinctive charm of a provincial Muslim city. One can hardly improve on the enthusiastic description of Evliya Celebi, who visited it in the seventeenth century.

The upper part of the town with Mount Olympus rising in the background is beautiful when seen from the plain of Filehdár, an hour's distance from it, and I can truly say that I have seen nothing like it during my travels. Brússa is a very devout town, abounding with Divines, expounders of the Korán and keepers of tradition, who are found no where else so numerous, excepting at Baghdád. Mount Olympus at the back of the town on the south side is a mine of living water, no less than one thousand and sixty well-known springs flow from it, and supply water in abundance to the palaces and houses. It abounds also in all kinds of flowers, particularly in syringa (Erghiwán), the annual assembly of Emír Sultán held in the season when the syringa is in perfection being much celebrated. The inhabitants being fair, the air good, the water full of holiness, contribute altogether, to render Brússa one of the most delicious spots on earth.

. . . . .

There are nine thousand shops. The Bezestán is a large building with four iron gates secured with iron chains; its cupola is supported by strong columns. It contains three hundred shops (doláb) in each of which merchants reside, who are as rich as the kings of Egypt. The market of the goldsmiths is outside the bezestán, and separate from it; the shops are all of stone. There are also the markets of the tailors, cotton-beaters, capmakers, thread merchants, drapers, linen merchants, cable merchants, and that called the market of the bride, where essence of roses, musk, ambergris, &c. are sold. The brains of the passers by are refreshed with the most delicious odours, and nobody is willing to leave it on account of the fragrance of the perfumes and the politeness of its merchants. These markets are established around the Bezestán, and the shops are arranged in rows. In each corner is a fountain supplying water out of two pipes. In the summer months the servants sprinkle the ground with water, so that the whole market resembles a serdáb or cooling place of Baghdád. The principal men of Brússa sit here during the hottest hours of the day. According to the descriptions of travellers there is no where to be found so pleasant a market place. The market of Haleb and of Ali Páshá at Adrianople are famous, but neither they, nor even those of Constantinople, are to be compared with the markets of Brússa. The saddlers, and the long market are the most crowded; and the one occupied by the sellers of roast meat near the rice khán is very elegant. None of the provisions at Brússa are sold by Infidels but all by true Moslims. The shops of the Sherbet-merchants are adorned with all sorts of cups, and in the summer-time they put flowers into the sherbet and also mix rosewater with it, which is not the custom any where else. The fruit merchants ornament their shops with branches bearing fruit. There are seventy-five coffee-houses each capable of holding a thousand persons, which are frequented by the most elegant and learned of the inhabitants; and three times a day singers and dancers execute a musical concert in them like those of Hossein Bikara. Their poets are so many Hassáns, and their story-tellers (Meddáh) so many Abúl-ma'álí. The one most famous for relating stories from the Hamzeh-námeh is Kúrbání Ali, and Sheríf Chelebí enchanted his hearers by those he told from the Sháh-námeh. Other story-tellers (Kissah Khán) were famous for reciting the tales of Abú Moslem the hatchet-bearer, which may be compared to the memoirs (Seir) of Weissi. All coffee-houses, and particularly those near the great mosque, abound with men skilled in a thousand arts (Hezár-fenn) dancing and pleasure continue the whole night, and in the morning every body goes to the mosque. These coffee-houses became famous only since those of Constantinople were closed by the express command of Sultán Murád IV. There are are also no less than ninety-seven Búza-houses, which are not to be equalled in the world; they are wainscoted with fayence, painted, each capable of accommodating one thousand men. In summer the Búza is cooled in ice, like sherbet; the principal men of the town are not ashamed to enter these Búza-houses, although abundance of youths, dancers and singers, girt with Brússa girdles, here entice, their lovers to ruin. The roads are paved with large flint-stones, a kind of paving not met with elsewhere; these stones are not the least worn by age, but they are dangerous for horses, who stumble on them because they are so hard and bright.

Evliya Celebi*

One of these fabulous markets, the Silk Bazaar, has recently been restored; its charming arcades are home to several attractive boutiques.

Lady Mary Wortley Montagu was to find the city little changed and just as attractive in its green and idyllic setting, and her countryman W. J. Hamilton also enthused, and not only about the quartzite granite and 'plutonic rocks' that compose the dominating presence of the town, Mt Olympus. Mrs Max Müller was equally enchanted.

We were up and out early in the morning, for the Mosques and Türbehs of Brûsa are very numerous, and the place is said to have a Mosque and a walk for every day in the year. The 'Great Mosque' is a perfect square, and is built on the plan of the earliest Mosques, very different from those of Constantinople, which are nearly all copied from St. Sophia, a square with apses on three sides. There are five aisles in the Great Mosque, and in the centre a large space is left unroofed so that the sun shines down into the central fountain. Except that the Minber or Friday pulpit is splendidly carved, this vast Mosque looked bare to us, after the more decorated Mosques of Stambûl. But we held our breath in wonder when we entered the Green Mosque, built by Muhammad I in 1420, the internal walls of which are entirely covered with old faïence of exquisite design, green being the chief colour. The doors, and the whole of what one might call a side chapel, were of carved white marble. There were formerly two tall minarets entirely covered with green faïence, but these were thrown down in the terrible earthquake of 1855, which destroyed much of the town, and in which over 1,000 people lost their lives. The Green Mosque stands on a platform facing the superb vale of Brûsa. Close by is the Türbeh of Muhammad I, the gem of the whole city, which was once covered outside as well as inside with faïence. Vefyk Pasha, who as governor of Brûsa did so much for the place, substituted green tiles for the outside faïence destroyed in 1855. The beauty of the designs (chiefly floral) of the faïence in the interior of this Mosque baffles one's power of description.

Mrs Max Müller, *Letters from Constantinople* (1897)

Bursa is perhaps a convenient centre for visiting the Roman sites of Bithynia, such as Iznik (Nicaea) and Izmit (Nicomedia). Many were the problems that faced the Roman governor Pliny in his period of duty in *c* AD 110–112, in controlling the expenditure of the municipalities on public buildings they deemed appropriate to their status as Roman cities; but weightiest of all was the steady growth of cells of Christians. The question of how to deal with practitioners of this proscribed religion is the subject of one of his most interesting and suggestive letters to the Emperor Trajan.

It is my invariable rule, Sir, to refer to you in all matters where I feel doubtful; for who is more capable of removing my scruples, or informing my ignorance? Having never been present at any trials concerning those who profess Christianity, I am unacquainted not only with the nature of their crimes, or the measure of their punishment, but how far it is proper to enter into an examination concerning them. Whether, therefore, any difference is usually made with respect to ages, or no distinction is to be observed between the young and the adult; whether repentance entitles them to a pardon; or if a man has been once a Christian, it avails nothing to desist from his error; whether the very profession of Christianity, unattended with any criminal act, or only the crimes themselves inherent in the profession are punishable; on all these points I am in great doubt. In the meanwhile, the method I have observed towards those who have been brought before me as Christians is this: I asked them whether they were Christians; if they admitted it, I repeated the question twice, and threatened them with punishment; if they persisted, I ordered them to be at once punished: for I was persuaded, whatever the nature of their opinions might be, a contumacious and inflexible obstinacy certainly deserved correction. There were others also brought before me possessed with the same infatuation, but being Roman citizens, I directed them to be sent to Rome. But this crime spreading (as is usually the case) while it was actually under prosecution, several instances of the same nature occurred. An anonymous information was laid before me, containing a charge against several persons, who upon examination denied they were Christians, or had ever been so. They repeated after me an invocation to the gods, and offered religious rites with wine and incense before your statue (which for that purpose I had ordered to be brought, together with those of the gods), and even reviled the name of Christ: whereas there is no forcing, it is said, those who are really Christians into any of these compliances: I thought it proper, therefore, to discharge them. Some among those who were accused by a witness in person at first confessed themselves Christians, but immediately after denied it; the rest owned indeed that they had been of that number formerly, but had now (some above three, others more, and a few above twenty years ago) renounced that error. They all worshipped your statue and the images of the gods, uttering imprecations at the same time against the name of Christ. They affirmed the whole of their guilt, or their error, was, that they met on a stated day before it was light, and addressed a form of prayer to Christ, as to a divinity, binding themselves by a solemn oath, not for the purposes of any wicked design, but never to commit any fraud, theft, or adultery, never to falsify their word, nor deny a trust when they should be called upon to deliver it up; after which it was their custom to separate, and then reassemble, to eat in common a harmless meal. From this custom, however, they desisted after the publication of my edict, by which, according to your commands, I forbade the meeting of any assemblies. After receiving this account, I judged it so much the more necessary to endeavour to extort the real truth, by putting two female slaves to the torture, who were said to officiate in their religious rites: but all I could discover was evidence of an absurd and extravagant superstition. I deemed it expedient, therefore, to adjourn all further proceedings, in order to consult you. For it appears to be a matter highly deserving your consideration, more especially as great numbers must be involved in the danger of these prosecutions, which have already extended, and are still likely to extend, to persons of all ranks and ages, and even of both sexes. In fact, this contagious superstition is not confined to the cities only, but has spread its infection among the neighbouring villages and country. Nevertheless, it still seems possible to restrain its progress. The temples, at least, which were once almost deserted, begin now to be frequented; and the sacred rites, after a long intermission, are again revived; while there is a general demand for the victims, which till lately found very few purchasers. From all this it is easy to conjecture what numbers might be reclaimed if a general pardon were granted to those who shall repent of their error.

Pliny, *Letters* X 97.

## Cyzicus (near Erdek)

The road eastwards leads us parallel to the shores of the Marmara, and at the apex of a triangular peninsula (where it joined the mainland) lay the ancient city of Cyzicus. This entered early into the legendary record as one of the ports of call of Jason and the Argonauts on their voyage to Colchis (the east coast of the Black Sea) to fetch the Golden Fleece. The mountain that lies inland from Cyzicus, Mt Dindymene, was one of the chief seats of the great mother goddess of Asia Minor, Cybele. Though the fertility she nurtured made the anchorage an attractive one, there were hazards too, as Apollonius describes.

> An ancient island in Propontis lies,
> That towering lifts its summits to the skies;
> Near Phrygia's corn-abounding coast it stands,
> And far-projecting all the main commands;
> An island this, save where the isthmus' chain
> Connects both lands, and curbs the boisterous main.
> Round its rough sides the thundering tempests roar,
> And a safe bay is formed on either shore.
> Aesepus' waters near the isthmus fall:
> And bordering tribes the mountain Arcton call.
> On this rough mountain, barbarous, fierce, and bold,
> Dwell mighty giants, hideous to behold;
> And, wonderful to tell! each monster stands
> With six huge arms, and six rapacious hands;
> Two pendent on their shaggy shoulders grow,
> And four deform their horrid sides below.
> The lowland isthmus, verging to the main,
> The Dolions till'd, and all the fertile plain.
> O'er these reigned Cyzicus the brave, the young,
> Who from the gallant warrior, Aeneus, sprung.
>
>                 . . . . .
>
> To this fair port, with gentle-breathing gales,
> This friendly shore, Thessalian Argo sails.

Inevitably, bitter battles ensue in which the Argonauts are eventually victorious. Jason's men thank the local goddess for their deliverance in the usual way:

> There, where his waters black Aesepus pours,
> Nepea's plain, and Adrasteia's towers.
> A vine's vast trunk adorned with branches stood,
> Though old, yet sound, and long had graced the wood:
> This trunk they hewed, and made, by Argus' skill,
> An image of the goddess of the hill;
> Which on the rocky eminence they placed,
> With the thick boughs of circling beeches graced.
> They rear an altar, then, on rising ground,

Of stones that readiest lay, and wide around
Dispose the branches of the sacred oak,
And Dindymus's deity invoke,
The guardian power of Phrygia's hills and woods;
The venerable mother of the gods.

. . . .

While on the burning victims Jason pours
Libations due, the goddess he implores
To smile propitious on the Grecian train,
And still the tempests of the roaring main.
Then Orpheus called, and youthful chiefs advance,
All clad in arms, to lead the martial dance;
With clashing swords they clattered on their shields,
And filled with festive sounds th'aerial fields.
Lost in these sounds was every doleful strain,
And their loud wailings for their monarch slain.
The Phrygians still their goddess' favour win
By the revolving wheel and timbrel's din.
Of these pure rites the mighty mother showed
Her mind approving, by these signs bestowed:
Boughs bend with fruit, Earth from her bosom pours
Herbs ever green, and voluntary flowers.
Fierce forest beasts forsake the lonely den,
Approach with gentleness, and fawn on men.
A pleasing omen, and more wondrous still,
The goddess gave: the Dindymean hill,
That ne'er knew water on its airy brow,
Bursts into streams, and founts perennial flow.
This wonder still the Phrygian shepherds sing,
And give the name of Jason to the spring.

    Apollonius of Rhodes, *Argonautica* I; tr. Francis Fawkes

A version of the Argonaut Dance was said by F. W. Hasluck to
be still performed here in 1910.

In the early Roman Empire the professional orator Aelius
Aristides favoured the now-flourishing city with one of the
encomia which he composed to order (several others survive,
on Athens and other places).

One would be uncertain as to whether most of the island has been
transferred here or remains in its place. But I think that all would
agree that this would be the offering of no other city or quarry than
your own. For their nature would not suffice. Formerly sailors used
to judge their position by the peaks of the islands, 'Here is Cyzicus',
'This is Proconnesus', and whatever other island one beheld. But

now the temple is equal to the mountains, and you alone have no need for beacons, signal fires, and towers for those putting into port. But the temple fills every vista, and at the same time reveals the city and the magnanimity of its inhabitants. And although it is so great, its beauty exceeds its size. If Homer and Hesiod had happened to be alive, I think that they would have readily transferred to here the tale about the Trojan wall and would have told how Poseidon and Apollo jointly designed and fashioned this work for the city, the former by providing rock from the depths of the sea and at the same time making it possible for it to be brought here, and the latter through his desire to adorn his city with such a great addition, as it is likely that a founder would do. You would say that each of the stones was meant to be the whole temple, and the temple the whole precinct, and again that the temple's precinct was big enough to be a city. If you wish to consider the comfort and luxury which it provides, it is possible to view this very great temple like three storied houses or like three decked ships, many times greater than other temples, and itself of a threefold nature. For part of the spectacle is subterranean, part on an upper story, and part in between in the usual position. There are walks which traverse it all about, underground and hanging, as it were made not as an additional adornment, but actually to be walks. There is no need to praise these things in speech, but they can be left to the geometricians and technical experts, at least to as many of these as are fully trained and capable of measuring so great a work, since I fear that not even all of these may be able to attain to accuracy in this matter. If someone should forego speaking about the temple itself, it is enough to express admiration for the engineering equipment and the transport, whose invention was prompted by the requirements of the temple, since they formerly did not exist among mankind.

Aelius Aristides, *Encomium of Cyzicus;* tr. C. A. Behr

In Roman times Cyzicus was indeed a prosperous port, adorned with many fine buildings, notably the Temple of Zeus completed and dedicated by the Emperor Hadrian in AD 167. J. P. Grelot enthused more about its secular amenities.

The ancient city of Cyzicum, which is one of the first that appears on the right hand upon the coast of Asia, was famous for the antiquity of its foundation, which it derives from the Argonauts, near five hundred years before the building of Rome: for its situation, which was in a lovely island joined to the shore on two large bridges; from its lofty towers and magnificent buildings, for the most part all of marble; from three great arsenals or magazines kept carefully in repair, and provided continually with plenty of all things necessary for the preservation of the inhabitants. The first was a storehouse of arms offensive and defensive. The second, of all sorts of tools, household furniture, and other necessaries, not only for the inhabitants, but for all that were subject to the jurisdiction of the city. And the third contained the granaries for corn, and other public provisions for the common benefit. . . . But of all those great advantages, which formerly it enjoyed, there remains nothing now but that of its situation.

J. P. Grelot, *A late voyage to Constantinople* (1683)

But the ruins of ancient Cyzicus suffered earlier and more devastatingly from the depredations of time and of builders than any other city of Asia Minor. When the indefatigable traveller Cyriac of Ancona visited Cyzicus in 1431 there were enough remains of the Temple of Poseidon for him to make some conjectures as to the size and layout of the building; but just over two centuries later John Covel found almost nothing left, and even W. J. Hamilton was able to deduce but little from the untidy hillock covered with holly oak.

We went to see ye ruines of Cyzico and indeed we received a great deal of satisfaction; for never was anything so exactly described, as Strabo hath done this. The ruines shew yt half stood on ye plain, and half on a rising hill. In ye low part not far from ye sea is a fine spring, which ye Greekes make an agiasma (dedication), perhaps it was Plinyes *fons Cupidinis* (Spring of Love), though we found another spring upon a rising hill to ye west of Cyzico, which is an agiasma also, and may be it, onely it runs nothing neare so fast as ye first; the poor Greekes have it in great esteem, we found many many rags there of poor votaryes repairing thither for one; I drank of both to see if I might find ye cure mentioned in Pliny wrought upon my self.

Perhaps neither is it, for we saw many rills and mills and there must be other springs.

. . . . .

A little farther from it towards the hills are found a most stately ruine which had been all of white marble, I guest it to have been of ye Corinthian order by ye head of a pillar there lying by, it had bene very large but was now broken and split to pieces. . . . It is very likely that this was ye famous temple of Nemesis or Adrasteia mentioned in Strabo; for they built those structures on low ground for fear of earthquakes.

John Covel; BM Add. MS 22914, f. 30 r-v. (5 April 1676/7)

On the whole, I must say that the loose and rubbly character of the buildings of Cyzicus little accords with the celebrity of its architects;

and although some appear to have been cased with marble, none of them give an idea of the solid grandeur of the genuine Greek style.

The destruction of all the public buildings, and the total desolation of the place, are in this instance the more remarkable, when we find that no modern town of importance has risen on its ruins; it may in a great measure be owing to the nature of the material of which these buildings were constructed. Although cased with the beautiful marble of the neighbouring hills, and of the quarries near Aidinjik, they are chiefly built of granite, and that of Cyzicus decomposes with great rapidity on exposure to the atmosphere. It appears to contain much felspar, producing alumina by its decomposition; and this has encouraged a rich vegetation, which either acts directly on the buildings themselves, or conceals them under an abundant verdure. The sand also blown up from the sea on each side of the isthmus appears to have done its share of the work: it is therefore probable that though few ruins of any importance are now visible, excavations properly conducted might produce very satisfactory results.

W. J. Hamilton*

In 1910 F. W. Hasluck produced perhaps the most thorough possible study of the remains of Cyzicus, but even he could determine little or nothing about the layout of the temple, whose vast labyrinthine foundations were regarded by the local villagers as the haunt of demons.

## Gelibolu (Gallipoli)

Gelibolu is a place of blood. It seems very far from living up to its ancient Greek name Kallipolis, Beautiful City; and is best remembered as the scene of terrible slaughter in the First World War as the allies tried in vain to establish themselves on the shore as a prelude to the push to Constantinople (which never came). A large war memorial commemorates the dead in this gloomy bare landscape. Those educated Englishmen who had the name of Achilles never far from their lips as they fought so close to where Achilles had battled to take Troy, might have remembered also a medieval legend of barbarism which is recounted by the Catalan soldier Ramon Muntaner (1265–1336).

In that gulf occurs the miracle that you will always find in it streaks of blood, the size of a boat's deck; some are larger, some smaller. And this gulf is always full of these streaks of fresh blood, but when you are outside this gulf you will find none. And the mariners gather up of this blood and carry it with them from one end of the world to the other as reliques. And this is caused by the blood of the Babes which was shed in that place, and so, from that time onwards, it is there and will always be there. And this is the real truth, for I have gathered some up with my own hands.

R. Muntaner, *Chronicle* (tr. 1921)

Two glimpses of Gallipoli in 1915 are enough to make one glad never to have been there.

We walked from the sea and passed immediately up the hill, through a field of tall corn filled with poppies, then another cornfield, then the fearful smell of death began as we came across scattered corpses. We mounted over a plateau and down through gullies filled with thyme where there lay about 4,000 Turkish dead. It was indescribable. One was grateful for the rain and grey sky. The smell was appalling. A Turkish Red Crescent man came and gave me some antiseptic wool with scent on it, and this they renewed frequently. There were two wounded in all that multitude of silence, crying in the gullies. The Turks were very distressed and Skeen strained a point to let them send water to the first wounded man who must have been a sniper crawling home. I walked over to the second, who lay with a high circle of dead that made a mound round him, and gave him a drink from my water bottle, but Skeen called to me to come on and I had to leave the bottle. Later a Turk returned it to me. Nazim, the Turkish Captain with me, said: 'At this spectacle even the most gentle must feel savage and the most savage must weep'. No one made offensive remarks except Howse, the Australian doctor.

The dead fill acres of ground, mostly killed in one big attack, but some recently. One saw the result of machine-gun fire very clearly; entire companies annihilated – not wounded, but killed, their heads doubled under them with the impetus of their rush and both hands clasping their bayonets.

Aubrey Herbert, Diary for 25th May 1915

Somebody turned round to offer me a cigar.

'You'd better light up this.'

And, as I paused for a moment in perplexity to wonder why I should exhaust by smoking what wind I had left, the smell of death floated over the ridge above and settled down upon us, tangible, it seemed, and clammy as the membrane of a bat's wing.

Immediately along the top of the ridge were the trenches of Quinn's Post with the Turkish trenches hardly twenty yards beyond. I clambered up on the parapet and stood there staring at the forbidden land which rolled away in grey-green bosky undulations as far as the eye could reach, and I remember thinking how much it reminded me of some serene estate over which brooded that im-memorial hush of the game-preserve. In the foreground was a narrow stretch of level scrub along which flags were stuck at intervals and a line of sentries, Australians and Turks, faced one another. Staff officers of both sides were standing around in little groups, and there was an atmosphere about the scene of local magnates at the annual sports making suggestions about the start of the obstacle race. Aubrey Herbert looked so like the indispensable bachelor that every country neighbourhood retains to take complete control of the proceedings on such occasions. Here he was, shuffling about, loose-gaited, his neck out-thrust and swinging from side to side as he went peering up into people's faces to see whether they were the enemy or not, so that, if they were, he could offer them cigarettes and exchange a few courtesies with them in their own language . . . and everywhere Turks digging and digging graves for some four thousand of their countrymen who had been putrefying in heaps along this narrow front for nearly a month of warm May air.

'I must trouble you to get off my parapet, Major. It's rather delicate,' said one of the men in the front trench to Orlo Williams, who had been surveying the scene through his glasses and by doing so nearly created an incident.

'And you've got your foot in an awkward place,' he called up to me. Looking down I saw squelching up from the ground on either side of my boot like a rotten mangold the deliquescent green and black flesh of a Turk's head.

'This parapet's pretty well made up of dead bodies,' said our friend below, putting out his hand to help me jump back into the trench, for he saw that I had had enough of it up there.

Compton Mackenzie, *Gallipoli Memories* (1929)

Turks suffered as heavily as the Australian troops in this long drawn out and futile battle.

### For the Fallen at Gallipoli

Soldier, you who have fallen for this earth
Your fathers may well lean down from heaven to kiss your brow.
You are great, for your blood saves the True Faith
Only the heroes of Bedr are your equals in glory.
Who can dig a grave that will not be too narrow for you?
If I say: 'Let us enshrine you in history,' it will not contain you
That book cannot hold your time of troubles
Only eternity can embrace you
If I were to set up the Ka'be as your headstone
If I could seize the revelation in my soul and write it as epitaph

If I could take the firmament with all its stars
And lay it as pall over your bloody coffin
And make a ceiling of purple clouds for your open tomb
And hang the seven lamps of the Pleiades
If, as you lie swathed in blood under this chandelier
I could detain the moonlight by your side
To stay till dawn as guardian of your tomb
If I could charge your chandelier with morning light
And wrap the silken sunset over your wounds –
Still I could not say: 'I have done something for your memory . . .'

                    Mehmet Akif Ersoy; tr. Bernard Lewis


## The Hellespont (Dardanelles)

Gelibolu marks the easternmost end of the Hellespont, named from Helle who fell in her flight from Orchomenos in Greece from the back of the Ram with the Golden Fleece on its way to Colchis, and was drowned in the sea. This tantalising stretch of water, narrow in reality but enormous in its significance as the division of Europe and Asia, aroused the hubris and the cruelty of the Persian King Xerxes I when he launched his attack on the Greeks in 480 BC.

To this shore, then, beginning at Abydos, they, on whom this task was imposed, constructed bridges, the Phœnicians one with white flax, and the Egyptians the other with papyrus. The distance from Abydos to the opposite shore is seven stades. When the strait was thus united, a violent storm arising, broke in pieces and scattered the whole work. When Xerxes heard of this, being exceedingly indignant, he commanded that the Hellespont should be stricken with three hundred lashes with a scourge, and that a pair of fetters should be let down into the sea. I have moreover heard that with them he likewise sent branding instruments to brand the Hellespont. He certainly charged those who flogged the waters to utter these barbarous and impious words: 'Thou bitter water! thy master inflicts this punishment upon thee, because thou hast injured him, although thou hadst not suffered any harm from him. And king Xerxes will cross over thee, whether thou wilt or not; it is with justice that no man sacrifices to thee, because thou art both a deceitful and briny river!' He accordingly commanded them to chastise the sea in this manner, and to cut off the heads of those who had to superintend the joining of the Hellespont.

                                        Herodotus, *Histories* VII

In the middle ages two castles were built at the mouth of the Dardanelles to guard the straits, the 'Old Castles' of Asia and Rumeli (in contrast to the new castles of the Bosphorus) on the sites of ancient Sestos and Abydos, homes respectively of Hero and Leander, where Byron emulated Leander's feat in swimming the straits and caught a cold. J. P. Grelot visiting the Dardanelles in the 1670s recalled the defeat of the Venetian Lazaro Mocenigo at Natoli-Eski Hisar in 1657, which baulked his plan to capture Constantinople. Grelot went on to discuss the legends of this strange corner of the Greek world.

They who now inhabit these castles are of much the same disposition, where, as in several other parts of Greece you shall find several of those old kind of sorceresses which they call Striglais, who being addicted to all sorts of mischief in their infancy, and despairing of any other allurement to purchase their love, put to sale the affections of others, of which they falsely vaunt themselves to be the mistresses; or else they seek the satisfaction of their hatred. They make use of several sorts of witchcraft, some they call Philtra, to create affection; other Ecthra, to procure hatred; others Vaskarmiais or phtarmiais, that deal in all sorts of fascinations and enchantments. These old hags practise after various manners, according to the mischief which they design; and altho' they go to work but by night and in secret, for fear of being apprehended by the Soubachi, and thrown into the sea with a stone about their necks, tied up in a sack; yet I shall here set down one remarkable passage, which was related to me by a person that lived upon the place concerning one of these witches that was taken in the act.

This same race of Circe, having a design to revenge themselves upon any one that has perhaps but given them cross language in the street, do it in this manner. They rise about midnight, and take three flint stones, over which they mumble for about half an hour certain words, which they teach to none but their scholars. Which being done, they put the stones in the fire till they are red hot, at what time they take them out again to light a little wax candle at each, which they place upon the feet of a three-legged stool, in a kind of imitation of the Trikirion of the Greek bishops. This done, they lay the three-legged stool across their heads, take up the three flints, by this time cold, and in this equipage forth they go into the street where the party lives, and being come to the first place where they find three ways to meet, they throw the three stones into the three different passages, believing, that by the help of such words which they utter at the same time that those fascinations will procure the mischief they intend.

J. P. Grelot, *A late Voyage to Constantinople*; tr. J. Philips (1683)

## The Troad

Troy is one of the most renowned names in western literature. Homer's tale of Troy stands at the fountainhead of the epic tradition, and no traveller from the Renaissance onwards who visited the Aegean shore of Turkey could approach its site without recollections of Achilles and Agamemnon, Hector, Priam and Paris welling up in his memory. To many, these heroes were almost as real as their neighbours. Not only Chateaubriand, but Alexander the Great visited Troy with a copy of Homer conveniently accessible. The romantic attraction of Troy has produced an unusually rich crop of responses in poets, travellers and archaeologists. What was it they came to seek?

It was the crime of Paris, the son of Priam King of Troy, that began the Trojan War. He eloped with Helen, the wife of King Menelaus of Sparta. Always a flighty youth, his new fancy entailed the desertion of his childhood sweetheart Oenone, who, as Tennyson imagined the scene, sought to assuage her sorrow by wandering on the high ridges of Mt Ida, which dominates the plain of windy Troy from far to the south-east.

> There lies a vale in Ida, lovelier
> Than all the valleys of Ionian hills.
> The swimming vapor slopes athwart the glen,
> Puts forth an arm, and creeps from pine to pine,
> And loiters, slowly drawn. On either hand
> The lawns and meadow ledges midway down
> Hang rich in flowers, and far below them roars
> The long brook falling through the cloven ravine
> In cataract after cataract to the sea.
> Behind the valley topmost Garfiarus
> Stands up and takes the morning; but in front
> The gorges, opening wide apart, reveal
> Troas and Ilion's columned citadel,
> The crown of Troas.
>                          Hither came at noon
> Mournful Œnone, wandering forlorn
> Of Paris, once her playmate on the hills.
> Her cheek had lost the rose, and round her neck
> Floated her hair or seemed to float in rest.
> She, leaning on a fragment twined with vine,
> Sang to the stillness, till the mountain-shade
> Sloped downward to her seat from the upper cliff.

'O mother Ida, many-fountained Ida,
Dear mother Ida, harken ere I die.
For now the noonday quiet holds the hill:
The grasshopper is silent in the grass:
The lizard, with his shadow on the stone,
Rests like a shadow, and the cicala sleeps.
The purple flowers droop; the golden bee
Is lily-cradled: I alone awake.
My eyes are full of tears, my heart of love,
My heart is breaking, and my eyes are dim,
And I am all aweary of my life.

'O mother Ida, many-fountained Ida,
Dear mother Ida, harken ere I die.'

Alfred, Lord Tennyson, *Oenone*

The most famous episode of the Trojan War was the cunning stratagem of Odysseus that brought about its conclusion: the trick of the Wooden Horse. This famous trick is commemorated in the modern monument of a wooden horse near the archaeological site of Troy. None of the many descriptions has ever matched that of Virgil in the second book of the Aeneid, where the exiled Aeneas recounts the tale to Queen Dido of Carthage.

The Greeks grew weary of the tedious war,
And by Minerva's aid, a fabric reared,
Which like a steed of monstrous height appeared:
The sides were planked with pine: they feigned it made
For their return, and this the vow they paid.
Thus they pretend; but in the hollow side,
Selected numbers of their soldiers hide:
With inward arms the dire machine they load;
And iron bowels stuff the dark abode.
In sight of Troy lies Tenedos, an isle
(While Fortune did on Priam's empire smile)
Renowned for wealth; but since, a faithless bay,
Where ships exposed to wind and weather lay.
There was their fleet concealed. We thought, for Greece
Their sails were hoisted, and our fears release.
The Trojans, cooped within their walls so long,
Unbar their gates, and issue in a throng
Like swarming bees, and with delight survey
The camp deserted, where the Grecians lay:
The quarters of the several chiefs they showed:

Here Phœnix, here Achilles, made abode;
Here joined the battles; there the navy rode.
Part on the pile their wondering eyes employ –
The pile by Pallas raised to ruin Troy.
Thymœtes first ('tis doubtful whether hired,
Or so the Trojan destiny required)
Moved that the ramparts might be broken down,
To lodge the monster fabric in the town.
But Capys, and the rest of sounder mind,
The fatal present to the flames designed,
Or to the watery deep: at least to bore
The hollow sides, and hidden frauds explore.
The giddy vulgar, as their fancies guide,
With noise say nothing, and in parts divide.
Laocoön, followed by a numerous crowd,
Ran from the fort, and cried from far, aloud:
'O wretched countrymen! what fury reigns?
What more than madness has possessed your brains?
Think you the Grecians from your coasts are gone?
And are Ulysses' arts no better known?
This hollow fabric either must inclose
Within its blind recess, our secret foes;
Or 'tis an engine raised above the town
To overlook the walls, and then to batter down.
Somewhat is sure designed by fraud or force:
Trust not their presents, nor admit the horse.'
Thus having said, against the steed he threw
His forceful spear, which, hissing as it flew,
Pierced through the yielding planks of jointed wood.
And trembling in the hollow belly stood.
The sides, transpierced, return a rattling sound; [wound.
And groans of Greeks inclosed come issuing through the
And had not Heaven the fall of Troy designed,
Or had not men been fated to be blind,
Enough was said and don t' inspire a better mind.
Then had our lances pierced the treacherous wood,
And Ilian towers and Priam's empire stood.
                    Virgil *Aeneid* II; tr. John Dryden


The complete disappearance of the city of Troy itself became a
commonplace, a lesson in the mutability of human affairs. The
Roman Ovid, the Byzantine Agathias, and even Edmund
Spenser returned to the same theme.

Troy, that art now nought but an idle name,
And in thine ashes buried low dost lie,
Though whilome far much greater then thy fame,
Before that angry Gods and cruell skie
Upon thee heapt a direfull destinie;
What boots it boast thy glorious-descent,
And fetch from heven they great genealogie,
Sith all thy worthie prayses being blent
Their ofspring hath embaste, and later glory shent?

Most famous Worthy of the world, by whome
That warre was kindled which did Troy inflame,
And stately towres of Ilion whilome
Brought unto balefull ruine, was by name
Sir Paris far renownd through noble fame;
Who, through great prowesse and bold hardinesse,
From Lacedæmon fetcht the fayrest Dame
That ever Greece did boast, or knight possesse,
Whom Venus to him gave for meed of worthinesse;

Fayre Helene, flowre of beautie excellent,
And girlond of the mighty Conquerours,
That madest many Ladies deare lament
The heavie losse of their brave Paramours,
Which they far off beheld from Trojan toures,
And saw the fieldes of faire Scamander strowne
With carcases of noble warrioures
Whose fruitlesse lives were under furrow sowne,
And Xanthus sandy bankes with blood all overflowne.

Edmund Spenser, The Faerie Queene

The desolation of the scene in the mid–nineteenth century is effectively conveyed by Charles Newton, already on his way to greater discoveries at Halicarnassus.

The country between the Dardanelles and Troy is covered with brushwood, without a village, and scarcely any cultivated land. Nothing breaks the monotony of the horizon but the vast tumuli which appear at intervals against the sky, marking the grave of some Homeric hero. In travelling through this country, we saw but few human beings. Instead of the paved roads of Mytilene thronged with fat and greasy citizens riding home on their mules, and with all manner of traffic between the populous villages, the roads in the plain of Troy have long strings of camels on their way to some far country, and an occasional horseman armed to the teeth. These are all the traces of humanity visible, except the Sclavonian herdsman, who, with pistols in his belt and accompanied by dogs more savage than himself, tends his vast flocks of sheep and goats; for now, as in the time of Horace,

*Priami Paridisque busto*
*Insultat armentum.*

C. T. Newton, *Travels and Discoveries in the Levant* (1865)

Lady Mary Wortley Montagu in a letter of 1718 summed up the realist's position on the site of Troy, but drew attention also to some more conspicuous landmarks near the coast which served more vividly as aide-memoires to the classically educated traveller.

All that is now left of Troy is the ground on which it stood; for, I am firmly persuaded, whatever pieces of antiquity may be found round it are much more modern, and I think Strabo says the same thing. However, there is some pleasure in seeing the valley where I imagined the famous duel of Menelaus and Paris had been fought, and where the greatest city in the world was situate; and 'tis certainly the noblest situation that can be found for the head of a great empire, much to be preferred to that of Constantinople, the harbour here being always convenient for ships from all parts of the world, and that of Constantinople inaccessible almost six months in the year, while the north wind reigns.

North of the promontory of Sigeum we saw that of Rhœteum, famed for the sepulchre of Ajax. While I viewed these celebrated fields of rivers, I admired the exact geography of Homer, whom I had in my hand. Almost every epithet he gives to a mountain or plain is still just for it; and I spent several hours in as agreeable cogitations as ever Don Quixote had on mount Montesinos. We sailed that night to the shore, where 'tis vulgarly reported Troy stood; and I took the pains of rising at two in the morning to view coolly those ruins which are commonly shewed to strangers, and which the Turks call *Eski Stamboul, i.e.,* Old Constantinople. For that reason, as well as some others, I conjecture them to be the remains of that city begun by Constantine. I hired an ass (the only voiture to be had there), that I might go some miles into the country, and take a tour round the ancient walls, which are of a vast extent.

These latter were the ruins of Alexandria Troas, the city founded by Alexander the Great to recall his visit to Troy; but most travellers, like Thomas Coryate in 1612, took them for the ruins of Troy. (See my *Literary Companion to Travel in Greece* (1984), 301f).

The tumuli near Kum Kale, the ancient Cape Sigeum, have been traditionally known as the tombs of Achilles and Patroclus, which they certainly are not though their origin is quite uncertain. Other heroes have also from time to time had their names attached to these barrows, and the population of the dead has fluctuated more remarkably than that of the living who have gone away. Antilochus, Ajax, and others have all been given homes in one or other of the tumuli.

As early as Roman times they were connected with the heroes of the Trojan War, and the Greek writer of the third century AD, Philostratus, had the vine dresser who is the main speaker of his dialogue *Heroicus* regale a visitor with tales of the gigantic bones found in them, and of the ghostly appearances of the heroes.

My grandfather knew that people like yourself are sceptical about the gigantic size of the heroes; he told me that the tomb of Ajax had been destroyed by the sea, close to which it lies, and that bones had become visible in it which belonged to a man eleven cubits tall. And he told me that the Emperor Hadrian on visiting Troy had these bones laid out and the grave remade in honour of Ajax; he even embraced and kissed the bones.

. . . .

The shepherds do not dare to visit the place at midday for the clatter of ghosts which rage in that place.

. . . .

The shepherds and goatherds still see on the plain of Troy great and divine beings, and they often portend some evil. If they appear covered in dust, they portend drought; if drenched in sweat, there will be rain and storms; if there is blood on their bodies and their weapons, they will send plagues to Ilion. But if none of these things is observed on the ghosts, they bring fine weather and the herdsmen sacrifice to them a lamb, a bull, a foal or whatever is appropriate. When blight descends on the cattle, they say it is from Ajax, because of the story that Ajax slaughtered the sheep in the belief that he was murdering the Achaeans after the judgment on the arms of Achilles. And no one pastures their sheep near his tomb for fear; for everything that grows there is noxious and harmful to flocks.

Philostratus, *Heroicus*; tr. R. S.

Alexander the Great, thinking the tomb of Achilles to be here, emulated the feat of Achilles in running three times around the tomb of Patroclus. He stripped naked and carried out the circuit of the tomb said to be Achilles' to the applause

of his assembled army. This feat established a further prece-
dent, and the Emperor Caracalla made sure on his visit to Troy
to do exactly as Alexander had done. Even Charles Cockerell,
the young architect who came this way in 1811, could not
resist the romantic urge to imitate the great heroes of Greece in
this way.

A more surprising enthusiast for these venerable if spurious
monuments was the Sultan Mehmed the Conqueror, the
victor of the siege of Constantinople. He managed to extract a
political point from his visit.

> How the Sultan examined the tombs of the
> heroes, as he passed through Troy, and how he
> praised and congratulated them

And he praised and congratulated them, their memory and their
deeds, and on having a person like the poet Homer to extol them. He
is reported to have said, shaking his head a little, 'God has reserved
for me, through so long a period of years, the right to avenge this city
and its inhabitants. For I have subdued their enemies and have
plundered their cities and made them the spoils of the Mysians. It
was the Greeks and Macedonians and Thessalians and Pelopon-
nesians who ravaged this place in the past, and whose descendants
have now through my efforts paid the just penalty, after a long
period of years, for their injustice to us Asiatics at that time and so
often in subsequent times.'

Critoboulos, *History of Mehmed the Conqueror*; tr. C. T. Riggs
(Princeton 1954)

When Hobhouse and Byron visited the Troad together in
1811, Byron could be induced to pay but little attention to the
antiquities: he preferred shooting snipe. But Hobhouse devoted a good deal of time to these tumuli and to some
fraudulent 'excavations' that had recently been carried out
there.

The son of Signor Solomon Ghormezano, French Consul at the
Dardanelles, was employed for two months, in the year 1787, in
opening the barrow, and worked at it alone, and by night, saying
that he was looking for a spring of water, 'so necessary to the
inhabitants of Giaur-Keui.' At length he discovered the place where
the relics were deposited. He immediately collected the whole, and
communicated his success to his employer, filling a large chest with
what he had found. This consisted of pieces of burned bones; pieces
of a large broken metal vase, with a small ornament round the rim;

some charcoal; a piece of calcined mortar of triangularly shaped metal [*sic*]; pieces of fine pottery, well painted with wreaths of flowers; some bits of large vases; small cups, some of them entire; a fragment of brass a foot and a half long, and in circumference as big as a quart bottle, weighing seven or eight pounds, which was at first called the hilt of a sword, but afterwards by Mr. De Choiseul declared to be the statue of a man, with a lion under each foot!!! And lastly, a small transparent piece of tube, a foot long and two inches in diameter, ornamented with chased or embossed branches, in good preservation.

'At the foundation of the barrow was a large slab, extending, as he supposed, over the whole surface, as, wherever he dug, he still found it: in the middle was a hole twelve feet square, around which was raised a wall three feet high, which was the sepulchre containing the relics; on the outside of this stone was strewed a quantity of lime, and of charcoal, supposed to be the ashes of the funeral pile.'

Now this is extracted from the account of the person who opened the barrow; but Mr. Le Chevalier says, 'towards the centre of the monument two large stones were found leaning at an angle, the one against the other, and forming a sort of tent, under which was presently discovered a small statue of Minerva, seated in a chariot with four horses, and an urn of metal, filled with ashes, charcoal, and human bones. This urn, which is now in the possession of the Comte de Choiseul, is encircled in sculpture with a vine-branch, from which are suspended branches of grapes, done with exquisite art.'

· · · ·

We have only the word of the Jew for the whole story; if, however, his account is true, the wonders of Mr. Le Chevalier must be fictions. The Minerva has, indeed, been modelled by Mr. Fauvel of Athens, and other specimens have been handed about, which have an appearance of extreme antiquity, but may have been found elsewhere, or have been manufactured at Paris. Both of the details cannot be correct; either the Jew is not to be believed, or Mr. Le Chevalier must have ventured at an imposture; for it is impossible to suppose that the fragments found by Ghormezano could have been metamorphosed by the heated imagination even of the most zealous antiquary into the Minerva and sepulchral urn of Mr. De Choiseul. It is now almost impracticable to collect any information on the subject at the spot; for the same secrecy is observed respecting the discovery at this time as at the period of the transaction.

J. C. Hobhouse, *Journey through Albania* (1813)

But the most vigorous efforts of the travellers were devoted to the attempt to establish the exact site of the lost city of Troy. Homer provided some tantalising clues in his description of

Achilles' pursuit of the Trojan prince Hector around the walls
of Troy.

> As Hector sees, unusual terrors rise,
> Struck by some god, he fears, recedes, and flies.
> He leaves the gates, he leaves the wall behind:
> Achilles follows like the winged wind.
> Thus at the panting dove a falcon flies
> (The swiftest racer of the liquid skies),
> Just when he holds, or thinks he holds his prey,
> Obliquely wheeling through the aërial way,
> With open beak and shrilling cries he springs,
> And aims his claws, and shoots upon his wings:
> No less fore-right the rapid chase they held,
> One urged by fury, one by fear impell'd:
> Now circling round the walls their course maintain,
> Where the high watch-tower overlooks the plain;
> Now where the fig-trees spread their umbrage broad,
> (A wider compass,) smoke along the road.
> Next by Scamander's double source they bound,
> Where two famed fountains burst the parted ground;
> This hot through scorching clefts is seen to rise,
> With exhalations steaming to the skies;
> That the green banks in summer's heat o'erflows,
> Like crystal clear, and cold as winter snows:
> Each gushing fount a marble cistern fills,
> Whose polish'd bed receives the falling rills;
> Where Trojan dames (ere yet alarm'd by Greece)
> Wash'd their fair garments in the days of peace.
> By these they pass'd, one chasing, one in flight:
> (The mighty fled, pursued by stronger might:)
> Swift was the course; no vulgar prize they play,
> No vulgar victim must reward the day:
> (Such as in races crown the speedy strife:)
> The prize contended was great Hector's life.
>
> Homer, *Iliad* 22; tr. Alexander Pope

It was those two springs that provided the focus of the
discussion. In antiquity it had been generally assumed that
Troy was on the same site as the Roman City of New Ilium,
but the local historian Demetrius of Scepsis insisted that
Homer's indications did not fit that site on the hill of Hisarlik.
Instead he placed Troy at a place called Callicolone where there
were two springs close together, and this view became

canonical through its adoption by the Augustan geographer Strabo. It was argued exhaustively by Robert Wood in 1750, and with definitive thoroughness by Jean-Baptiste Lechevalier in 1791. Troy was universally taken to be at Callicolone, which was now called Pınarbaşı.

Edward Daniell Clarke in 1801 was the first to question seriously the identification, placing Troy instead of Ciplak, not far from Hisarlik. This is how he eliminated the claims of Pınarbaşı. At the first spring,

We first tried the water with our hands; it felt warm, and even the rock near and above the surface of the water was sensibly affected by heat. We then had recourse to our thermometer: it was graduated according to the scale of *Celsius*; but we shall give the result according to the corresponding elevation of *Fahrenheit*, being more adapted to common observation in *England*. When exposed to the external air, the mercury stood at 48°; or sixteen degrees above the freezing point. We then placed it in one of the crevices whence the water issued, so as to immerse both the tube and the scale: in two minutes, the mercury rose to 62°, and it there remained. We then tried the same experiment in all the other crevices; and found the heat of the water the same, although the temperature of the external air was lowered to 47°. From hence we proceeded to the hot spring of M. *Chevalier*; and could not avoid being struck by the plausible appearance it offereed, for those who wished to find here a *hot* and a *cold* spring, as *fountains* of the *Scamander*. It gushes perpendicularly out of the earth, rising from the bottom of a *marble* and *granite* reservoir, and throwing up as much water as the famous fountain of *Holywell* in *Flintshire*. Its surface seems vehemently boiling; and during cold weather, the condensed vapour above it causes the appearance of a cloud of smoke over the well. The *marble* and *granite* slabs around it are of great antiquity; and its appearance, in the midst of surrounding trees, is highly picturesque. The mercury had now fallen, in the external air, to 46°, the sun being down; but when the thermometer was held under water, it rose as before, to 62°. Notwithstanding the warmth of this spring, fishes were seen sporting in the reservoir. When held in the stream of either of the two channels which conduct the product of these springs into a marsh below, the temperature of the water was diminished, in proportion to its distance from the source whence it flowed. We repeated similar observations afterwards, both at midnight, and in the morning before sun-rise; but always with the same results. Hence it is proved, that the *fountains* of *Bonarbashy* are all of them *warm* springs; and there are many such springs, of different degrees of temperature, in all the district through which the *Mender* flows, from *Ida* to the *Hellespont*.

E. D. Clarke *Travels*,★ ch. 5.

In 1822 Charles Maclaren published an argument for Hisarlik: it would have been impossible to run three times round Balı Dağ in heavy armour, as Homer had said the heroes did; and Pınarbaşı was invisible from the crest of Mt Ida from whence Zeus was said to have watched the progress of the war; and there were two springs at Hisarlik too. Byron tired of the argument, and mocked 'the European youth Whom to the spot their schoolboy feelings bear'; but the ground was now ready for the dramatic intervention of Heinrich Schliemann, who followed a dream and made it reality by excavating the city he claimed had haunted him since childhood.

In conclusion, I flatter myself with the hope that, as a reward for my enormous expenses and all my privations, annoyances, and sufferings in this wilderness, but above all for my important discoveries, the civilised world will acknowledge my right to re-christen this sacred locality; and in the name of the divine Homer I baptize it with that name of immortal renown, which fills the heart of everyone with joy and enthusiasm: I give it the name of TROY and ILIUM, and I call the acropolis, where I am writing these lines, by the name of *Pergamus of Troy*.

Heinrich Schliemann, *Troy and Its Remains*;

tr. L. Dora Schmitz (1875)

# CHAPTER THREE

# Ionia and Lydia

The seaboard of Asia Minor is littered with the skeletons of magnificent cities. From Troy in the north to Xanthus in the south, the names are a roll-call of the proud origins of Western thought and of the wealth that Roman rule brought to Anatolia. Ephesus, Miletus and Colophon, where philosophy was born; Cnidus of the famous Aphrodite; Didyma of the oracles, Priene of the town planners, Pergamon the capital of the cultured Attalid dynasty: all these cities rose in the fifth century BC, flourished first modestly and then, under Rome, magnificently. The rivers silted up the sea, landlocking their harbours and burying their buildings; Christians superseded pagans, despite flurries under philhellenes like Hadrian and Julian; and the cities declined into medieval villages, the victims for a millennium of Sassanians and Saracens, Seljuk and Ottoman Turks, Gauls and Goths. Crippled by onslaught they sank into reedy desolation about their towering temples and theatres, until travellers came from Europe to redeem them from oblivion.

Most visitors to the Aegean coast of Turkey and its hinterland will make their headquarters at Izmir or at Kuşadası, or perhaps the now popular resort of Bodrum. The most central is Kuşadası; Izmir is the best centre for Pergamum and Teos, Bodrum for the more southerly sites. The sites have accordingly been arranged in three groups around each of these centres. The whole of this area had the closest connection with Greece in the classical period and many cities remained Greek throughout the Ottoman domination and until the exchange of populations between Greece and Turkey in 1922. Most of the travellers in modern times were mainly on the hunt for

classical and Christian echoes, and distinctively Turkish culture and tales show a correspondingly slight presence in their
annals.

## Izmir

We start at Izmir, 'Infidel Smyrna', which first enters history
as one of seven contenders to be the birthplace of Homer, and
in modern times was one of the most hospitable points on the
Turkish coast for the visiting giaour. In its nineteenth-century
heyday it was a prosperous merchant city with a predominantly Greek bourgeoisie. But few travellers would spend
time on its prosaic aspects when such a wealth of curiosities
was to be encountered. Here, for a start, is George Wheler, the
young divine and botanical enthusiast who travelled with the
learned Jacob Spon and added to his *Journey into Greece*, beside
Spon's learning, his own 'weeds and divine reflections'.

About Smyrna are abundance of camelions; which is an animal
something resembling a lizard; but hath his back gibbous, like a hog;
and its feet are divided like the claws of a wood-pecker, or parrot;
two claws before, and three behind; which are not separated from
each other, until near the ends. A long tail it hath, like a rat, and is
ordinarily as big; but it hath very little, or no motion with its head.
They are in great abundance about the old walls of the castle; where
they breed, and lie in holes, and heaps of ruins. Several we saw; and
two we kept twenty days at least: in which time we made the
following observations upon them.

  Their colour useth to be green, darker toward the back, and lighter
towards the belly, inclining to a yellow, with spots sometimes of a
reddish colour, and sometimes whitish. But the green would often
change into a dark dirt-colour, without any appearance of
green. . . . This changing of colours is given to this creature by
nature, for its preservation. . . . When it sees itself in danger to be
caught, it opened its mouth and hissed like a snake. In a small time
after I put it into my handkerchief, it turned the same colour, white,
with some spots and a little tincture of red. This little one changed its
colour more nimbly than others that were greater.
                           ·   ·   ·   ·

  Of its excrement I remarked nothing: but my comrade telleth, that
a person of curiosity at Lyons, assured him from his own observations, that although the camelion did eat little, or nothing; yet it
nevertheless made much excrement.
                       ·   ·   ·   ·

And this is what I observed of this wonderful animal; which thus challengeth praise for its creator, the lord of all wonder.

Here are abundance of Pellicans . . . ·

George Wheler, *Journey into Greece* (1682)

Smyrna was the base of operations for the expedition of the Society of Dilettanti led by Richard Chandler in 1764.

Chandler, in his account of the neighbourhood of Smyrna, mentions a supposed cave of Homer, pointed out to him near the upper aqueducts of Megalos Paradeisos, and which he says he visited. This cave, into which I descended amidst brambles and weeds, is a long narrow passage, excavated in the soft calcareous tuff which has been deposited by a neighbouring spring, and in which are a few impressions of the leaves of recent plants. The gallery is evidently the remains of an ancient aqueduct, for the purpose of conveying the water through the projecting promontory, where the rock was too precipitous to carry it round. It resembles, both in shape and appearance, those which are seen in the hills in the neighbourhood of Rome, and its antiquity is probably not very great.

W. J. Hamilton*

This cave was visited in 1699 by the young antiquary Edmund Chishull, who was moved by it to an effusion of Latin verse no doubt welcomed by its recipient, his former schoolmaster at Winchester College:

> No Nymph can boast
> More learned gods than Smyrna, Homer's city.
> Hearken, ye sons of Wykeham! in a shady vale
> I read in his great Iliad, and I slept
> At Meles' sounding Cave, when suddenly
> The hallowed shade of reverend Homer stood
> Before me, solved the towns' dispute, and said
> 'Harm not the holy turf on which the bard once wrote!'
>     I rise, and honouring the aged father,
> At once made for the town at Tmolus' foot.
> Here once stood Gyges' palace, Croesus', Sardis' king,
> Where father Hermus flows and nourishes the fields,
> And golden Pactolus slides from his caves.
>         Iter Poeticum, in *Antiquitates Asiaticae* (1728); tr. R. S.

Travellers seem always to have been fascinated by Smyrna, which blended prosperity and cosmopolitanism with all the fascination of the East. The studious traveller W. J. Hamilton and Miss F. M. Skene, the daughter of the Scottish painter of

Greek scenes James Skene, responded alike to the colour and variety of the bazaars, to the allurements of the Western opera as well as the eternal image of the caravan of camels.

In modern Smyrna, the objects most deserving of attention are the bazaars, which, though inferior to those of Constantinople, are in some respects more remarkable. Goods of different kinds are sold in different parts, arranged in wooden booths spread over a large extent of ground. The narrow road or path between them is covered in, and sometimes boarded under foot. At night they are regularly locked up and guarded by watchmen. One long row of booths is occupied by the sellers of dried fruits, where baskets of raisins, figs, dates, apricots, and plums are arranged in inviting piles; whilst a neigh-bouring gallery is occupied by shops, solely devoted to the manufac-ture of the wooden drums or boxes in which the figs of Smyrna are sent to Europe. Fresh fruit is usually sold in the streets and open market-places. In another part are the bazaars for ancient arms, matchlocks, yataghans, and pistols, with other curiosities, and objects of virtú. Pipes are sold in another quarter, and one gallery, called the English bazaar, is occupied by cotton goods, and printed calicoes chiefly from Manchester.

But perhaps the most striking object there is the great variety of curious and gay costumes, various even amongst the different classes of Turks; but still more so from the heterogeneous nations that swarm and congregate in this busy quarter. The grave and stately Turkish merchant or shopkeeper, in his ample robes, and squatting on his shop-board, contrasts with the strong, active, and almost gigantic *hamal* or porter, bending beneath a burthen which it seems scarcely possible for the human back to sustain; though I have been informed that it is not unusual for them to carry a load of twelve or fourteen cwt. Their dress is as simple as that of the other is osten-tatious, with bare legs and white drawers, and a wisp of cotton-cloth rolled round their dirty fez or red skull-cap. Again, the Xebeque from the mountains, and the banks of the Mæander, with bare legs and white drawers fitting tight to his thighs, but made preposter-ously loose behind, with his high and gaudy turban bedecked with tassels and fringes, is a very different being from the Euruque or Turcoman, clad in sombre brown, tramping along in heavy-shod iron boots, and driving on his camels and asses laden with charcoal for sale. Then the Armenians and Levantines, with their huge kalpaks and flowing robes, their dark complexions, and clean-shaved chins, are as different from the mean-looking fair-haired Jews, with bare foreheads, long-pointed beards, and rather open necks, as anything can well be imagined: it is extraordinary how many fair effeminate-looking persons there are amongst the Jews of

Smyrna. Again, what a striking difference we see between the proud chavasse with his splendid arms, his dagger, pistols, and silver-mounted yataghan, and the bandy-legged, half-starved tactico (regular infantry soldier), with his ugly, useless fez and blue tassel, looking half angry and half ashamed of his ill-made and un-mahometan dress! Hard by is a long train of Turkish women, silently shuffling along in their yellow slippers, whose spectral dress forms a striking variety to the party-coloured figures by which they are surrounded. Their faces are invisible, being concealed by a black silk mask, which strangely clashes with the white shroud or cloak thrown over their heads, and which almost envelopes their bodies in its ample folds. It is rare indeed that any other part of their dress can be seen but the hem of a robe or the tip of a yellow boot.

W. J. Hamilton*

The Bridge of the Caravans, is long and narrow, built over a rapid, winding stream, and connecting the town with a much frequented road leading into the interior of the country. For this reason, it is constantly the scene of that most beautiful pageant of Eastern manners, from which it derives its name, as there is an almost unceasing succession of caravans passing over it. It is surrounded by a vast number of lofty and luxuriant trees, which renders the moving picture hourly to be seen on it, still more striking. First, distinctly heard in the intense stillness of the air, comes the low tinkle of the camel bells, and then, appearing and vanishing again among the waving branches, the long undulating procession is seen to wind along the road. As they ascend the bridge, the varied objects of striking interest, which form as a whole so picturesque a scene, are gradually displayed in slow succession; then descending on the other side, the train is lost among the green woods and projecting rocks, till, long after, it may be seen, like a dark serpent winding over the brow of the hill. At the head of the line, walks the demure and modest little donkey, leading, without bit or bridle, the whole procession, and under whose guidance alone, his magnificent com-panions will consent to move a step; and, meekly following him, a string of some eighteen or twenty camels move along with slow majestic step, wreathing their long necks with their own peculiar and graceful movement, and looking with their half-shut eyes as gentle and mild, as in reality they are vicious and dangerous. The drivers who guide them by the voice alone, are mounted on their backs; the flowing draperies of their oriental dresses gathered round them, as they sit with folded arms musing thoughtfully. These men are all from the interior, true children of the desert, over whom no breath of civilisation has passed; and as they emerged from the thick wood, and one by one threw back the white bernous from their dark countenances, to examine the evening sky, there was something in the calm look with which they fixed their clear black eyes upon the pale star rising in the far horizon, that seemed to reveal to me how different must be the whole aspect of the world to them, from what it is to men who dwell in cities in contact with each other, in a thick atmosphere of humanity as it were, instead of drawing their inspirations from nature alone as these do, and that, the vast solemn nature of the desert.

F. M. Skene, *Wayfaring Sketches* (1847)

## Bergama

The ruins of ancient Pergamum lie some way north-east of Izmir, atop a precipitous mountain nearly a thousand feet above the plain. Pergamum was one of the most illustrious cities of the Hellenistic period. Its splendour coincided with the reign of the Attalid dynasty, named after Attalus who became king in 241 BC. His son Eumenes II was responsible for the erection of most of the buildings that adorn the acropolis, including the massive Altar of Zeus, a thank-offering for victory whose reliefs of the Battle of Gods and Giants were one of the most powerful works of Pergamene art. He also built the Library which presented such a powerful challenge to that of King Ptolemy in Alexandria that the latter forbade the export of papyrus on which books were copied. Nothing daunted, the Pergamenes responded by inventing parchment (it is named after them) as an alternative medium for the copying of books.

Eumenes' great-nephew Attalus III was the last king of Pergamum. Regarding absorption into the Roman Empire as inevitable, he bequeathed his possessions (ie. his kingdom) to Rome, and in 133 BC the Attalid kingdom became the Roman province of Asia. And the Library? Mark Antony gave it as a present to Cleopatra, and it foundered in the wreck of that great love and bid for world supremacy.

Pergamum was ruined in the middle ages by one of the earthquakes that plagued Asia Minor, and when the future Emperor Theodore II Lascaris visited it in the fifteenth century it could only arouse a nostalgic admiration for the achievements of those Hellenes of a millennium and a half ago.

We arrived at Pergamos, a city as it were celestial, a dwelling not for spirits, but for men as a protection against demons (who these may be, must be surmised). It is hard to view thoroughly, and no less hard to ascend. It is full of theatres, these being so aged and wasted by time that the brilliance is to be seen as it were in a glass. . . . It is full everywhere of the majesty of the Hellenic spirit, and the vestiges of their wisdom: the city itself demonstrates this in its disdain for us, mere latecomers to the greatness of its ancestral glory. For these buildings are overwhelming compared with the structures of today – although Aristotle writes that, in general, everything is less than wonder leads us to suppose. Walls rise up no less high than the brazen heaven, great in artistry. Through the middle runs a river, bridged by spreading arches. By the governor of the poles!, one would hardly think them made by hand, but as it were of a piece with the earth and of solid stone. If Phidias or any sculptor should see them, he would be amazed at their regularity and purity of line. Among the buildings are low cells (kelludria?), which appear to be the refuse of perished dwellings, and fill the beholder's sight with pain. . . . On either side of the walls of the great theatre stand cylindrical towers, vying with each other in the smoothness of their stonework, and girdled with zones. These could never be the work of hands, or the conception that of a modern mind: they astonish the onlooker. . . . Looking at the citadel, how did we despond, how did we leap and dance, transported in joy mixed with pain and weeping through our delight.

Theodore II Lascaris, *Letters*; tr. R. S.

The Great Altar, which had been one of the Seven Wonders of the World, was buried underground. The only memory of it that remained was the description in Revelation 2 of Pergamum as the Throne of Satan – an appropriate designation for a monument that celebrated war in heaven. In the nineteenth century travellers could see only the massive city walls and some other fragments, which were rapidly disappearing to be re-used in building. It was one man with an obsession, the engineer Carl Humann, who recovered this monument for posterity. His correspondent, the director of the Berlin museum, recognised from his description of some reliefs that he had discovered the great relief of the Gods and Giants that had adorned the Altar of Zeus. Stone by stone Humann and his team brought the great work to light.

When I had blasted the wall down so far that we were close up to it I personally carefully removed stone after stone and found the neck and chin, then the left cheek and the eye. When I saw the eye I cried out: '*That's a dead man!*' For this statue, although completely and beautifully sincere, definitely had the emaciated and stark look of death. I am telling you this because it shows that one can set no great store by my *artistic* critical faculty. Eventually the statue was completely excavated and turned out to be a beautiful youth with curly hair, stretched out, the breast high and drum-like (25 centimetres) the right arm, unfortunately broken, raised, the left hanging down, the head slightly inclined to one side, the mouth half open, not distorted by pain, but rather by fatigue, as though asleep; only the wide-open, rolled back eyes showed that we were looking at a man killed in battle. Strength and beauty were here united in most marvellous harmony. To the left a leg belonging to another statue is visible.

.   .   .   .

I hope it is not just the ecstasy of discovering something oneself which leads me to say that we have here a masterpiece of sculpture. My sketches drawn in the courtyard with frozen fingers, can only give you an inaccurate impression of the beauty of these pieces.

Carl Humann, *Der Pergamon-Altar*; tr. C. M. Kaine

The relief was transported in its entirety to Berlin, where it was reconstructed and put on exhibition with other monumental structures from the Middle East such as the Great Gate of Babylon, in what is now the Pergamon Museum in East Berlin.

## Siğaçik

Siğaçik is the site of ancient Teos, memorable in poetry as the grave of the cheerful and gracious poet of love and wine Anacreon. A life of pleasant comfort at the court of the tyrant Polycrates of Samos ended when the latter was crucified as the result of a treacherous Persian plot; but his grave reflects the atmosphere of his poetry, and he was evoked by his younger contemporary Simonides, and by the youthful Goethe as a fellow-hedonist.

> Mother of purple grapes, soul-soothing vine,
> Whose verdant boughs their graceful tendrils twine:
> Still round this urn, with youth unfading, bloom,
> The gentle slope of old Anacreon's tomb.
> For so the unmixed-goblet-loving sire,
> Touching the livelong night his amorous lyre,

Even low in earth, upon his brows shall wear
The ruddy clustering crowns they branches bear,
Where, though still fall the sweetest dews, the song
Distilled more sweetly from that old man's tongue.

Simonides, tr. H. H. Milman

Here where the briar rose blooms, where vines and laurels
   entangle,
  Here where the turtledove moans, here where the grasshopper
   trills,
What is this grave on which all the immortal gods have besprinkled
  Beauty and vigorous green? Here is Anacreon at peace.
Springtime, summer and autumn the god-loved poet enjoyed;
  Forever under this hill, winter is kept from his bones.

Goethe; tr. R. S.

Teos was one of the first sites visited by Richard Chandler's expedition to study the antiquities of Ionia, one of the foremost attractions of which was the Temple of Dionysus here.

In the morning we crossed the isthmus to Teos, now called Bodrun.[1] We found this city almost as desolate as Erythræ and Clazomene. The walls, of which traces are extant, were, as we guessed, about five miles in circuit; the masonry handsome. Without them, by the way, are vaults of sepulchres stripped of their marble, as it were forerunners of more indistinct ruin. Instead of the stately piles, which once impressed ideas of opulence and grandeur, we saw a marsh, a field of barley in ear, buffaloes ploughing heavily by defaced heaps and prostrate edifices, high trees supporting aged vines, and fences of stones and rubbish, with illegible inscriptions, and time-worn fragments. It was with difficulty we discovered the temples of Bacchus; but a theatre in the side of the hill is more conspicuous. The vault only, on which the seats ranged, remains, with two broken pedestals in the area . . .

The city-port is partly dry, and sand-banks rise above the surface of the water. On the edge are vestiges of a wall, and before it are two small islets. On the left hand, or toward the continent, is a channel, which seemed artificial, the water not deep. I saw a boy wade across it . . . Beyond it, on the shore before Sevri-hissar, which stands inland, are four or five tall barrows.

The heap of the temple of Bacchus lay in the middle of a corn field, and is overrun with bushes and olive-trees. It was one of the most celebrated structures in Ionia. The remains of it have been engraved

---

[1] Chandler seems to be confused, unless *bodrun* ('cellar, vault') was a local name for the ruins.

at the expense of the society of Dilettanti, and published, with its history, in the *Ionian Antiquities*; and a beautiful portico has since been erected at the seat of the right hon. lord le Despenser, near High Wycomb [sic], under the inspection of Mr. Revett, in which the exact proportions of the order are observed.

The town has long been deserted. It has no ruins of churches, to prove it existed under the Greek emperors; nor of mosques or baths, to show it was frequented by the Turks. In the time of Anacreon the Teians migrated, from a love of liberty, to Thrace, but some afterwards came back, and the city reflourished. They are now utterly gone, and it is likely never to return. The site is a wilderness; and the low grounds, which are wet, produce the iris, or flag, blue and white. This flower is stamped on the money of Teos. We saw cranes here stalking singly in the corn and grass, and picking up and gorging insects and reptiles; or flying heavily with long sticks in their mouths to the tops of trees, and of the remoter houses and chimneys, on which they had agreed to fix their habitation.

Richard Chandler, *Travels in Asia Minor* (1775)

## Ephesus

### Ephesus

And where stands Ephesus, in days gone by
Pride of the East, Ionia's radiant eye,
Boasting the shrine to famed Diana reared,
Earth's wonder called, that myriad hearts revered?
There spreads Selinus' lake beneath the hill,
And flows unchanged the Cayster's willowed rill;
These speak the city near, – through waving grass,
O'er blackened stones, we slowly laboring pass;
Across our way the timid leveret springs;
Woke from his sleep, the snake uncoils his rings.
No street we tread, but climb a grass-grown mound, –
What! is this Ephesus that moulders round?
The embattled walls that swept o'er Lepre's side,
To shapeless ruin crushed, have stooped their pride:
Where stood that early church Paul loved so well,
No cross, no tomb, no stone remains to tell.
Diana's fane that, glassed in depths below,
From bronze and silver cast a starry glow,
With statues, colonnades, and courts apart,
And porphyry pillars, each the pride of art, –
Have Time's stern scythe, man's rage, and flood and fire,
Left naught for curious pilgrims to admire?

A few poor footsteps now may cross the shrine,
Cell, long arcade, high altar, all supine;
Bound with thick ivy, broken columns lie,
Through low rent arches winds of evening sigh,
Rough brambles choke the vaults where gold was stored,
And toads spit venom forth where priests adored.

The shivering bolt of ruthless ruin falls
On pleasure's haunts, as well as priestly walls:
See! in the circus, where gay chariots pressed
Their rapid race, the plover builds her nest.
Ten thousand voices rang from yonder hill,
There, clothed with moss, sweep circling benches still,
But e'en the peasant shuns that spot in fear,
So deep the voiceless calm, its look so drear.
Poor actors! Greek or Roman, where are they,
That toiled and laughed to make their fellows gay?
Down the long stream of sable Lethe tost,
Their graves unknown, and e'en their memories lost.

Yet, Ephesus! while desolate and lorn,
And though thy starless night shall know no morn,
Cold is the breast of him who looks on thee,
And feels no thrill of solemn ecstasy.
As musing now we walk thy desert bound,
The heart leaps up as at a trumpet's sound,
For here, e'en here, – name never to expire, –
Paul taught his church, and breathed his words of fire;
These very stones his foot perchance hath trod,
These roofless walls have heard his prayers to God.
There did Demetrius raise his heathen cry
'Gainst him who led men's wandering thoughts on high,
Showed the dark errors of their baseless dreams,
Poured on the spirit's night celestial beams,
And cheered us with the hope, when worms shall prey
On this poor form consigned to slow decay,
The soul, with added powers and new-fledged plume,
Shall spring to life and joy, beyond the tomb.

Ay, Paul's bright fame, above the fame of kings,
On these sad ruins dazzling lustre flings.
But chief tradition points to yon rude tower,
Where passed in bonds the apostle's lonely hour,
And pious hands have reared in later day
These fretted Gothic walls, and arches gray:
Within this cell – hush, heart! thy fluttering fears –

To Fancy's eye his godlike form appears:
What solemn thought that lofty brow displays!
What holy fervor in that lifted gaze!
Monarchs! behold a greater far than ye;
Conquerors! to Christ's brave champion bend the knee!

Nicholas Michell

This poem of the Cornish poet Nicholas Michell (1807–1880) incorporates most of the details that have made Ephesus famous in history. A modest Greek city in the fifth century BC, its chief fame was as birthplace of Heraclitus 'the weeping philosopher' whose dark and enigmatic pronouncements continue to tease the minds of historians of ancient philosophy. Heraclitus would have been able to admire the Temple of Artemis in his native city which counted as one of the wonders of the ancient world; burnt down one night in the year Alexander the Great was born by a madman called Herostratus who hoped thereby to make himself famous for ever, it was rebuilt on the same site and according to the same designs though in the newer hellenistic style. This was the temple that Pliny the Elder saw when the city was in its heyday, under the Roman Empire.

Chandler's discussion is as good a summary as any of the ancient traditions of the temple, though by his time all trace of it had vanished.

The worship of the great goddess Diana had been established at Ephesus in a remote age. The Amazons, it is related, sacrificed to her there, on their way to Attica, in the time of Theseus; and some writers affirmed, the image was first set up by them under a tree. The vulgar afterwards believed it fell down from Jupiter. It was never changed, though the temple had been restored seven times.

This idol, than which none has been ever more splendidly enshrined, was of a middling size, and of very great antiquity, as was evident from the fashion, it having the feet closed. It was of wood, which some had pronounced cedar, and other ebony. Mutianus, a noble Roman, who was the third time consul in the year of our Lord seventy-five, affirmed from his own observation, that it was vine, and had many holes filled with nard to nourish and moisten it, and to preserve the cement. It was gorgeously apparelled; the vest embroidered with emblems and symbolical devices; and, to prevent its tottering, a bar of metal, it is likely of gold, was placed under each hand. A veil or curtain, which was drawn up from the floor to the ceiling, hid it from view, except while service was performing in the temple.

The priests of the goddess were eunuchs, and exceedingly respected by the people. The old institutions required that virgins should assist them in their office, but, in process of time, these, as Strabo has remarked, were not all observed.

. . . .

It may be imagined, that many stories of the power and interposition of the goddess were current and believed at Ephesus. The most striking evidence of the reality of her existence, and of her regard for her suppliants, was probably furnished by her supposed manifestations of herself in visions. In the history of Massiliæ, now Marseilles, it is related, that she was seen by Aristarche, a lady of high rank, while sleeping, and that she commanded her to accompany the Greek adventurers, by whom that city was founded. Metagenes, one of the architects of her temple at Ephesus, had invented a method of raising the vast stones to the necessary height, but it did not succeed so well as was expected, with a marble of prodigious size, designed to be placed over the doorway. He was excessively troubled, and, weary of ruminating, fell asleep, when he beheld the goddess, who bade him be comforted, she had been his friend. The next day the stone was found to have settled, apparently from its own weight, as he wished.

Richard Chandler, *Travels in Asia Minor* (1775)

Ephesus was the home of wonder workers: the Emperor Vespasian's private magician was an Ephesian. So Ephesus made a natural setting for one of the miracles of the mysterious sage of the first century AD Apollonius of Tyana. Part literary pundit, part holy man, Apollonius represented a type not infrequent in the high Empire, and was the subject of a fascinating biography by Philostratus.

In Ephesus, however, the plague had arrived and nothing proved effective against it. They sent an embassy to Apollonius, therefore, hoping to make him the curer of their misfortune. He decided to make the journey without delay, and after merely saying, 'Let us go', he was in Ephesus, imitating, I suppose, Pythagoras's famous miracle of being in Thurii and Metapontum both at once. He summoned the Ephesians together, and said, 'Don't worry. I will end the plague today.'

So saying, he led them all, young and old, towards the theatre where the statue of the Averter stands. There they found what appeared to be an old beggar, pretending to have his eyes closed. He carried a bag and a lump of bread in it, and had ragged clothing and a wrinkled face. Apollonius made the Ephesians stand around the man, and said, 'Collect as many stones as possible and throw them at this outcast.' The Ephesians were puzzled by his meaning and shocked at the thought of killing someone who was a visitor and so destitute, and the man also pleaded with them, saying everything to gain their pity. But Apollonius urged the Ephesians relentlessly to crush the man and not let him escape. When some of them hit him from a distance and the man, who had appeared to have his eyes closed, suddenly opened them and showed them to be full of fire, the Ephesians realized it was a spirit and threw so many stones that a pile of them built up over him. After a while Apollonius told them to remove the stones and to discover the beast that they had killed. When they uncovered the man they thought they had stoned, he had vanished; instead they saw a dog resembling a Molossian hound but the size of the largest lion, crushed by the stones and spewing foam like a dog with rabies. The statue of the Averter, in the shape of Hercules, stands near the spot where the apparition was stoned.

Philostratus, *Life of Apollonius of Tyana*, Book IV

It was at about the time of Apollonius' sensational descent on Ephesus that a wholly fictional character, Eumolpus in Petronius' Satyricon, was telling one of the most renowned tales with Ephesus as its location.

'There was once upon a time at Ephesus a lady of so high repute for chastity that women would actually come to that city from neighbouring lands to see and admire. This fair lady having lost her husband, was not content with the ordinary signs of mourning, such as walking with hair dishevelled behind the funeral car and beating her naked bosom in presence of the assembled crowd; she was fain further to accompany her lost one to his final resting-place, watch over his corpse in the vault where it was laid according to the Greek mode of burial, and weep day and night beside it. So deep was her affliction, neither family nor friends could dissuade her from these austerities and the purpose she had formed of perishing of hunger. Even the Magistrates had to retire worsted after a last but fruitless effort. All mourned as virtually dead already a woman of such singular determination, who had already passed five days without food.

'A trusty handmaid sat by her mistress's side, mingling her tears with those of the unhappy woman, and trimming the lamp which stood in the tomb as often as it burned low. Nothing else was talked of throughout the city but her sublime devotion, and men of every station quoted her as a shining example of virtue and conjugal affection.

'Meantime, as it fell out, the Governor of the Province ordered certain robbers to be crucified in close proximity to the vault where the matron sat bewailing the recent loss of her mate. Next night the soldier who was set to guard the crosses to prevent anyone coming and removing the robbers' bodies to give them burial, saw a light shining among the tombs and heard the widow's groans. Yielding to curiosity, a failing common to all mankind, he was eager to discover who it was, and what was afoot. Accordingly he descended into the tomb, where beholding a lovely woman, he was at first confounded, thinking he saw a ghost or some supernatural vision. But presently the spectacle of the husband's dead body lying there, and the woman's tear-stained and nail-torn face, everything went to show him the reality, how it was a disconsolate widow unable to resign herself to the death of her helpmate. He proceeded therefore to carry his humble meal into the tomb, and to urge the fair mourner to cease her indulgence in grief so excessive, and to leave off torturing her bosom with unavailing sobs. Death he declared was the common end and last home of all men, enlarging on this and the other commonplaces generally employed to console a wounded spirit. But the lady, only shocked by this offer of sympathy from a stranger's lips, began to tear her breast with redoubled vehemence, and dragging out handfuls of her hair, to lay them on her husband's corpse.

'The soldier however, refusing to be rebuffed, renewed his adjuration to the unhappy lady to eat. Eventually the maid, seduced doubtless by the scent of the wine, found herself unable to resist any longer, and extended her hand for the refreshment offered; then with energies restored by food and drink, she set herself to the task of breaking down her mistress's resolution. "What good will it do you," she urged, "to die of famine to bury yourself alive in the tomb, to yield your life to destiny before the Fates demand it?

'"Think you to pleasure thus the dead and gone?

'"Nay! rather return to life, and shaking off this womanly weakness, enjoy the good things of this world as long as you may. The very corpse that lies here before your eyes should be a warning to make the most of existence."

'No one is really loath to consent, when pressed to eat or live. The widow therefore, worn as she was with several days' fasting, suffered her resolution to be broken, and took her fill of nourishment with no less avidity than her maid had done, who had been the first to give way.

'Now you all know what temptations assail poor human nature after a hearty meal. The soldier resorted to the same cajolements which had already been successful in inducing the lady to eat, in order to overcome her virtue. The modest widow found the young

soldier neither ill-looking nor wanting in address, while the maid
was strong indeed in his favour and kept repeating:

> "Why thus unmindful of your past delight,
> Against a pleasing passion will you fight?"

'But why make a long story? The lady showed herself equally
complaisant in this respect also, and the victorious soldier gained
both his ends. So they lay together not only that first night of their
nuptials, but a second likewise, and a third, the door of the vault
being of course kept shut, so that anyone, friend or stranger, that
might come to the tomb, should suppose this most chaste of wives
had expired by now on her husband's corpse. Meantime the soldier,
entranced with the woman's beauty and the mystery of the thing,
purchased day by day the best his means allowed him, and as soon as
ever night was come, conveyed the provisions to the tomb.

'Thus it came about that the relatives of one of the malefactors,
observing this relaxation of vigilance, removed his body from the
cross during the night and gave it proper burial. But what of the
unfortunate soldier, whose self-indulgence had thus been taken
advantage of, when next morning he saw one of the crosses under his
charge without its body! Dreading instant punishment, he acquaints
his mistress with what had occurred, assuring her he would not
await the judge's sentence, but with his own sword exact the penalty
of his negligence. He must die therefore; would she give him
sepulture, and join the friend to the husband in that fatal spot?

'But the lady was no less tender-hearted than virtuous. "The Gods
forbid," she cried, "I should at one and the same time look on the
corpses of two men, both most dear to me. I had rather hang a dead
man on the cross than kill a living." So said, so done; she orders her
husband's body to be taken from its coffin and fixed upon the vacant
cross. The soldier availed himself of the ready-witted lady's expedient, and next day all men marvelled how in the world a dead
man had found his own way to the cross.'

                            Petronius, *Satyricon*; tr. Oscar Wilde

The fictional chef d'oeuvre of Petronius must be almost
contemporaneous with perhaps the most famous of historical
events in Ephesus, the arrival of the Apostle Paul to preach the
gospel of Christ and to inveigh against the religion of Artemis,
Diana of the Ephesians.

The story (Acts of the Apostles 19.24–41) is well known:
the silversmiths rose up in riot against the new teaching, because their chief employment was in making silver shrines for
Diana. The 'chiefs of Asia' were obliged to intervene to calm

the people. (I suppose Paul won in the end – for where are all those silver shrines now? Destroyed, melted down by the avaricious or the intolerant.)

Christian Ephesus rapidly accumulated its plethora of legends, most of which are attached to sites still visited at the present day, for example the cave of the Seven Sleepers:

Among the insipid legends of ecclesiastical history, I am tempted to distinguish the memorable fable of the SEVEN SLEEPERS; whose imaginary date corresponds with the reign of the younger Theodosius and the conquest of Africa by the Vandals. When the emperor Decius persecuted the Christians, seven noble youths of Ephesus concealed themselves in a spacious cavern in the side of an adjacent mountain; where they were doomed to perish by the tyrant, who gave orders that the entrance should be firmly secured with a pile of huge stones. They immediately fell into a deep slumber, which was miraculously prolonged, without injuring the powers of life, during a period of one hundred and eighty-seven years. At the end of that time, the slaves of Adolius, to whom the inheritance of the mountain had descended, removed the stones, to supply mate-rials for some rustic edifice; the light of the sun darted into the cavern, and the seven sleepers were permitted to awake. After a slumber, as they thought, of a few hours, they were pressed by the calls of hunger; and resolved that Jamblichus, one of their number, should secretly return to the city, to purchase bread for the use of his companions. The youth (if we may still employ that appellation) could no longer recognise the once familiar aspect of his native country; and his surprise was increased by the appearance of a large cross, triumphantly erected over the principal gate of Ephesus. His singular dress and obsolete language confounded the baker, to whom he offered an ancient medal of Decius as the current coin of the empire; and Jamblichus, on the suspicion of a secret treasure, was dragged before the judge. Their mutual inquiries produced the amazing discovery that two centuries were almost elapsed since Jamblichus and his friends had escaped from the rage of a Pagan tyrant. The bishop of Ephesus, the clergy, the magistrates, the people, and, as it is said, the emperor Theodosius himself, hastened to visit the cavern of the Seven Sleepers; who bestowed their benediction, related their story, and at the same instant peaceably expired. The origin of this marvellous fable cannot be ascribed to the pious fraud and credulity of the *modern* Greeks, since the authentic tradition may be traced within half a century of the supposed miracle. James of Sarug, a Syrian bishop, who was born only two years after the death of the younger Theodosius, has devoted one of his two hundred and thirty homilies to the praise of the young men of Ephesus. Their legend, before the end of the sixth century, was translated from the Syriac into the Latin language, by the care of Gregory of Tours. The hostile communions of the East preserve their memory with equal reverence; and their names are honourably inscribed in the Roman, the Abyssinian, and the Russian calendar. Nor has their reputation been confined to the Christian world. This popular tale, which Mahomet might learn when he drove his camels to the fairs of Syria, is introduced, as a divine revelation, into the Koran. The story of the Seven Sleepers has been adopted, and adorned, by the nations, from Bengal to Africa, who profess the Mahometan religion; and some vestiges of a similiar tradition have been discovered in the remote extremities of Scandinavia. This easy and universal belief, so expressive of the sense of mankind, may be ascribed to the genuine merit of the fable itself. We imperceptibly advance from youth to age, without observing the gradual, but incessant, change of human affairs, and, even in our larger experiences of history, the imagination is accustomed, by a perpetual series of causes and effects to unite the most distant revolutions. But, if the interval between two memorable æras could be instantly annihilated; if it were possible, after a momentary slumber of two hundred years, to display the *new* world to the eyes of a spectator, who still retained a lively and recent impression of the *old*; his surprise and his reflections would furnish the pleasing subject of a philosophical romance. The scene could not be more advantageously placed than in the two centuries which elapsed between the reigns of Decius and of Theodosius the younger. During this period, the seat of government had been transported from Rome to a new city on the banks of the Thracian Bosphorus; and the abuse of military spirit had been suppressed by an artificial system of tame and ceremonious servitude. The throne of the persecuting Decius was filled by a succession of Christian and orthodox princes, who had extirpated the fabulous gods of antiquity; and the public devotion of the age was impatient to exalt the saints and martyrs of the Catholic church on the altars of Diana and Hercules. The union of the Roman empire was dissolved; its genius was humbled in the dust; and armies of unknown Barbarians, issuing from the frozen regions of the North, had established their victorious reign over the fairest provinces of Europe and Africa.

Edward Gibbon, *Decline and Fall of the Roman Empire*, ch. 33

The Virgin Mary and John the Baptist were supposed to have come to Ephesus after the Crucifixion, thus conferring on the city a peculiar sanctity reflected in the tale recorded by

Ramon Muntaner (1265–1336), the soldier who joined the Catalan expedition against Greece.

And in the said place, Ephesus, is the tomb which monsenyer Saint John the Evangelist entered when he had taken leave of the people; and then a cloud as of fire was seen, in which, it is believed, he ascended to Heaven, body and soul. And this would well seem to be so, from the miracle which is seen every year at his tomb; namely, that on Saint Stephen's day, ever year, at the hour of vespers, there comes out of the tomb (which is four-cornered and stands at the foot of the altar and has a beautiful marble slab on the top, full twelve palms long and five broad) and in the middle of the slab there are nine very small holes, and out of these holes, as vespers are being begun on Saint Stephen's day (on which day the vespers are of Saint John) manna like sand comes out of each hole and rises full a palm high from the slab, as a jet of water rises up. And this manna issues out, and it begins to issue out, as I have told you, when vespers are begun to be sung on Saint Stephen's day, and it lasts all night and then all Saint John's day until sunset. There is so much of this manna, by the time the sun has set and it has ceased to issue out, that, altogether, there are of it full three cuarteras of Barcelona. And this manna is marvellously good for many things; for instance, he who drinks it when he feels fever coming on will never have fever again. Also, if a lady is in travail and cannot bring forth, if she drinks it with water or with wine, she will be delivered at once. And again, if there is a storm at sea and some of the manna is thrown in the sea three times in the name of the Holy Trinity and Our Lady Saint Mary and the Blessed Saint John the Evangelist, at once the storm ceases. And again, he who suffers from gall stones, and drinks it in the said names, recovers at once. And some of this manna is given to all the pilgrims who come there; but it only appears once a year.

R. Muntaner, *Chronicle* (tr. 1921)

Even more dramatic was the discovery of a house supposed to be that of the Virgin Mary. A Bavarian nun, Catharina Emmerich, who lived in the first part of the nineteenth century, used frequently to see visions relating to the Virgin and her earthly homes. She habitually wrote down the details. One day the vision vouchsafed her, shortly before the Feast of the Assumption, described in remarkable detail the site of a house on a hill a little south of ancient Ephesus where the Virgin had lived out her last years (until the age of 64, according to another of Catharina's visions). Excavators who tested the truth of her reports were amazed to discover a house in precisely this location and of apparently sufficient antiquity to be authentic. (The same cannot be said of the 'prison of St Paul' pointed out now at Ephesus, which is of medieval date.) Yet Catharina was quite uneducated and had certainly never seen a description even of the general topography of Ephesus.

Mary did not live in Ephesus itself, but in the country near it where several women who were her close friends had settled. Mary's dwelling was on a hill to the left of the road from Jerusalem some three and a half hours from Ephesus. This hill slopes steeply towards Ephesus; the city as one approaches it from the south-east seems to lie on rising ground immediately before one, but seems to change its place as one draws nearer. Great avenues lead up to the city, and the ground under the trees is covered with yellow fruit. Narrow paths lead southwards to a hill near the top of which is an uneven plateau, some half-hour's journey in circumference, overgrown, like the hill itself, with wild trees and bushes. It was on this plateau that the Jewish settlers had made their home. It is a very lonely place, but has many fertile and pleasant slopes as well as rock-caves, clean and dry and surrounded by patches of sand. It is wild but not desolate, and scattered about it are a number of trees, pyramid-shaped, with big shady branches below and smooth trunks.

John had had a house built for the Blessed Virgin before he brought her here. Several Christian families and holy women had already settled here, some in caves in the earth or in the rocks, fitted out with light woodwork to make dwellings, and some in fragile huts or tents. They had come here to escape violent persecution. Their dwellings were like hermits' cells, for they used as their refuges what nature offered them. As a rule, they lived at a quarter of an hour's distance from each other. The whole settlement was like a scattered village. Mary's house was the only one built of stone. A little way behind it was the summit of the rocky hill from which one could see over the trees and hills to Ephesus and the sea with its many islands. The place is nearer the sea than Ephesus, which must be several hours' journey distant from the coast. The district is lonely and unfrequented. Near here is a castle inhabited by a king who seems to have been deposed. John visited him often and ended by converting him. This place later became a bishop's see. Between the Blessed Virgin's dwelling and Ephesus runs a little stream which winds about in a very singular way.

· · · ·

The little house stood near a wood among pyramid-shaped trees with smooth trunks. It was very quiet and solitary. The dwellings of the other families were all scattered about at some distance. The whole settlement was like a village of peasants.

Catharina Emmerich, *Life of the Blessed Virgin Mary* (1897)

By the middle ages not only had the temple of Artemis sunk into the marsh from which it was only resurrected in the 1860s; the rest of Roman Ephesus was ruined, fallen a prey to the successive waves of Persians, Seljuks, Ottomans and earthquakes which devastated medieval Asia Minor. A small modern town grew up at Selcuk, which was by now an inland site as the river had carried down so much silt that the coastline had moved several miles westwards. Without its maritime raison d'être the city had degenerated. It was a ruin when William Lithgow visited it in 1611.

A hundred and fifty years later the Dilettanti were here. Like Lithgow, Chandler had to rely more on what he had read than on what he could see to fill out his description, but the picture of the present town is sufficiently wretched.

The Ephesians are now a few Greek peasants, living in extreme wretchedness, dependence, and insensibility; the representatives of an illustrious people, and inhabiting the wreck of their greatness; some, the substructions of the glorious edifices which they raised; some, beneath the vaults of the stadium, once the crowded scene of their diversions; and some, by the abrupt precipice, in the sepulchres, which received their ashes. We employed a couple of them to pile stones, to serve instead of a ladder, at the arch of the stadium and, to clear a pedestal of the portico by the theatre from rubbish. We had occasion for another to dig at the Corinthian temple; and sending to the stadium, the whole tribe, ten or twelve, followed; one playing all the way before them on a rude lyre, and at times striking the sounding-board with the fingers of his left hand in concert with the strings. One of them had on a pair of sandals of goat-skin, laced with thongs, and not uncommon. After gratifying their curiosity, they returned back as they came, with their musician in front.

Such are the present citizens of Ephesus, and such is the condition to which that renowned city has been gradually reduced. It was a ruinous place when the emperor Justinian filled Constantinople with its statues, and raised his church of St. Sophia on its columns. Since then it has been almost quite exhausted. Its streets are obscured and overgrown. A herd of goats was driven to it for shelter from the sun at noon; and a noisy flight of crows from the quarries seemed to insult its silence. We heard the partridge call in the area of the theatre and of the stadium. The glorious pomp of its heathen worship is no longer remembered; and Christianity, which was there nursed by apostles, and fostered by general councils, until it increased to fulness of stature, barely lingers on in an existence hardly visible.

Richard Chandler, *Travels in Asia Minor* (1775)

Mark Twain, on his tour with the Innocents abroad, was well enough impressed by Ephesus: so much so that he almost forgets to poke fun.

I wish to say a brief word of the aspect of Ephesus.

On a high, steep hill, toward the sea, is a gray ruin of ponderous blocks of marble, wherein, tradition says, St. Paul was imprisoned eighteen centuries ago. From these old walls you have the finest view of the desolate scene where once stood Ephesus, the proudest city of ancient times, and whose Temple of Diana was so noble in design and so exquisite of workmanship that it ranked high in the list of the Seven Wonders of the World.

Behind you is the sea; in front is a level green valley (a marsh, in fact) extending far away among the mountains; to the right of the front view is the old citadel of Ayassalook, on a high hill; the ruined Mosque of the Sultan Selim stands near it in the plain (this is built over the grave of St. John, and was formerly a Christian Church); further toward you is the hill of Pion, around whose front is clustered all that remains of the ruins of Ephesus that still stand; divided from it by a narrow valley is the long, rocky, rugged mountain of Coressus. The scene is a pretty one, and yet desolate – for in that wide plain no man can live, and in it is no human habitation. But for the crumbling arches and monstrous piers and broken walls that rise from the foot of the hill of Pion, one could not believe that in this place once stood a city whose renown is older than tradition itself. It is incredible to reflect that things as familiar all over the world today as household words belong in the history and in the shadowy legends of this silent, mournful solitude. We speak of Apollo and of Diana – they were born here; of the metamorphosis of Syrinx into a reed – it was done here; of the great god Pan – he dwelt in the caves of this hill of Coressus; of the Amazons – this was their best prized home; of Bacchus and Hercules – both fought the warlike women here; of the Cyclops – they laid the ponderous marble blocks of some of the ruins yonder; of Homer – this was one of his many birthplaces; of Cimon of Athens; of Alcibiades, Lysander, Agesilaus – they visited here; so did Alexander the Great; so did Hannibal and Antiochus, Scipio, Lucullus, and Sylla; Brutus, Cassius, Pompey, Cicero, and Augustus; Antony was a judge in this place, and left his seat in the open court, while the advocates were speaking, to run after Cleopatra, who passed the door; from this city these two sailed on pleasure excursions, in galleys with silver oars and perfumed sails, and with companies of beautiful girls to serve them and actors and musicians to amuse them; in days that seem almost modern, so remote are they from the early history of this city, Paul the Apostle preached the new religion here, and so did John, and here it is supposed the former was pitted against wild beasts, for in 1 Corinthians, xv. 32, he says:

'If after the manner of men I have fought with beasts at Ephesus,' etc.,

when many men still lived who had seen the Christ; here Mary Magdalen died, and here the Virgin Mary ended her days with John, albeit Rome has since judged it best to locate her grave elsewhere; six or seven hundred years ago – almost yesterday, as it were – troops of mail-clad Crusaders thronged the streets; and to come down to trifles, we speak of meandering streams and find a new interest in a common word when we discover that the crooked river Meander, in yonder valley, gave it to our dictionary. It makes me feel as old as these dreary hills to look down upon these moss-hung ruins, this historic desolation. One may read the Scriptures and believe, but he cannot go and stand yonder in the ruined theater and in imagination people it again with the vanished multitudes who mobbed Paul's comrades there and shouted, with one voice, 'Great is Diana of the Ephesians!' The idea of a shout in such a solitude as this almost makes one shudder.

It was a wonderful city, this Ephesus. Go where you will about these broad plains, you find the most exquisitely sculptured marble fragments scattered thick among the dust and weeds; and protruding from the ground or lying prone upon it are beautiful fluted columns of porphyry and all precious marbles; and at every step you find elegantly carved capitals and massive bases and polished tablets engraved with Greek inscriptions. It is a world of precious relics, a wilderness of marred and mutilated gems. And yet what are these things to the wonders that lie buried here under the ground? At Constantinople, at Pisa, in the cities of Spain, are great mosques and cathedrals whose grandest columns came from the temples and palaces of Ephesus, and yet one has only to scratch the ground here to match them. We shall never know what magnificence is until this imperial city is laid bare to the sun.

The finest piece of sculpture we have yet seen and the one that impressed us most (for we do not know much about art and cannot easily work up ourselves into ecstasies over it) is one that lies in this old theater of Ephesus, which St. Paul's riot has made so celebrated. It is only the headless body of a man, clad in a coat of mail, with a

Medusa head upon the breastplate, but we feel persuaded that such dignity and such majesty were never thrown into a form of stone before.

What builders they were, these men of antiquity! The massive arches of some of these ruins rest upon piers that are fifteen feet square and built entirely of solid blocks of marble, some of which are as large as a Saratoga trunk and some the size of a boardinghouse sofa. They are not shells or shafts of stone filled inside with rubbish, but the whole pier is a mass of solid masonry. Vast arches that may have been the gates of the city are built in the same way. They have braved the storms and sieges of three thousand years, and have been shaken by many an earthquake, but still they stand. When they dig alongside of them, they find ranges of ponderous masonry that are as perfect in every detail as they were the day those old Cyclopian giants finished them. An English company is going to excavate Ephesus – and then!

Mark Twain, *The Innocents Abroad* (Hartford, Connecticut, 1869)

After so much (almost) seriousness he launches into a lively and highly diverting account of the legend of the Seven Sleepers.

And the English company that was to excavate Ephesus? That was one man, the engineer John Turtle Wood, with whatever labourers he could obtain with the resources supplied by the British Museum, eager to acquire fine works of art. But Wood's interest was less in exhibitable treasures than in ascertaining the site of the Temple of Artemis. This, after many years of frequently frustrating labour, he eventually did. His attempts are described more fully in my book, *Land of Lost Gods*; suffice it to point out here the unusual difficulty of the task on a site where the water table had risen since antiquity and the temple site was more or less permanently waterlogged. Things were no better when at the turn of the century another expedition from the British Museum under David Hogarth (the archaeological mentor of Lawrence of Arabia) made a further attempt to recover substantial remains of the temple.

The waters guarded their trust. That winter is still remembered in Anatolia for its rains and the fevers which followed. When I returned to the site near the end of March, I looked out over a lake below whose unruffled surface the pedestal lay drowned too deep for any one but a diver to rob its core. Its upper stones, said the Ephesians, would not emerge till late summer. What was to be done? Except by the help of a very powerful steam pump, the water could not be drained out of a great hollow, many feet below the general level of the plain and hardly higher than the surface of the distant sea. I left a contractor to clear away the upper part of Wood's great rubbish heaps, which still blocked the two ends of the site, and went back to Smyrna.

To make a long story short, an engine and pump were lent by the Ottoman Railway Company and three weeks later dragged to the edge of our pit; and after we had cut a passage seaward for the strong stream which its twelve-inch pipe would disgorge, it was set to work to lower the lake. But we were only at the beginning of difficulties. The free water was sucked up in a few hours; but the drainage of the lower levels, which was dammed by deep and massive foundation walls, could not be collected fast enough to keep the great pipe free of air, and clear of mud. If the engine stopped, the water ceased to flow towards it, and in the lapse of a night the pond would rise nearly as high again as at the first. In the end we had no choice but to spend many days in cutting a network of channels through the foundations and in deepening the pool below the pipe by hauling out great rubble blocks which had been bedded down by the builders of the latest temple. The men, who had to wade to their middles under a hot sun, fell sick of fevers, and I myself began to feel none too well. On the last day of April I took to my bed, and after fighting my malady for a week, went down to Smyrna in high fever and was put to bed in the Seamen's Hospital for other ten days. Thus it was not till May was half gone that, with drainage channels dug, the central area of the temple fenced against inflow, and a second and smaller pump rigged over the treasure-spot, we could hunt again for jewels.

They appeared one after another in the sieves just as they had done five months before; and when the clean bottom sand had been scraped out of the four corners of the pedestal, we had added nearly five hundred trinkets. But now I found that I cared for none of these things. The fever had left me unstrung, and I longed for nothing but the moment when I might scrape Diana's mud off my feet for the last time. Every evening I hoped against hope that the lode would be exhausted next day.

·   ·   ·   ·

In one case only did we seem to light on anything buried with intention. This was a little jar, set upright in an angle of the lowest foundations and once sealed with a covering, whose binding-cord still clung to the clay. My men were no longer in their first innocence, and dealers in contraband waited at noon and night to tempt them. He who first sighted this jar, as he was scraping slime into his basket, looked stealthily about him; but I was at his back, poor fellow, ready to lift his prize myself, and I still see his sad eyes as nineteen electrum coins of the earliest mintage of Lydia fell out of his pot.

D. G. Hogarth, *Accidents of an Antiquary's Life* (1910)

## Pamukkale (Hierapolis)

The curious town of Pamukkale lies a little to the east of Kuşadası; they offer one striking attraction to the tourist, and that has never been better described than by Richard Pococke.

The warm waters here are the greatest natural curiosities in Asia; they rise to the south of the theatre in a deep basin, and are very clear: they are only tepid, have the taste of the Pyrmont waters, but are not so strong, and must have in them a great quantity of sulphur; they do not drink them, though I could not perceive either salt or vitriol in the taste of them to make them unwholesome. The springs flow so plentifully that they make a considerable stream; it is observed by the ancients that these waters were excellent for dyeing, and that the roots of the trees at this place gave a tincture equal to the scarlet or purple, and now there are shrubs growing about the hill, the roots of which are incrusted with a petrification of these waters, which might be used in dyeing. The water now runs in channels about three feet wide, which are incrusted on each side to the thickness of about half a foot. The side of the hill, where the water runs, is covered with a white incrustation, and the channels which conveyed it through the city into the plain are entirely filled up, as well as the arches of the aqueduct, all appearing like the solid rock; and I observed towards the brow of the hill some hollow parts, where the rain water has settled, around which there are partitions of a white sulphurous incrustation, probably occasioned by the motion of the water in windy weather; and in some parts there are little heaps, which appear like white salt, but are solid stone. In one part, where the water runs down the hill, it forms a most beautiful hanging petrification like rock work; the side of the hills below appearing as white as snow; and possibly they might call this place Pambouk-Kalesi (the cotton castle) from the resemblance of its whiteness to that of cotton.

. . . .

Another great curiosity here was what they called Plutonium, a cave, out of which a vapour exhaled, that was mortal to animals, like that at Piermount, and, I suppose, for the same reason, the waters here being of the same nature. They promissed to show me this place, but brought me to a deep hole full of water near the basin, which was more strongly impregnated with the mineral, but it had no manner of effect on a bird which I put on the water.

Richard Pococke, *Description of the East* (1743–5)

## Didim (Didyma)

An easy journey by road south from Kuşadası lies the village of Didim, the site in antiquity of the Oracle of Apollo administered by a family called the Branchidae. The temple is a vast enclosure surrounded by the usual stylobate and columns, on a massive scale; the actual place of consultation was a smaller edifice in the centre of the main enclosure, to which access was gained through the mysterious passages descending from the main front platform of the temple.

This ancient oracle had been honoured by kings: though Xerxes had taken the bronze image of Apollo to adorn his capital at Ecbatana (Hamadan), King Seleucus had returned it two centuries later. Emperors like Trajan and Julian had given resources to adorn and refurbish the temple, until it was closed for ever by Theodosius' edict of AD 385 which banned extispicy and other forms of pagan prophecy.

Some of the oracles were known from inscriptions in Chandler's day, though many more have been recovered in this century by the excavations of Theodor Wiegand and Bertrand Haussoullier. Though unimpressive if one is seeking world-shattering revelations, the oracular responses testify to the preoccupations and often overwhelming anxieties of those who consulted it.

Your prophet Damianos inquires: having instructed him through your sacred oracle to establish in your holy sanctuary an altar of the most holy goddess Soteira by the altar of the most reverend and fruitful Demeter, he begs you to act as law-giver of the properly spoken hymnic address to her.

The god decreed:

We call upon Soteira at our most holy supplication to meet us with mercy, along with mother Deo.

Few of these were known when Chandler and the Dilettanti visited the city, still buried in rubble as it had fallen in earthquakes many centuries before, and in fact functioning in part as the foundation of a small village.

The temple of Apollo was . . . two miles and a half, from the shore . . . It is approached by a gentle ascent, and seen afar off; the land toward the sea lying flat and level. The memory of the pleasure which this spot afforded me will not be soon or easily erased. The columns yet entire are so exquisitely fine, the marble mass so vast and noble, that it is impossible perhaps to conceive greater beauty and majesty of ruin. At evening, a large flock of goats, returning to the fold, their bells tinkling, spread over the heap, climbing to browse on the shrubs and trees growing between the huge stones. The whole mass was illuminated by the declining sun with a variety of rich tints, and cast a very strong shade. The sea, at a distance was smooth and shining, bordered by a mountainous coast, with rocky island. The picture was as delicious as striking. A view of part of the heap, with plates of the architecture of this glorious edifice, has been engraved and published, with its history, at the expense of the society of Dilettanti.

We found among the ruins, which are extensive, a plain stone cistern, covered, except an end, with soil; many marble coffins, unopened, or with the lids broken; and one, in which was a thigh bone; all sunk deep in earth; with five statues, near each other, in a row, almost buried. In the stubble of some Turkey wheat were a number of bee-hives, each a long hollow trunk of wood headed like a barrel, piled in a heap. An Armenian, who was with me, on our putting up a hare, to my surprise slunk away. This animal, as I was afterwards informed, is held in abomination by that people, and the seeing it accounted an ill omen.

The temple of Apollo Didymæus seeming likely to detain us some time, we regretted the entire solitude of the spot, which obliged us to fix our quarters at Ura. Our Armenian cook, who tarried there with our baggage, sent us provisions ready dressed, and we dined under a shady tree by the ruins. Our horses were tied, and feeding by us. Our camel-leader testified his benevolence and regard, by frequent tenders of his short pipe, and of coffee, which he made unceasingly, sitting cross-legged by a small fire. The crows settled in large companies round about, and the partridge called in the stubble.

At our return in the evening to Ura, we found two fires, with our kettles boiling, in the open air, amid the huts and thickets. A mat was spread for us on the ground by one of them. The Turks of Ura, about fourteen in number, some with long beards, sitting cross-legged, helped to complete the grotesque circle. We were lighted by the moon, then full, and shining in a blue cloudless sky. The Turks smoked, talked, and drank coffee with great gravity, composure, and deliberation. One entertained us with playing on the Turkish guitar and with uncouth singing. The thin-voiced women, curious

to see us, glided as ghosts across the glades, in white, with their faces
muffled. The assemblage and the scene was uncommonly wild, and
as solemn as savage . . .

Richard Chandler, *Travels in Asia Minor* (1775)

Didim was until the twentieth century a mainly Greek
village. It was at that time called Yeronda. With the exchange
of populations following on the Smyrna debacle of 1922, the
village became entirely depopulated and also fell a victim to
the vengeful vandalism of the victorious Turks. Saturnino
Ximenez wrote an evocative description in his book of 1925,
*Asia Minor in Ruins*, which seems to be unknown to most of
the major libraries of Britain (I eventually tracked it down in
the classics faculty library in Cambridge).

I could easily imagine the scene before the Exodus of 1922. The
people would be gathering to discuss business and to sip coffee, a
yard or so from the Temple of Apollo. On moonlight nights the
columns of the Didymeion must have thrown a spell of enchantment
over this delightful spot. But today the well is dry, the houses open
to every wind, the tables and benches smashed to pieces, the
Cafeneion is no more; only the plane trees still offer the shade of their
boughs. In the school-house the looters seem to have been attacked
by a sort of frenzy, for everything was smashed, torn, trampled
upon. We picked up some leaves of a book in Greek telling the story
of St Thyrsus, a Christian of Didymi, who suffered martyrdom at
Miletus. Pictures, exercise books, breviaries, all were torn to shreds.
The houses in the square had gardens planted with flowers and
shrubs, and on one of the shrubs were red paper roses, relics no
doubt of a family festivity. The vegetable life went on in the midst of
death; the myrtles and oleanders brightened the little gardens;
bunches of grapes hung from their trellises; the fig trees yielded their
fruit. In the churchyard lay several trunks which the refugees had
carried there, thinking they would be in sanctuary; but the lids had
been torn off and nothing was left of the contents; even the locks had
been removed. We went into the church, and I hardly know how to
describe the scene of devastation that met our eyes. We had to make
our way over heaps of boards, seats, ornaments, ikons, crosses,
lamps, lecterns, all in pieces and thrown about anyhow. From the
wooden ikonostasia, crudely carved and painted in various colours,
the sacred images had been torn away; the marble altar was split in
two.

The description seems like a scene from another world.
Didim has returned now to its village peace; new houses, a

new restaurant have sprung up, the ruins have been cleared, and in this cheerful and welcoming village there is no hint of that tragedy of lives uprooted and wrecked of only sixty-odd years ago.

## Bodrum (Halicarnassus)

*The City*

I arose early this morning. I woke up the sea
A man had caught a squid, he was holding it up
I bent down to look at his eyes, they were blue and round.
He heaved when breathing like a heavy labourer.
Three men sat drinking tea and reading the sky.
One was describing the south wind, acting out
The part. 'In B.C. Bodrum there were only the quarters
Of Salmachis and Zephyria', said another.
I thought of the Dorians and of the great Alexander
Of the Castle of Saint Peter, the Chevalier de Naillac.
At six the sun came up, we all disappeared.

Ilhan Berk; tr. Nermin Menemencioglu

The great period of Halicarnassus was the reign of Mausolus, the fourth century BC ruler of Caria whose capital was at Halicarnassus and who gave his name to every grandiloquent tomb that has ever been erected since the one he built for himself and which was completed after his death by his widow. His name became a byword in antiquity and after for the futility of the attempt to perpetuate one's fame by structures of perishable material – by anything other than deeds and the fame that attends them.

In vain do earthly princes, then, in vain,
Seek with pyramides to heaven aspired,
Or huge colosses built with costly pain . . .
To make their memories for ever live;
For how can mortal immortality give?
Such one Mausolus made, the world's great wonder,
But now no remnant doth thereof remain . . .
But Fame with golden wing aloft doth fly,
Above the reach of ruinous decay,
And with brave plumes doth beat the azure sky.

Edmund Spenser, *The Ruins of Time*

The Mausoleum was shattered by an earthquake at the beginning of the fifteenth century, thus providing a convenient source of worked stone when the Knights of St John arrived shortly afterwards to build their Castle of St Peter which still dominates the bay of Bodrum. A few reliefs were still visible to whet the appetite of archaeologically minded travellers, but it was far from easy to gain access to them.

Some years ago, a French frigate, being at Boodroom, the commander expressed a great desire to see the marbles in the fortress; but the then governor absolutely refused to admit him without direct orders from the Porte. The commander had interest; the ambassador was set to work; and in a short time the frigate returned, bearing the necessary ferman. The governor put it to his forehead, in acknowledgement of its authority, and declared his readiness to proceed. Arrived at the outer gate, 'Effendy,' said the governor, 'the orders of my imperial master must be implicitly obeyed.' 'Let me in, then,' exclaimed the impatient captain. 'Undoubtedly,' replied the Turk, 'for so I am enjoined to do by the ferman; but as it contains no directions about your coming out again, you will perhaps forgive this momentary pause, before we pass the drawbridge.' The French commandant, not chusing to put such hazardous irony to the test, departed.

Capt. Beaufort, *Karamania* (1817)

In the event it was Charles Newton, the keeper of antiquities at the British Museum, who with the enthusiastic assistance of Lord Stratford de Redcliffe, the British ambassador to the Porte, was enabled to excavate ancient Halicarnassus and the ruins of the Mausoleum. But many obstacles had to be overcome as he advanced his dig closer and closer to the houses of the little village below the castle. Eventually a single house stood square in his path.

It was evident that this house must be bought; but how this could be managed was not so clear, for I knew from long experience how difficult it is to deal with an Oriental. I therefore called in to my aid my old friend Mehemet Chiaoux, who had so kindly allowed me to dig in his field, and empowered him to conduct the negotiation. His first attempts were not very successful, for the old Turk whose house stood in my way had a termagant wife, who objected strongly to our proceedings. One day when we were engaged in an experiment how near to the foundations we could venture to dig without undermining the house, a long gaunt arm was suddenly thrust through the shutters from within, and a discordant female voice screeched out some unpleasant Turkish imprecations on our heads.

Mehemet Chiaoux, who happened to be standing close to the window, with his back to the house, beat a hasty retreat, with a very discomposed and uncomfortable expression of countenance. It was only after some days that he told me that the old lady had taken this opportunity of dropping some burning cinders down his back, between his shirt and his skin.

Old Suliman, the husband of this formidable dame, was a trembling decrepit old man, who, though he had been a famous wrestler in his day, and could still tell tales of the prowess of his youth, stood in bodily fear of his wife. In a weak moment he allowed us to dig in his garden: we soon came to a young fig-tree, which it was absolutely necessary to remove. While we were bargaining for the price of this tree, down it came suddenly, having been maliciously undermined by my workmen. Poor old Suliman got a beating that day, and our stalwart sapper, Corporal Jenkins, standing on the edge of a trench, was suddenly upset into it ignominiously by a well-aimed blow from a chopping-block, hurled at his head from the window. We paid no attention to these little interruptions, but continued to dig on, till having at length worked all round Suliman's house, and left it standing like an island in a sea of rubble, I thought the time was come for a definite offer. After much parleying, the price was fixed at £20. I waited on old Suliman in his own house, with the money in my hand, and found myself in the awful presence of Mrs. Suliman, who looked like the first cousin of the Eumenides. The wrinkles on her mahogany face were such as Juvenal describes:

> 'Quales, umbriferos ubi pandit Tabraca saltus,
> In vetula scalpit jam mater simia bucca.' ·

The poor old man gazed wistfully on this treasure, as if he had never seen as much money in his life. 'It is not enough!' said the stern old hag. I immediately swept up my little heap of gold and withdrew. This prompt measure had more effect than hours of parleying, and I got the house two days afterwards.

Newton concludes his account of the excavation by reproducing a letter which had been picked up in the streets of Bodrum and handed to him. 'It bears no signature; but the writer is evidently one of the sailors of the *Supply*.'

'Dear father and moter, with gods help i now take up my pen to right these few lines to you hopeing to find you in good health & sperits as thank god it leaves me at present. Dear father of all the drill that a

seaman was put to i think the Supply's company have got the worst,
for here we are at Boderumm a useing the peke madock & shovel.
nevur was there such a change from a sea man to a navy; yes by
George we are all turned naveys sumetimes a diging it up &
sometimes a draging it down to the waters edge & then imbarking it.
Dear father this is the finest mable that ever i saw; we get on so very
slow that i fear we shall be hear a long time; the city of Ninevea as
been sunk such a long time that we find nothing but mable; every
thing els is compleatley roted away. what is most to be seen is the
crockery ware that they used in those days; their is upwards of a
hundred turks & Greeks mixt together; they have dug up to lions,
but they are very much broken about from lying so long in the
ground or by the shok of the earthquake when the place was
destroyed. Dear father we have pleanty of frute one sorte and
another, we have almons figs grapes pomegranets & melons, but i
doant know whether melons are counted frute or vegetable, we eat
them raw & so do every one els here. We have them in great plenty,
they are by far the best frute that we can get here; i have one now on
my right hand has big has a peck, or measure; the best of it is we
cannot manage to eat more than half a dozen at the time but they are
the best thing a man can eat when he is thirsty. Dear father we have
had one male since we have bean here; i am a frade that the answers to
my letters are lost, if so it was my fault – send me word of Eliza, the
first chance i was sadley disopainted, i hoped to get intelegence of
eliza. Dear father i will write every male from here, send me Georges
and Charlotte adressis; give my kind love to her & tell her i have got
a keepsake for her & saley; rember me to Jessy tell him i hope to
have a turkish curieau for him. i think i shall bring him a gravestone
they are very romantict and hansom; mind give my kind love to
mother. god bless you direct to Boderumm malta or elsewhere
Mediteriaien.'

Charles T. Newton, *Travels and Discoveries in the Levant* (1865)

All difficulties were trifles to the Victorian explorer; and
Newton successfully unearthed many massive marbles, including several stone lions and a human figure generally
identified with Mausolus himself, which is now in the British
Museum. Perhaps Mausolus's fame has defeated the grave
after all?

## Cnidus

Another site to which Newton devoted considerable attention
was nearby Cnidus, at the end of the Resadiyel peninsula

almost facing Bodrum across the Gulf of Cos. Though his
finds consisted mainly of the gigantic stone lion and the fine
statue of Demeter in the British Museum, it was not for these
that any ancient visitor would have made the pilgrimage
to Cnidus. For a pilgrimage it was, to visit the temple of
Aphrodite which housed the most famous female nude statue
of antiquity, the Aphrodite of Praxiteles. This seems to have
been guaranteed to arouse passion to an unusual degree, as a
story attributed to Lucian shows.

Now, as we had decided to anchor at Cnidus to see the temple of
Aphrodite, which is famed as possessing the most truly lovely
example of Praxiteles' skill, we gently approached the land with the
goddess herself, I believe, escorting our ship with smooth calm
waters. The others occupied themselves with the usual preparations,
but I took the two authorities on love, one on either side of me, and
went round Cnidus, finding no little amusement in the wanton
products of the potters, for I remembered I was in Aphrodite's city.
First we went round the porticos of Sostratus and everywhere else
that could give us pleasure and then we walked to the temple of
Aphrodite. Charicles and I did so very eagerly, but Callicratidas was
reluctant because he was going to see something female, and would
have preferred, I imagine, to have had Eros of Thespiae instead of
Aphrodite of Cnidus.
  And immediately, it seemed, there breathed upon us from the
sacred precinct itself breezes fraught with love. For the uncovered
court was not for the most part paved with smooth slabs of stone to
form an unproductive area but, as was to be expected in Aphrodite's
temple, was all of it prolific with garden fruits. These trees, luxuriant
far and wide with fresh green leaves, roofed in the air around them.
But more than all others flourished the berry-laden myrtle growing
luxuriantly beside its mistress and all the other trees that are endowed
with beauty. Though they were old in years they were not withered
or faded but, still in their youthful prime, swelled with fresh sprays.
Intermingled with these were trees that were unproductive except
for having beauty for their fruit – cypresses and planes that towered
to the heavens and with them Daphne, who deserted from Aphrodite and fled from that goddess long ago. But around every tree crept
and twined the ivy, devotee of love. Rich vines were hung with their
thick clusters of grapes. For Aphrodite is more delightful when
accompanied by Dionysus and the gifts of each are sweeter if blended
together, but, should they be parted from each other, they afford less
pleasure. Under the particularly shady trees were joyous couches for
those who wished to feast themselves there. These were occasionally

visited by a few folk of breeding, but all the city rabble flocked there on holidays and paid true homage to Aphrodite.

When the plants had given us pleasure enough, we entered the temple. In the midst thereof sits the goddess – she's a most beautiful statue of Parian marble – arrogantly smiling a little as a grin parts her lips. Draped by no garment, all her beauty is uncovered and revealed, except in so far as she unobtrusively uses one hand to hide her private parts. So great was the power of the craftsman's art that the hard unyielding marble did justice to every limb. Charicles at any rate raised a mad distracted cry and exclaimed, 'Happiest indeed of the gods was Ares who suffered chains because of her!' And, as he spoke, he ran up and, stretching out his neck as far as he could, started to kiss the goddess with importunate lips. Callicratidas stood by in silence with amazement in his heart.

The temple had a door on both sides for the benefit of those also who wish to have a good view of the goddess from behind, so that no part of her be left unadmired. It's easy therefore for people to enter by the other door and survey the beauty of her back.

And so we decided to see all of the goddess and went round to the back of the precinct. Then, when the door had been opened by the woman responsible for keeping the keys, we were filled with an immediate wonder for the beauty we beheld.

. . . .

When we could admire no more, we noticed a mark on one thigh like a stain on a dress; the unsightliness of this was shown up by the brightness of the marble everywhere else. I therefore, hazarding a plausible guess about the truth of the matter, supposed that what we saw was a natural defect in the marble. For even such things as these are subject to accident and many potential masterpieces of beauty are thwarted by bad luck. And so, thinking the black mark to be a natural blemish, I found in this too cause to admire Praxiteles for having hidden what was unsightly in the marble in the parts less able to be examined closely. But the attendant woman who was standing near us told us a strange, incredible story. For she said that a young man of a not undistinguished family – though his deed has caused him to be left nameless – who often visited the precinct, was so ill-starred as to fall in love with the goddess. He would spend all day in the temple and at first gave the impression of pious awe. For in the morning he would leave his bed long before dawn to go to the temple and only return home reluctantly after sunset. All day long would he sit facing the goddess with his eyes fixed uninterruptedly upon her, whispering indistinctly and carrying on a lover's complaints in secret conversation.

. . . .

In the end the violent tension of his desires turned to desperation and he found in audacity a procurer for his lusts. For, when the sun was now sinking to its setting, quietly and unnoticed by those present, he slipped in behind the door and, standing invisible in the inmost part of the chamber, he kept still, hardly even breathing. When the attendants closed the door from the outside in the normal way, this new Anchises was locked in. But why do I chatter on and tell you in every detail the reckless deed of that unmentionable night? These marks of his amorous embraces were seen after day came and the goddess had that blemish to prove what she'd suffered. The youth concerned is said, according to the popular story told, to have hurled himself over a cliff or down into the waves of the sea and to have vanished utterly.

Ps – Lucian, *Affairs of the Heart*

Alas, though copies of the type are still in existence, this provocative work is lost for ever. The remains seen by the first modern visitor to describe Cnidus, Lord Charlemont in 1749, were less alluring though bathed in the dazzling charm of the Aegean; a good deal of wishful thinking was necessary to identify the temple of Aphrodite.

Above the theatre, a little higher up the hill, we discovered the beautiful remains of a magnificent temple, richly ornamented, and of the Corinthian Order. Its materials are of the whitest marble, probably Parian from its purity and its grain. Several capitals and cornices finely wrought, but above all a pediment of excellent workmanship and exquisite taste, though somewhat impaired by time, clearly evinced that it had been built in the best age, and in the purest style of architecture. This was perhaps the temple of Cnidian Venus, which Praxiteles enriched with that famous statue of the goddess, universally esteemed by the ancients, his masterpiece, and the noblest effort of the art, which has rendered Cnidos renowned through the world, and brought strangers from all parts to visit it.

Lord Charlemont, *Travels in Greece and Turkey* (1785)

Optimists can still hope that echoes of that statue's beauty may reach across the centuries to us: now that the site is being excavated by Professor Iris Love, much may be hoped for.

At the time when this work was ordered, Cos too commissioned from Praxiteles a clothed Aphrodite, whose success was not equal to that of the naked Phryne, and indeed the city fell into debt and was unable to pay. Both are lost; but out of the sea last year, entangled in a fisherman's net, between Cos and Cnidus, a bronze head was rescued, in whose beauty the age of Praxiteles is echoed. The veil has been eaten and encrusted by the water; the metal has broken away where the rise of the breasts begins; but the face is intact. It is not like any other Greek head that I know: it has the long, bony oval of the Mediterranean, and curved nose and features that promise to be fine in age. There is the quality of a Renaissance Madonna, a compassion rare in the ancient world; and this sentiment is wrought with delicacy not in but through the features, so that the goddess expresses a pity beyond human pity – and yet is aloof and not involved. She is in the museum of Smyrna, shut in a cage of glass – a sad degradation for beauty that should need no other than itself to protect it. Whether it was the sight of it so captive; or the presence of the unattainable which perhaps the fingers of the sculptor felt without his knowledge; or mere loveliness, rising for the comfort of men from her deep bays, I cannot tell; but I stood rooted and speechless before the statue from the sea.

Freya Stark, *The Lycian Shore* (1956)

## Muğla

The town of Muğla has no such antique associations, but was the subject of a particularly interesting description of a contest of professional bards in the mid-nineteenth century, which to a classically schooled reader must inevitably arouse echoes of the blind bard Homer, himself an Ionian. The observer would clearly believe that nothing had changed in millennia.

I had once the good fortune to witness an Ashik (Aşık) contest. It was in the fine town of Mooghla, near the southwest corner of Asia Minor. An Ashik had come in that day, and the public cryer had challenged the town in his name to furnish an antagonist worthy to be its champion. Evening came. The field of contest was the interior court of the great Khan, whose stone galleries shone with the bonfires which had been lighted below in honour of the occasion. Many of the citizens had taken their seats around the court, and the caffigi was busy running here and there among the solemn and silent crowd, giving to one a pipe, to another a cup of coffee, and to a third a narguileh. One side of the central platform was occupied by the musicians; on the other, the rivals sat facing each other; and it was easy to perceive, by the vacant turning of the eyeballs of one of them, that, like Homer, the great Ashik of antiquity, he was totally blind. After a prelude by stringed instruments, his voice was heard pouring forth a brilliant couplet upon the silent night, in rich and manly strains; and, when he closed, the suppressed hum of the audience told that his eloquence was appreciated. The musicians struck up the air and hardly had their last note been heard, when the city champion in fair and fitting strains boldly sang his reply to the opening challenge. Thus they went on for some time, the improvised couplets flying across from one to the other rival; and, for a while, it seemed doubtful who would remain master of the field. Ere long, however, the man of Mooghla's voice began to lag behind in its replies; he was more and more at a loss for fitting words to match his antagonist's strains; while the Ashik, growing bolder and more excited by the prospect of victory, pressed closer upon his foe, who was finally silenced and surrendered to his unquestioned superior. The Ashik went on, pouring forth, in a triumphal tone, couplet after couplet of rich, melodious song, and apparently unconscious of all else. In the darkness of blindness, he sang at the top of his voice, like the nightingale of the neighbouring vale at midnight, with all the luxury of conscious superiority, and closed with a new laurel on his brow, a new theme of triumph for his life-long wanderings.

H. J. van Lennep, *Travels in little-known parts of Asia Minor* (1870)

## Lydia: Sardis

Turning north again, we direct our steps towards the inland kingdom of Lydia, which reached its greatness under King Croesus in the sixth century BC. This king preferred accommodation with the Greeks living to the west rather than attempting to extend his kingdom to the Aegean shore. He seems to have been a great respecter of Greek culture, sending dedications to Delphi at frequent intervals, and contributing handsomely to the construction of the temple of Artemis at Ephesus. Such philhellenism naturally earned him the approbation of the Greeks, among whom he became a hero. His meeting with Solon of Athens has passed into legend, thanks to the pen of Herodotus.

On his arrival he was hospitably entertained by Crœsus, and on the third or fourth day, by order of the king, the attendants conducted him round the treasury, and showed him all their grand and costly contents; and when he had seen and examined every thing sufficiently, Crœsus asked him this question: 'My Athenian guest, your great fame has reached even to us, as well of your wisdom as of your travels, how that as a philosopher you have travelled through various countries for the purpose of observation; I am therefore desirous of asking you, who is the most happy man you have seen?' He asked this question, because he thought himself the most happy of men. But Solon, speaking the truth freely, without any flattery, answered, 'Tellus the Athenian.' Crœsus, astonished at his answer, eagerly asked him, 'On what account do you deem Tellus the happiest?' He replied, 'Tellus, in the first place, lived in a well-governed commonwealth; had sons who were virtuous and good; and he saw children born to them all, and all surviving: in the next place, when he had lived as happily as the condition of human affairs will permit, he ended his life in a most glorious manner. For coming to the assistance of the Athenians in a battle with their neighbours of Eleusis, he put the enemy to flight, and died nobly. The Athenians buried him at the public charge in the place where he fell, and honoured him greatly.'

When Solon had roused the attention of Crœsus by relating many and happy circumstances concerning Tellus, Crœsus, expecting at least to obtain the second place, asked, whom he had seen next to him. 'Cleobis,' said he, 'and Biton, for they being natives of Argos, possessed a sufficient fortune, and had withal such strength of body, that they were both alike victorious in the public games; and moreover the following story is related of them: when the Argives were celebrating a festival of Juno, it was necessary that their mother should be drawn to the temple in a chariot; but the oxen did not come from the field in time, the young men therefore, being pressed for time, put themselves beneath the yoke, and drew the car in which their mother sat; and having conveyed it forty-five stades, they reached the temple. After they had done this in sight of the assembled people, a most happy termination was put to their lives; and in them the Deity clearly showed, that it is better for a man to die than to live. For the men of Argos, who stood round, commended the strength of the youths, and the women blessed her as the mother of such sons; but the mother herself, transported with joy both on account of the action and its renown, stood before the image and prayed, that the goddess would grant to Cleobis and Biton, her own sons, who had so highly honoured her, the greatest blessing man could receive. After this prayer, when they had sacrificed and partaken of the feast, the youths fell asleep in the temple itself, and never awoke more, but met with such a termination of life. Upon this the Argives, in commemoration of their piety, caused their statues to be made and dedicated at Delphi.'

Thus Solon adjudged the second place of felicity to these youths. But Crœsus, being enraged, said, 'My Athenian friend, is my happiness then so slighted by you as nothing worth, that you do not think me of so much value as private men?' He answered, 'Crœsus, do you inquire of me concerning human affairs – of me, who know that the divinity is always jealous, and delights in my confusion? For in lapse of time men are constrained to see many things they would not willingly see, and to suffer many things *they would not willingly suffer*. Thus, then, O Crœsus, man is altogether the sport of fortune. You appear to me to be master of immense treasures, and king of many nations; but as relates to what you inquire of me, I cannot say, till I hear you have ended your life happily. For the richest of men is not more happy than he that has a sufficiency for a day, unless good fortune attend him to the grave, so that he ends his life in happiness. Many men, who abound in wealth, are unhappy; and many, who have only a moderate competency, are fortunate. He that abounds in wealth, and is yet unhappy, surpasses the other only in two things; but the other surpasses the wealthy and the miserable in many things. The former indeed is better able to gratify desire, and to bear the blow of adversity. But the latter surpasses him in this; he is not indeed equally able to bear misfortune or *satisfy* desire, but his good fortune wards off these things from him; and he enjoys the full use of his limbs, he is free from disease and misfortune, he is blessed with good children and a fine form, and if, in addition to all these things, he shall end his life well, he is the man you seek, and may justly be called happy; but before he die we ought to suspend our judgment, and not pronounce him happy, but fortunate. Now it is impossible for any one man to comprehend all these advantages: as no one country suffices to produce every thing for itself, but affords some and wants others, and that which affords the most is the best; so no human being is in all respects self-sufficient, but possesses one advantage, and is in need of another; he therefore who has constantly enjoyed the most of these, and then ends his life tranquilly, this man, in my judgment, O king, deserves the name of happy. We ought therefore to consider the end of every thing, in what way it will terminate; for the Deity having shown a glimpse of happiness to many, has afterwards utterly overthrown them.'

When he spoke thus to Crœsus, Crœsus did not confer any favour on him, and holding him in no account, dismissed him; since he considered him a very ignorant man, because he overlooked present prosperity, and bade men look to the end of every thing.

Herodotus, *Histories* I

Solon the Athenian was of course proved right, for Croesus' kingdom was conquered by the Persians, who were preparing to enslave Croesus and his family. The tale is taken up in a beautiful ode by the Cean poet Bacchylides.

. . . once, even the ruler of horse-taming Lydia, Croesus
was protected by Apollo of the golden sword
when, by the fated judgment of Zeus,
Sardis was taken by the Persian sword.

And he, when he came to the far from hoped-for day of weeping
would not wait for slavery,
but built a pyre before his bronze-walled house
and there he ascended with his virtuous wife
and his daughters, weeping piteously;
and he stretched his arms to the sky and cried
'Spirit of too much power,
where now is the grace of the gods?
Where is the lord, the son of Leto?
The house of Alyattes crumbles,
the golden eddies of Pactolus run red with blood,
the women are dragged in shame from their splendid chambers.
All that I loved is hateful; sweet now to die.'

He spoke, and ordered the man of Ohrmazd
to kindle his dwelling of wood.
The girls wailed, and stretched their hands to their mother.
For the death that stands visible before him is most hateful to man.

But, as the brilliant power of fire began to shoot through the
    faggots,
Zeus, setting above Croesus a black cloud,
quenched the yellow fire.

Nothing is unbelievable, which the mind of god chances on.
Then Apollo the Delian born
brought the old man to the people beyond the North Wind,
and gave him a home there with his slim-ankled daughters
– for his piety, because more than all mortals
he had sent gifts
to holy Pytho.

from Bacchylides, *Ode* 3; tr. R. S.

The remains of Sardis are at the village of Sart Mustafa, and
have attracted the attention of many travellers in modern
times. One of the earliest was Thomas Smith, a fellow of
Magdalen College, Oxford, and chaplain of the Levant Company who arrived in Smyrna in February 1670. He was not
greatly enamoured of his Turkish hosts – 'The Turks are justly
branded with the character of a barbarous nation . . .', and so
on for thirty pages – not least because he had narrowly escaped
having his throat cut upon Mt Olympus near Bursa by a group
of Janissaries. Robbers lurked everywhere. Like Wheler, he
was moved by the desolate state of the former Seven Churches
of Asia. Sardis, he wrote:

(retaining somewhat of its name still, though nothing of its ancient glory, being called by the Turks Sart) is situated at the foot of the famous mountain Tmolus on the north side of it, having a spacious and delightful plain before it, watered with several streams that flow from the neighbouring hill to the south east, and with the Pactolus, arising from the same, on the east, and increasing with its waters the stream of Hermus, with which it runs; now a pitiful and beggarly village, the houses few and mean; but for the accommodation of travellers, it being the road for the caravans that come out of Persia to Smyrna with silk, there is a large Chane built in it, as is usual in most towns that are near such publick roads, or have any thing of trade.

. . . .

   To the southward of the town at the bottom of a little hill, the castle lying eastward of them are very considerable ruines still remaining, which quickly put us in mind of what Sardes was, before earthquakes and war had caused those horrid desolations there.

Thomas Smith, *Remarks upon the Manners . . . of The Turks*
(Oxford 1678)

The ubiquitous W. J. Hamilton has also left us a fine description of the site and its setting in a plain dotted with the giant molehills of the tombs of the kings of Lydia, which the Turks call Bin Tepe, the Thousand Hills. Chief of these tumuli is the tomb of Alyattes.

It took us about ten minutes to ride round its base, which would give it a circumference of nearly half a mile. Towards the north it consists of the natural rock, a white horizontally stratified earthly limestone, cut away so as to appear as part of the structure. The upper portion is sand and gravel, apparently brought from the bed of the Hermus. Several deep ravines have been worn by time and weather in its sides, particularly on that to the south; we followed one of these, as affording a better footing than the smooth grass, as we ascended to the summit. Here we found the remains of a foundation nearly eighteen feet square, on the north of which was a huge circular stone ten feet in diameter, with a flat bottom and a raised edge or lip, evidently placed there as an ornament on the apex of the tumulus. Herodotus says that phalli were erected upon the summit of some of these tumuli, of which this may be one; but Mr Strickland supposes that a rude representation of the human face might be traced on its weatherbeaten surface. In consequence of the ground sloping to the south, this tumulus appears much higher when viewed from the side of Sardis than from any other. It rises at an angle of about 22°, and is a conspicuous object on all sides.

   It is impossible to look upon this collection of gigantic mounds, three of which are distinguished by their superior size, without being struck with the power and enterprise of the people by whom they were erected, and without admiring the energies of the nation who endeavoured to preserve the memory of their kings and ancestors by means of such rude and lasting monuments. Hitherto, indeed, they appear to have escaped the destroying hand of conquerors; but the time and means at our disposal would not allow of our making any attempt to penetrate into the interior of any of these royal sepulchres; an undertaking, however, which would probably richly reward the speculator or the antiquary.

W. J. Hamilton, *Travels and Researches in Asia Minor* (1852)

Since 1958 a team from Cornell and Harvard Universities has excavated the ancient city of Sardis and has recovered much fine pottery, metalwork and even wall-paintings from the site. Some of the letters of the director of the dig, George Hanfmann, give an attractive picture of the conditions of an archaeological expedition in Turkey today.

Cambridge    September 17, 1958

I had meant to write this letter at Sardis, but our last days 'on location' proved to be extremely hectic. The big schoolroom and the schoolyard were a chaos of boxes, wheelbarrows, pickaxes, and more boxes. We were working feverishly to pack part of our finds for shipment to the museum at Manisa, another lot was to be stored in the village, and all of the excavation equipment was to be 'winterized' and stowed away. The weather, which had treated us to temperatures of 110–115° during the last two weeks of the campaign, made an aboutface. Rain began to pour steadily and cold winds blew from the heights of Tmolus, disrupting our plans for out-of-doors packing. Nor was this the only disruption. Every couple of hours or so, a taxi with journalists would drive up and we would be cajoled into posing with our trophies – such as were not yet packed up. Our first move was always to explain that we had *not* found the treasure of Croesus, and, indeed, believed that Cyrus had taken it long ago. Now the belief that the treasure of Croesus still lies hidden at Sardis is almost an article of faith with many people in Turkey; and when the Associated Press carried a dispatch that we had found the site of the city of Croesus, there was a rush to see what we had done with the treasure. Indeed, the first intimation we had was the appearance at midnight of two armed state troopers, who stated that they had been dispatched by higher authorities to guard the treasure, and asked why our commissioner had not reported the find and its contents. Our genial Kemal Bey replied with greatest good humor that if the

gentlemen would show him the treasure, he would be the first to
report its contents in detail.

### 1960

On August 21, a whirlwind and dust storm within a matter of
minutes made night of day. It must have been in a storm like this that
Apollo miraculously concealed and carried away Croesus from the
fire death. The storm was followed by a downpour of several hours
which flooded most of our excavations and nearly wiped out our
deep pits. Fortunately, work on these had already stopped, but some
of the Lydian areas near the House of Bronzes remained lakes that
slowly turned to mud. We were considering where we might
borrow pumps, but eventually things dried out, and we were able to
finish the planned digging and clean up most of the mud from this
deluge.

### Summer 1966

For several days a small detachment of workmen supervised alternately by Metin Kunt and myself have been at work starting to clear
an imposing grave complex some fifty feet long. It is a beautifully
built unit with a long entrance corridor, a long chamber, and a square
chamber at the end. All were left in considerable chaos by our illicit
brethren.

This is perhaps as good a time as any to describe the situation,
which is, indeed, hard to understand. Briefly, being outside the law,
and inside the right – the wet – season, the illicit diggers hold all the
trump cards. They go around with long heavy irons which pierce the
ground and test for either hollows or big hefty stones. Their record
at Duman Tepe – the ridge and twin mounds they tackled in
February and March – was remarkable: six hits and two errors. The
romantic and sinister image of invaders from nowhere digging in the
dark of the night was discredited by the amount of work done, the
apparent knowledge of local conditions, and the statement of one of
the landowners that seventy or eighty people were working at one
time.

The law requires report of any antiquities found within a week,
but unless a person is caught while digging, nothing happens. And
nobody feels like intefering. The landowners merely shrug their
shoulders and say, 'Why should I want a hole in my head?' The
gendarmerie says they would never get there in time on foot over a
distance of fifteen miles through the mud. It is obvious that local
people must be involved. However, when asked they always speak
of a mysterious shepherd, who had appeared, dug, and disappeared.

It is different when it comes to legal digging. We must go to
officials, get official messages to village mayors and guards, and

promise to indemnify the owners should their crops suffer any damage. There is one cold comfort in all this. Every known investigation since 1850 has indicated that all Bin Tepe tombs have been opened, entered, and reentered time and again, from possibly as early as Hellenistic through quite modern times. The find mentioned above is what ancient and medieval graverobbers left or overlooked. On the other hand, our purpose is to secure knowledge about this unique and grandiose cemetery as a whole, about its development, about the religious and social aspects involved; and even this evidence is being destroyed both by illicit digging and agricultural activities.

G. M. A. Hanfmann, *Letters from Sardis* (1972)

Ephesus, Hierapolis, Sardis; the remaining four of the Seven Churches of Asia were Thyateira, Colossae, Laodicea and Philadelphia. We leave the Ionian hinterland with the comments of Thomas Smith and George Wheler on two more of them. We may feel fortunate that the decline of the Seven Churches has not, after all, been the last word on the historical fate of fertile Ionia.

## Philadelphia

Philadelphia is called by the Turks Alah Shehr or the fair city. . . . A city formerly of as great strength as beauty, having had three strong walls towards the plain. . . . Defended by them, but more by the valour of its inhabitants, it maintained its liberty, and held out against Ur-chan and Morat the first, when all the lesser Asia had been over-run by the Ottoman forces; but at last in the reign of Bayazid the first, whom the Turks call Yilderim or Lightning, after a long distance the Philadelphians having made several sallies, but all in vain, to remove and raise the siege, it was forced to submit to the fate of other cities, and became a prey to the barbarous Conqueror, who was not wanting in cruelty to express his revenge and furious rage against the distressed citizens for daring to withstand so long his victorious arms: there being about a mile and a half out of town to the south, a thick wall of men's bones confusedly cemented together on the stones; in all probability raised by his command: (for sure none but a Barbarian would have done it) in complyance perchance with some rash vow that he had made, when he lay fretting and storming before it. The Churches felt the terrible effects of his fury as well as the inhabitants; most of them being demolished and turned into dunghills.

Thomas Smith, *Remarks upon the Manners . . . of the Turks*
(Oxford 1678)

## Laodicea

The doom of Laodicea seemeth to have been yet more terrible than any of the rest: for it is now utterly destroyed, and forsaken of men, an habitation only for wolves, foxes and chacals, a den of dragons, snakes and vipers. And that because the Lord hath executed the judgment, that he hath spoken, upon her: that all the world might know, and tremble at the fierce anger of God against impertinent, negligent and careless sinners. For such was the accusation of the luke warm Laodiceans, that grew proud, and self-conceited, thinking themselves better than they were. Wherefore, because they were neither hot, nor cold, they were loathsom to God; and he therefore assured them, He would *spit them out of His Mouth*. The ruins show it to have been a great city.

George Wheler, *A Journey into Greece* (1682)

# CHAPTER FOUR

# Central Anatolia

## Ankara

Ankara, the capital of Turkey since 1923, was probably founded not long after 1000 BC by the Phrygians. When Alexander the Great conquered the Persian Empire in 323 BC the city acquired its first known name, Ancyra, the Greek for anchor. Soon after this it was settled by Galatians, invaders from what is now France, and by the time of the Emperor Augustus it was an important city which the Emperor honoured with a temple inscribed with the record of his achievements, in Greek. This has survived the battering of ages and the inscription was a source of fascination to all travellers.

Joseph Pitton de Tournefort had done his homework when he visited the city in 1701, and pronounced it one of his favourites in all Asia.

Angora, or Angori, as some pronounce it, which the Turks call Engour, delighted us more than any other city in the Levant. We imagined the blood of those brave Gauls, who formerly possessed the country about Toulouse, and between the Cevennes and the Pyrenees, still ran in the veins of the inhabitants of this place. Those generous Gauls, confined in their own country too much for their courage, set out to the number of 30,000 men, to go and make conquests in the Levant, under the conduct of many commanders, of whom Brennus was chief. Whilst this general ravaged Greece, and plundered the temple of Delphos of its immense riches, twenty thousand men of this army marched into Thrace with Leonorius, who, as a Gaul, doubtless called himself Leonorix. . . . The Gauls spread terror all over Asia, even to Mt Taurus, as we learn from Titus Livy, whom I follow closely in this expedition. . . . There being three sorts of Gauls among them, they divided their conquests in such manner, that one sort fixed upon the coast of the Hellespont; another inhabited Aeolia and Ionia; and the most famous, who were called Tectosages, penetrating further, extended themselves to the River Halys, one day's journey from Angora, which is the ancient Ancyra.

. . . .

The Emperor Augustus did, no doubt, beautify Ancyra, seeing Tzetzes calls him the founder of it; and it was probably in acknowledgement that the inhabitants consecrated to him the greatest monument ever yet in Asia. You shall judge, my lord, of the beauty of this building by the design of it, which you commanded me to take. It was all of white marble, in large pieces; and the corners of the vestibulum, which yet remain, are alternately of one piece, returning with a corner, in a manner of a square; the sides or legs of which are three or four feet long. These stones are moreover cramped together with pieces of copper, as appears by the hollows in which they lay. The chief walls are still thirty or five and thirty feet high. The front is entirely destroyed; there remains only the door by which they went out of the vestibulum into the house. This door, which is square, is two feet high, and nine feet two inches wide; and its posts, which are each of one piece, are two feet three inches thick. On the side of this door, which is full of ornaments, was cut above seventeen hundred years ago the life of Augustus in fine Latin, and handsome characters. The inscription is in three columns on the right and left: but besides the defaced letters, 'tis full of great hollows, like those wherein they cast bullets for cannon. These hollows, which have been made by the peasants, to get out the pieces of copper with which the stones were cramped together, have destroyed half the letters. The facings of stone are of an oblong square, very neat, jutting out one inch. Without reckoning the vestibulum, this building is within-side fifty-two feet long, and thirty-six and a half wide. There remain still three grated windows of marble, with great squares like those of our windows. I don't know how these were finished, whether with a transparent stone, or with glass.

One sees within the circumference of this building the ruins of a Christian church, near two or three sorry houses, and some cowhouses. This is what the monument of Ancyra is come to.

This temple of Rome and Augustus had first been observed by the French scholar Laisné late in 1670. He would not trouble to copy the remains of the inscription, so damaged by 'time and the barbarism of the Turks', but Tournefort made a copy. Later finds have supplemented the text from Ancyra, and the published text is one of our most valuable sources for the history of Augustus' reign.

With the growing instability on the decline of Roman power, Ancyra changed rulers many times:

The situation of Angora in the middle of Asia has frequently exposed it to great ravages. It was taken by the Persians in 611, in the time of Heraclius, and ruined in 1101, by that dreadful army of Normans or Lombards, as M du Cange will have it, commanded by Tzitas and the Count de S Gilles, who was afterwards known by the name of Raimond, Count of Toulouse and Provence. . . . The Tartars made themselves masters of Ancyra in 1239. It was afterwards the chief seat of the Ottomans; for Orthogul, father of the famous Ottomans, settled himself here.

J. P. de Tournefort, *Voyage into the Levant*; tr. J. Ozell (1741)

When Bayezid became Ottoman Sultan his power was such that even the Emperor of Byzantium had to fall at his feet. To preserve the peace the Emperor Manuel II Palaeologus had to present himself as a vassal in December 1391 at Bayezid's court, where he was received with all the supercilious indifference that was to become familiar to later visitors to the Ottoman court. His letter to the Sultan is pitiful:

How is it possible that I should be in want, I who, for a long time now, have been leading such a great army into a strange land in winter – though many call the land a friendly one? Add to this the shortage of victuals and the need to buy these at great expense, which has absorbed almost all our attention, as in the enemy territory we have used up all the supplies we brought with us from home. How will my comrades feel, who are familiar neither with the customs nor the language nor the religion, and in a well-governed city can hardly buy the remnants of the goods on sale in the market, where indeed they must virtually fight with you, if by brute force they are to snatch something from the hands of the secondhand goods merchants? Consider in addition the haughtiness, the contempt of those who hold the highest ranks next to the Sultan, the greed, the insatiability, the readiness to demand, the savage nature, the mutual envy, the anger of each one of them against the foreigners, the hatred, if they should not leave them their possessions and return home denuded of everything. This too must not be passed over: the daily hunt, the succeeding immoderation at table, the swarms of actors, the groups of flautists, the choruses of singers, the masses of dancers, the noise of cymbals, the rowdy laughter that follows the drinking of wine – does it not mean that those who make such

behaviour their constant companion, are indeed stupid? It is only
circumstances which compel us to undertake such a difficult task,
enveloped though we are in so much misfortune; it is the result of
your and your sons' valorous pride. For I do not see *you* going
directly from the midday meal to the evening meal (like those who
are considered happy among you), and from this to sleep and then
again to the midday meal in a perpetual cycle, so that their life
consists of sloth and excess, in no way becoming to men. Oh that
this evil connection could be broken! But everything that breaks it
is 'of no value', that is, nothing that is better and more honourable,
but only the opposite. If, then, your wisdom, understanding and
humility did not give me courage to speak, you may be sure that I
should give up the task at once.

Manuel Paleologus, Letters; tr. R. S.

Those tales of luxury are corroborated by the Greek historians. It was that hedonism that proved Bayezid's downfall,
as Tournefort relates.

Angora was fatal to the Ottoman, and the battle which Tamerlane
obtained there over Bajazet, had well nigh destroyed their empire.
Bajazet, the haughtiest man in the world, too confident in himself,
left his camp to go a-hunting. Tamerlane, whose troops began to
want water, laid hold on this opportunity and rendering himself
master of the small river which ran between the two armies, three
days after forced Bajazet to give him battle, to prevent his army from
dying of thirst. His army was cut to pieces, and the Sultan taken
prisoner, the 7th of August 1401.

J. P. de Tournefort, op. cit.

Gibbon's account of the battle of Angora is vivid, and the
tale inspired Marlowe too.

Firm in his plan of fighting in the heart of the Ottoman kingdom, he
avoided their camp; dexterously inclined to the left; occupied
Cæsarea; traversed the salt desert and the river Halys; and invested
Angora; while the sultan, immoveable and ignorant in his post,
compared the Tartar swiftness to the crawling of a snail; he returned
on the wings of indignation to the relief of Angora; and, as both
generals were alike impatient for action, the plans round that city
were the scene of a memorable battle, which has immortalised the
glory of Timour and the shame of Bajazet. For this signal victory,
the Mogul emperor was indebted to himself, to the genius of the
moment, and the discipline of thirty years. He had improved the
tactics without violating the manners, of his nation, whose force still
consisted in the missile weapons, and rapid evolutions, of a numer-

ous cavalry. From a single troop to a great army, the mode of attack was the same: a foremost line first advanced to the charge, and was supported in a just order by the squadrons of the great vanguard. The general's eye watched over the field, and at his command the front and rear of the right and left wings successively moved forwards in their several divisions, and in a direct or oblique line; the enemy was pressed by eighteen or twenty attacks; and each attack afforded a chance of victory. If they all proved fruitless or unsuccessful, the occasion was worthy of the emperor himself, who gave the signal of advancing to the standard and main body, which he led in person. But in the battle of Angora, the main body itself was supported, on the flanks and in the rear, by the bravest squadrons of the reserve, commanded by the sons and grandsons of Timour. The conqueror of Hindostan ostentatiously shewed a line of elephants, the trophies, rather than the instruments, of victory: the use of the Greek fire was familiar to the Moguls and Ottomans; but, had they borrowed from Europe the recent invention of gunpowder and cannon, the artificial thunder, in the hands of either nation, must have turned the fortune of the day. In that day, Bajazet displayed the qualities of a soldier and a chief; but his genius sunk under a stronger ascendant; and, from various motives, the greatest part of his troops failed him in the decisive moment.

Edward Gibbon, *Decline and Fall of The Roman Empire*, ch. 65

### Bajazeth. Tamburlaine

*Baj.* Now shalt thou feel the force of Turkish arms,
Which lately made all Europe quake for fear.
I have of Turks, Arabians, Moors, and Jews,
Enough to cover all Bithynia.
Let thousands die: their slaughter'd carcasses
Shall serve for walls and bulwarks to the rest;
And as the heads of Hydra, so my power,
Subdu'd shall stand as mighty as before.
If they should yield their necks unto the sword,
Thy soldiers' arms could not endure to strike
So many blows as I have heads for thee.
Thou know'st not, foolish-hardy Tamburlaine,
What 'tis to meet me in the open field,
That leave no ground for thee to march upon.
*Tamb.* Our conquering swords shall marshal us the way
We use to march upon the slaughter'd foe,
Trampling their bowels with our horses' hoofs,
Brave horses bred on the white Tartarian hills.
My camp is like to Julius Caesar's host,
That never fought but had the victory;

Nor in Pharsalia was there such hot war
As these my followers willingly would have.
Legions of spirits, fleeting in the air,
Direct our bullets and our weapons' points,
And make your strokes to wound the senseless air;
And when she sees our bloody colours spread,
Then Victory begins to take her flight,
Resting herself upon my milk-white tent.
But come, my lords, to weapons let us fall;
The field is ours, the Turk, his wife, and all.
    *Exit with his followers.*
*Baj.* Come, kings and bassoes, let us glut our swords,
That thirst to drink the feeble Persians' blood.


But later:

*Baj.* Great Tamburlaine, great in my overthrow,
Ambitious pride shall make thee fall as low,
For treading on the back of Bajazeth,
That should be horsed on four mighty kings.
*Tamb.* Thy names and titles and thy dignities
Are fled from Bajazeth and remain with me,
That will maintain it 'gainst a world of kings.
Put him in again.
    *They put him into the cage.*
*Baj.* Is this a place for mighty Bajazeth?
Confusion light on him that helps thee thus.
*Tamb.* There, while he lives, shall Bajazeth be kept,
And, where I go, be thus in triumph drawn;
And thou, his wife, shall feed him with the scraps
My servitors shall bring thee from my board,
For he that gives him other food than this,
Shall sit by him, and starve to death himself:
This is my mind, and I will have it so.
Not all the kings and emperors of the earth,
If they would lay their crowns before my feet,
Shall ransom him, or take him from his cage.
The ages that shall talk of Tamburlaine,
Even from this day to Plato's wondrous year,
Shall talk how I have handled Bajazeth.
These Moors, that drew him from Bithynia
To fair Damascus, where we now remain,
Shall lead him with us whereso'er we go.
Techelles, and my loving followers,
Now may we see Damascus' lofty towers,

Like to the shadows of Pyramides
That with their beauties graced the Memphian fields.
The golden stature of their feather'd bird,
That spreads her wings upon the city walls,
Shall not defend it from our battering shot.
The townsmen mask in silk and cloth of gold,
And every house is as a treasury;
The men, the treasure, and the town are ours.

Christopher Marlowe, Tamburlaine

The historian is more sceptical of this memorable piece of cruelty.

The *iron cage* in which Bajazet was imprisoned by Tamerlane, so long and so often repeated as a moral lesson, is now rejected as a fable by the modern writers, who smile at the vulgar credulity. They appeal with confidence to the Persian history of Sherefeddin Ali, which has been given to our curiosity in a French version, and from which I shall collect and abridge a more specious narrative of this memorable transaction. No sooner was Timour informed that the captive Ottoman was at the door of his tent, than he graciously stepped forwards to receive him, seated him by his side, and mingled with just reproaches a soothing pity for his rank and misfortune. 'Alas!' said the emperor, 'the decree of fate is now accomplished by your own fault: it is the web which you have woven, the thorns of the tree which yourself have planted. I wished to spare, and even to assist, the champion of the Moslems: you braved our threats; you despised our friendship; you forced us to enter your kingdom with our invincible armies. Behold the event. Had you vanquished, I am not ignorant of the fate which you reserved for myself and my troops. But I disdain to retaliate; your life and honour are secure; and I shall express my gratitude to God by my clemency to man.'

Edward Gibbon, *Decline and Fall of The Roman Empire*, ch. 65

By 1701, things had quieted down a bit in Angora.

Angora, at present, is one of the best cities in Anatolia, and everywhere shows marks of its ancient magnificence. One sees nothing in the streets but pillars and old marbles. . . . The walls of the city are low, and furnished with very sorry battlements. They have indifferently made use of pillars, architraves, capitals, bases and other ancient pieces, intermingled with masonry, to build the wall, especially in the towers and gates, which nevertheless are not at all the more beautiful; for the towers are square, and the gates plain.

.　.　.　.

They breed the finest goats in the world in the champaign of Angora. They are of a dazzling white, and their hair, which is fine as silk, naturally curled in locks of eight or nine inches long, is worked up into the finest stuffs, especially camlet: but they don't suffer these fleeces to be exported unspun, because the country people gain their livelihood thereby. . . . The thread made of this goats' hair is sold from four livres to twelve or fifteen livres the oque.

J. P. de Tournefort, *op.cit.*

Tournefort duly provided an illustration of one of those famous goats, which also attracted the attention of other writers.

One of the minor mysteries of Asia is the popularity of Plato (in the guise of the Muslim sage Iflatun) in legend. Many miracles were attributed to him throughout Asia Minor as well as in Constantinople (where Galen was nearly as popular a magician of legend), and his name was attached to wonder-working wells and the like. One such near Angora is described by F. W. Hasluck (*Annual of the British School at Athens*, 18 [1911–12]), 265ff, who refers to the late medieval account by Haci Khalfa:

To the east of Angora, not far from the river Kyzyl, there is a ruined Christian temple. Here there is a well, now dry, but of such potency that if any one who is troubled in the head looks into it, while wrapped in a winding sheet, he either leaves the building of sound mind, or dies on the spot. But anyone who tries this when of sound mind will see nothing there, but will at once perceive a strong odour of sulphur. Next to the well is a cemetery, which is called Dementium.

Mustafa Ibn 'Abd Allah (Haci Khalfa), *Gihan Numa*; Latin tr. M. Norberg (Gothenburg 1818); tr. R.S.

## Phrygia

The ancient kingdom of Phrygia stretches westwards from Ankara, and its capital is at Gordium. The city was named after the legendary founder Gordius, whose story is canonically told by John Lydgate.

> *Gordius*
>
> After his wedding he wex fortunate,
> The chronicle can bear me well record:
> There fell in Phrygia a sudden great debate
> Among the commons, and mortal discord,

Knowing no means to bring them at accord,
Till their gods by notable providence
Taught them a way to appease their violence,

How that debate should among them last
Until the time they had chosen a king.
And they began cry and pray their gods fast,
By some sign or miracle out showing,
To give to them a manner knowledging,
That they might, to their notable increase,
Choose such one that should them set in peace.

They had answer, to wait and be well ware,
To set spies by busy attendance,
On whom they met riding in a chair
To Jove's temple to do his observance,
And him rescue, by gods ordinance,
Upon his head, without more tarrying,
To set a crown in Phrygia to reign as king.

And Gordius in his car riding
Toward the temple, they on the way him met;
And awaiting chose him to be their king,
And solemnly home they did him fete;
Upon his head a rich crown they set.
And he to them so equal was and meet,
That he them brought in rest and quiet.

Thus to the crown Gordius did attain,
By tokens showed unto his great avail.
And their discords and strifes to restrain,
He to his lieges gave notable counsel,
That they should with royal apparel
Go take his car, as he did them devise,
And offer it up in most lowly wise

In the temple that was consecrate
To Jupiter, a most solemn place.
And more to make the offering fortunate,
They should it set, without longer space,
Before the goddess that was called Grace,
Which by miracles their hearts to appease,
Set all the people in quiet and in ease.

John Lydgate, *Fall of Princes* IV 1758 ff

It was on that throne that the semi-legendary King Midas
was also to sit – he who asked of the gods that everything he

touched should turn to gold, and then hungered and thirsted among viands that gleamed yellow and drink that froze to bright metal in his hand.

The legend of the wagon was alluded to by Arrian, the historian of Alexander the Great.

There was also another traditional belief about the wagon: according to this, the man who undid the knot which fixed its yoke was destined to be the lord of Asia. The cord was made from the bark of the cornel tree, and so cunningly was the knot tied that no one could see where it began or where it ended. For Alexander, then, how to undo it was indeed a puzzle, though he was none the less unwilling to leave it as it was, as his failure might possibly lead to public disturbances. Accounts of what followed differ: some say that Alexander cut the knot with a stroke of his sword and exclaimed, 'I have undone it!', but Aristobulus thinks that he took out the pin – a sort of wooden peg which was driven right through the shaft of the wagon and held the knot together – and thus pulled the yoke away from the shaft. I do not myself presume to dogmatize on this subject. In any case, when he and his attendants left the place where the wagon stood, the general feeling was that the oracle about the untying of the knot had been fulfilled. Moreover, that very night there was lightning and thunder – a further sign from heaven; so Alexander, on the strength of all this, offered sacrifice the following day to the gods who had sent the sign from heaven and proclaimed the Loosing of the Knot.

Arrian, *Campaigns of Alexander*

## Konya

'Everything comes to an end, even the road from Akserai to Konya'
Gertrude Bell, letter of 16 July 1907 (*Letters*, 251)

Konya, ancient Iconium, is one of the oldest continuously occupied towns in the World with traces of habitations dating back nearly nine millennia. In Phrygian legend it was the first place to emerge after the flood. In classical times it was known as Eikonion (Iconium), and quickly acquired a Greek foundation legend.

Perseus came to Lycaonia, and vanquished the opposition of the people by the power of the Gorgoneion, which turned his enemies to stone. He then made a village called Amandra into a Greek city, and called it Iconium from the eikon or image of the Gorgon, which he received there before the victory. This seems to point to Divine help granted to him before the battle began. He erected in front of the new city a statue representing himself holding up the Gorgon's head; and this statue (the authorities say) is standing there to the present day. The coins show us the same statue which these authorities mention, and which was doubtless an ornament of the city; there can be little doubt that it was a Hellenistic work modelled after the famous statue of Perseus by the great Attic sculptor of the fifth century BC, Myron.

W. M. Ramsay, *Cities of St Paul* (1907)

It is of course best known to Western readers for its place in the story of St Paul:

And it came to pass in Iconium, that they went both together into the synagogue of the Jews, and so spake, that a great multitude both of the Jews and also of the Greeks believed. But the unbelieving Jews stirred up the gentiles, and made their minds evil affected against the brethren. Long time therefore abode they speaking boldly in the Lord, which gave testimony unto the word of grace, and granted signs and wonders to be done by their hands. But the multitude of the city was divided: and part held with the Jews, and part with the apostles. And when there was an assault made both of the Gentiles, and also of the Jews with their rulers, to use them despitefully, and to stone them, they were ware of it, and fled unto Lystra and Derbe, cities of Lycaonia, and unto the region that lieth round about: and there they preached the gospel.

And there sat a certain man at Lystra, impotent in his feet, being a cripple from his mother's womb, who never had walked: the same heard Paul speak: who stedfastly beholding him, and perceiving that he had faith to be healed, said with a loud voice, Stand upright on thy feet. And he leaped and walked. And when the people saw what Paul had done, they lifted up their voices, saying in the speech of Lycaonia, The gods are come down to us in the likeness of men. And they called Barnabas, Jupiter; and Paul, Mercurius, because he was the chief speaker. Then the priest of Jupiter, which was before their city, brought oxen and garlands unto the gates, and would have done sacrifice with the people. Which when the apostles, Paul and Barnabas heard of, they rent their clothes, and ran in among the people, crying out, and saying, Sirs, why do ye these things? We also are men of like passions with you, and preach unto you that ye should turn from these vanities unto the living God, which made heaven, and earth, and the sea, and all things that are therein: who in past times suffered all nations to walk in their own ways. Nevertheless, he left not himself without witness, in that he did good, and gave us rain from heaven, and fruitful seasons, filling our hearts with food and gladness. And with these sayings scarce restrained they the people, that they had not done sacrifice to them.

Acts of the Apostles, 14. 1–18

Though some classical and Ottoman fortifications remain, the chief interest of Konya lies in the convent of the Mevlevi or Whirling Dervishes, built here by Sultan Selim I. This order of Dervishes was founded in 1231 by Jelal-ud-Din Rumi, a Persian from Balkh who at the age of six was already accustomed to the visits of angels and demons.

One day he astounded his playmates by giving a jump, and disappearing into the skies. On his return, 'greatly altered in complexion and changed in figure', he explained that he had been conveyed there by 'a legion of beings clothed in green mantles', who had shown him 'strange things of a celestial character, and on your cries reaching us they lowered me down again to the Earth'. The dervish is thus compared to the bird which flies upwards above the roof, a creature exalted above common men and freed from worldly cares and anxieties.

                          J. P. D. B. Kinross, *Within Taurus* (1954)

The ritual of the Whirling Dervishes was described by many travellers, most of whom saw it in Constantinople rather than its native home. Dickens' friend Albert Smith was typical of many:

Having put off our shoes, we entered an octagonal building, with galleries running round it, and standing places under them, surrounding the railed enclosure in which the dervishes were to dance, or rather spin. One division of this part of the building was put aside for Christians, the others were filled with common people and children. When I arrived, one old dervish, in a green dress, was sitting at one point of the room, and twenty-four in white, were opposite to him. A flute and drum played some very dreary music in the gallery. At a given signal they all fell flat on their faces, with a noise and precision that would have done honour to a party of pantomimists; and then they all rose and walked slowly round, with their arms folded across their breasts, following the old green dervish, who marched at their head, and bowing twice very gravely to the place where he had been sitting, and to the spot opposite to it. They performed this round two or three times. Then the old man sat down, and the others, pulling off their cloaks, appeared in a species of long petticoat, and one after the other began to spin. They commenced revolving precisely as though they were waltzing by themselves; first keeping their hands crossed on their breast, and then extending them, the palm of the right hand, and the back of the left being upwards. At last, they all got into play, and as they went round and round, they put me in mind of the grand party we have seen on the top of an organ, where a *cavalier seul* revolves by himself, and bows as he faces the spectators.

They went on for a long time without stopping – a quarter of an hour, perhaps, or twenty minutes. There was something inexpressibly sly and offensive in the appearance of these men, and the desire one felt to hit them hard in the face became uncomfortably dominant. At the end of their revolutions, they made another obeisance to the old man, and all this time the players in the orchestra howled forth a kind of hymn. This ceremony was repeated three or four times, and then they all sat down again and put their cloaks on, whilst another dervish, who had walked round and round amongst the dancers, whilst they were spinning, sang a solo. During this time, their faces were all close to the ground. This done, they rose and marched before the old green dervish once more, kissing his hand as they passed, and the service concluded, occupying altogether about three-quarters of an hour.

Albert R. Smith, *A Month at Constantinople* (1850)

Gertrude Bell responded enthusiastically to the convent when she visited it on May 13, 1905:

Konia contains the mother house of the Dervishes and the founder of the order, Jelal ed Din Rumi the great Persian, is buried there. My visit to his tomb was a real pilgrimage for I know some of his poems and there are things in them that are not to be surpassed. He lies under a dome tiled with blue, bluer than heaven or the sea, and adorned inside with rich and sombre Persian enamel and lacquer and on either side of him are rows and rows of the graves of the Chelebis, the Dervish high priests and his direct descendants – all the Chelebis who have been ministers and over each is the high felt hat of the order with a white turban wrapped round it. Beyond the tomb are two great dancing halls with polished floors and the whole is enclosed in a peaceful garden, fountains and flowers set round with the monastic cells of the order. So he lies, Jelal ed din Rumi, and to my mind the whole quiet air was full of the music of his verses: 'Ah listen to the reed as it tells its tale: Listen, ah, listen, to the plaint of the reed.' 'They reft me from the rushes of my home, my voice is sad with longing, sad and low.' (But the Persian is the very pipe, the plaintive pipe of the reed, put into words and there is nothing so invades the soul.)

Letter of 13, May 1905

The mystical teachings of Rumi were based on a questioning of experience that reduced certainty to a minimum, consciousness to a void into which truth could enter:

*I am the Life of My Beloved*

What can I do, Muslims? I do not know myself.
I am no Christian, no Jew, no Magian, no Musulman.
Not of the East, not of the West. Not of the land, not of the sea.
Not of the Mine of Nature, not of the circling heavens,
Not of earth, not of water, not of air, not of fire;
Not of the throne, not of the ground, of existence, of being;
Not of India, China, Bulgaria, Saqseen;
Not of the kingdom of the Iraqs, or of Khorasan;
Not of this world or the next: of heaven or hell;
Not of Adam, Eve, the gardens of Paradise or Eden;
My place placeless, my trace traceless.
Neither body nor soul: all is the life of my Beloved
                          from Idries Shah, *The Way of the Sufi* (1968)

Much of the teaching of the Dervishes took the form of
tales, like parables. Naturally, many of the Dervish tales were
set in Konya, like this one which tells of Rumi's wisdom.

### The Merchant and the Christian Dervish

A rich merchant of Tabriz came to Konia, looking for the wisest man
there, for he was in trouble. After trying to get advice from the
religious leaders, the lawyers and others, he heard of Rumi, to whom
he was taken.

He took with him fifty gold pieces as an offering. When he saw the
Maulana in the audition-hall, he was overcome with emotion.
Jalaludin said to him:

'Your fifty coins are accepted. But you have lost two hundred,
which is why you are here. God has punished you and is showing
you something. Now all will be well with you.'

The merchant was amazed at what the Maulana knew. Rumi
continued:

'You have had many troubles because one day in the far west of
Christendom you saw a Christian dervish lying in the street. You
spat at him. Go to him and ask forgiveness, and give him our
salutations.'

As the merchant stood terrified at this reading of his mind,
Jalaludin said: 'Shall we show him to you now?' He touched the wall
of the room, and the merchant saw the scene of the saint in the
market place in Europe. He reeled away from the Master's presence,
completely nonplussed.

Travelling as fast as he could to the Christian sage, he found him
lying prostrate on the ground. As he approached him, the Frankish
dervish said: 'Our Master Jalal has communicated with me.'

The merchant looked in the direction in which the dervish was pointing, and saw, as in a picture, Jalaludin chanting such words as these: 'Whether a ruby or a pebble, there is a place on His hill, there is a place for all . . .'

The merchant carried back the greetings of the Frankish saint to Jalal, and settled down in the community of the dervishes at Konia.

from Idries Shah, *Tales of the Dervishes* (1967)

## Akşehir

Not far from Konya to the north west is Akşehir, famous as the home of Nasreddin Khoja, the wise fool of Turkish legend. He lived in the time of Tamburlaine, and several cycles of tales attached themselves to his person. The following is typical:

### Nasreddin Khoja Dividing Five Eggs

During the invasion of Turkey by Tamerlane, the great despot came to Akshehir, where Nasreddin Khoja lived. As Tamerlane entered the city, he saw Nasreddin Khoja sitting by the side of the road watching the procession. Khoja was wearing a blanket wrapped around his head as a turban, and this called Tamerlane's attention to him. Tamerlane ordered that the man be brought before him.

'Who are you?' he asked Khoja.

'I am the god of the earth,' answered Khoja.

'Since you are the god of the earth, perhaps you can enlarge the eyes of this attendant of mine. See what very small eyes he has.'

'I wonder,' answered Khoja, 'whether I did not make it plain to you or whether you just did not understand me. I am not the god of the heavens who can do such things. If you want something done above the waist, ask him; anything below the waist is in my sphere.'

Tamerlane talked for a good while with Nasreddin Khoja, and he was very pleased with his wit. He sent him away finally, but a few days later he ordered him brought back for his amusement. One of the emperor's wives had cooked five eggs, and he invited Khoja to join them in a meal. He said to Nasreddin Khoja, 'I want you to divide these five eggs fairly among the three of us.'

Without hesitating, Khoja took the five eggs and said, 'Here is one for you, your majesty, and since you have two below your waist, that makes a total of three eggs for you. This one is mine, and that makes three for me too. And the other three are for your wife, for she has none below the waist.'

from W. S. Walker, *Tales Alive in Turkey* (1966)

The tomb of the Khoja may be seen to this day at Ak Shehir, in the vilayet of Konia. In the middle of a field or graveyard – I am not sure which, for I saw the site in mid-winter when everything was deep in snow – is a small domed building, partly open at the sides; under the dome is a tomb above which hangs the enormous green turban, about the size of an ordinary umbrella, which the Khoja wore in his lifetime. A small hole is left in the masonry of the grave, as he insisted on having a window through which he could look out on the world of men, and a slab which bears his name gives the year of his death as 1366 A.H, equivalent to about 1950 AD, by which inscription he is said to have meant to puzzle future generations.

Odysseus (Charles Eliot), *Turkey in Europe* (1900)

## Cappadocia: Göreme

Just to the west of Kayseri are the famous rock-hewn churches and monasteries of the Cappadocian Fathers, who followed the rule of St Basil (AD 329–79) and who continued for a thousand years here until the Seljuk conquest. The fantastic conical rocks formed from the lava flows of now extinct volcanoes spread across the landscape like so many spires and turrets, – the locals call them fairy chimneys, peri bacaları (Freely, 239). Each is pitted with the carving of cells, chapels and dwellings. They are the most extensive museum of Byzantine painting anywhere, though in the nineteenth century this was scarcely of interest to travellers who saw in it only a barbaric art. It was not until 1907 that the paintings were studied seriously. The Oxford geographer H. F. Tozer was interested only in the carved architecture and the history of its inhabitants.

What especially attracted our attention was the great difficulty – in some cases impossibility – of access to these habitants. Here and there they may have been reached by a passage on the inside, for in one place we saw a staircase running up into the rock, though to the foot of this, strange to say, there was no approach; but in most instances the entrances to the caves were far out of reach, and in precipitous places. The most probable idea that suggested itself was that they had been reached by ladders or scaffoldings attached to the rocks, which may have been movable, as is the case in some Greek monasteries at the present day, with a view to greater security. The desire of concealment was clearly an influential motive with those who dwelt here, for in the places nearer to the ground which we entered, the passages were sometimes not more than three feet high, and the staircases were very narrow and winding.

The first chamber to which we were conducted had evidently been a refectory. It was oblong in shape, and excavated to some depth; and in the walls at various points were niches, intended apparently to receive lamps, which must have been frequently needed, for the light only entered through the door. On the left-hand side, running nearly the whole length of the room, was a narrow stone table, hewn out of the rock, and detached everywhere except at its base; it was rounded at the inner end, where seemed to be the seat of honour. A stone bench ran all round it, which equally formed part of the native rock. The roof was flat, and about fifteen feet high. . . . Passing on from this we came to a church, which was entered by a vestibule, vaulted above, and decorated half-way up the side walls with a blind arcade of horseshoe arches. At the further end of this there is a narrow passage, leading by a winding flight of stairs into the church, which is twenty-four feet long, and quite concealed in the bowels of the rock. The arrangement of this church, and of all the others we visited, and to a great extent their architecture, was thoroughly Byzantine, for the form was that of a Greek cross, and it had two cupolas, supported on six columns, two of which were engaged in the wall of the *iconostasis*, or altar-screen, which in places of worship of the Greek Church separates the sanctuary from the rest of the building. On the front of the screen were two seats, and another within it as well as the altar. Four columns had been knocked away, but their capitals remained, all cut out of the tufa; and here too the arches were horseshoed, as indeed we found them to be almost universally in these structures. The whole place was covered with frescoes in the Byzantine style, and these were in the main well preserved, owing to the dryness of the air, though many had been intentionally defaced, probably by the Mahometans. The execution was good for Byzantine paintings, and often more spirited and original than what is usually found in that style.

. . . . .

It is not too much to say that the sides of this long valley are filled with similar traces of its former occupants. The entire region may be described as one sepult monastic dwelling-place – a Byzantine Pompeii. And after seeing it we are naturally led to inquire what period it dates from, and what was the history of its inhabitants. But here we are left almost entirely to conjecture, for there are no documents relating to it, no annalists that mention its existence, and no inscriptions on its walls. There is one name, however, from which it seems difficult wholly to dissociate it, that of St. Basil. That eminent saint, who was born at the neighbouring Caesareia, and at one time of his life taught rhetoric there, and finally became bishop of that see, has been always regarded by the monks of the Eastern Church, and is still regarded by them, as the founder of their rule.

Living as he did in the middle of the fourth century A.D., in the
ecclesiastical affairs of which period he played a prominent part, he
was a great man in a great age; and it is no slight glory to Cappadocia
that it should have produced in one generation three such distinguished persons as him and his brother, Gregory of Nyssa, and his
friend, Gregory of Nazianzus. He was at once strong and tender; a
learned divine, and at the same time a vigorous administrator; and
notwithstanding the weakness of his health throughout his life, he
both practised severe asceticism and exercised a powerful influence
over his contemporaries. He seems to have been impressed with the
evils attendant on the hermit life, which up to that time had been
the regular form of monasticism, and accordingly he instituted the
coenobite system, or organisation of monks in communities.

H. F. Tozer, *Turkish Armenia and Eastern Asia Minor* (1881)

## The Hittites

The Hittites are one of the most remarkable discoveries of the
last century of archaeology. From a people known only from
references in the Old Testament as one of a number of
apparently localised tribes interfering with the progress of the
people of Israel, they have been revealed as the rulers of one of
the most magnificent and powerful empires of bronze age
Anatolia. Their racial affiliation too has been an eye-opener:
previously assumed to be Semites like their neighbours, their
language, when it was deciphered by F. Hrozny in 1915,
proved to be Indo-European, related rather to the languages of
the Greeks and Persians than to any of their Middle Eastern
neighbours.

Hittites are traceable in Asia Minor from about 2500 BC,
when they first settled at the site later known as Hattusas, the
capital of the later Empire, at Boğazkale north of Yozgat.
After a period of destruction in the eighteenth century BC, the
Hittite Old Kingdom was established and existed for about
three centuries before imperial aggrandisement turned it into
an Empire. This Empire controlled much of Eastern Turkey
and northern Syria until it was overthrown by invading tribes,
perhaps Thracians, about 1180 BC.

Near to the capital at Hattusas was the national sanctuary of
the 'thousand gods' of the Hittites at Yazılıkaya. This seems to
have been largely erected in the reign of King Tudhaliyas IV
(1250–20 BC) who is portrayed in the friendly embrace of the

gods in the remarkable series of rock-cut reliefs. A recently discovered text, quoted by John Freely in his guide to Turkey (p. 268) has strengthened the presumption that this was the scene of the celebration of the Hittites' New Year festival:

In honour of the Weather God at the beginning of the New Year a great festival of Heaven and Earth was celebrated. All the gods assembled and entered into the house of the Weather God. Whichever god harbours anger in his soul shall chase the evil anger from his soul. Now eat at this feast, drink! Satisfy your hunger and quench your thirst. Hail to the King and Queen! Hail to the Heaven and Earth and the grain!

## Boğazkale and Yazılıkaya

None of this could have been known to Charles Texier who discovered the reliefs of Boğazkale and Yazílíkaya in 1834. Though the excitement of his discovery gleams through the long description, the conclusions he draws are an object lesson to archaeologists who might be tempted to conclude too readily from insufficient evidence, or to assume that any new discovery can necessarily be fitted into the framework of existing knowledge. The Hittites changed the map of Near Eastern history. Excavations began at Boğazkale in 1906 under Hugo Winckler, and in time led to the interpretation of the language, mentioned above. New discoveries, for example of links with Mycenaean Greece, make them into an ever more fascinating factor in the bronze age world.

It was on July 28 that we discovered at the village of Boghaz keui the imposing ruins of which answer completely the question (of the site of ancient Pterium). Since that time the obscure Turkish village has become famous among the learned; its ruins have been visited by a great number of travellers, many dissertations have been written on the subjects represented in the bas-reliefs which have been so marvellously preserved through the centuries; we have accomplished our task, we have returned to the light a city forgotten for twenty-five centuries. . . . The existence of the ruins revealed an Asia hitherto unknown, opened a new era in Oriental studies, and was, in the words of one academician, the source of discoveries whose conclusions no one could predict.

. . . . .

The plateau on which the ruins of the temple are situated is terminated on the north by a chalk mountain covered with bushes, which is still in a state of wild and uncultivated nature. On the southern side, the land cultivated by the inhabitants forms a few insignificant undulations.

.    .    .    .

The interest which attached for me to these ruins became still greater when I learnt that about two miles from the city there was a tall enceinte in the rock, around which are sculpted bas-reliefs representing a subject relating to events today completely forgotten, but which must have been of great significance in the history of these peoples.

The road which leads to this enceinte leads through uncultivated country; no traces of building are to be seen; the place appears never to have been inhabited. Today it is equally deserted, and the peasants were afraid to find themselves there at the onset of night. Nothing in the environs indicates the existence of a monument of such importance. The monument of Yasili kaia (the written stone), as the inhabitants call it, is perfectly preserved . . . It forms an almost square room, and on the steep rocks are bas-reliefs in several scenes, about the height of a man.

.    .    .    .

All these reliefs belong evidently to a single subject, and portray a great political or religious event, celebrated in the annals of these peoples. But they are not the only works of this kind on view, there are many other sculptured tablets in other parts of the enceinte, and all seem to me to belong directly to the theme of the main relief.

.    .    .    .

A careful examination of this monument demonstrates that it is not the work of one of the peoples who inhabited Western Asia. The resemblance of the figure mounted on a lion to Babylonian sculpture leads to the conjecture that it represents one of the principal divinities revered by the Medes or Assyrians.

.    .    .    .

It can be counted as incontestable that the human figures in these reliefs are all wearing the costume of the Sacae. . . . The festivals of the Sacae were celebrated not only in this part of Media but in Babylon itself. The description of Athenaeus, after Berossus, does not resemble that of Strabo; but the name is the same. It is possible that the ceremonies were modified as they moved away from the country of their origin. . . . it was the custom that the slaves should give orders to their masters. . . . This proves that the institution of these festivals was anterior to the reign of Cyrus, and when one sees the extreme importance attached by the peoples to their celebration, one cannot be surprised that they perpetuated their memory by a monument.

Charles Texier, *Asie Mineure* (1835); tr. R. S.

Marie Wiegand, the wife of the archaeologist Theodore Wiegand, who visited the monuments of Phrygia in June 1908, gives an evocative description of the setting of Yazılıkaya.

Between Arslan Kaya and Yazilikaya, we continued briskly through tall pine forests, climbing and descending, passing long columns of ox-carts with wheels of solid oak: they could be detected for miles by their distinctive sound. Often they clattered like church bells being rung in disorder, often they sounded like wild beasts, and every time we met one it was loaded with fine tree trunks or with planks, which are often brought many days' march by railway. The people only march about three hours a day; then they unharness their beasts and let them graze, with the carts arranged in a circle. . . . The incredible wealth of timber, combined with a civilisation quite other than must have existed at earlier times in this region, shows itself today in a whole series of customs. So the well-buckets are carved of solid logs; the pitchers which hang from every cart and which the workers carry into the fields are hewn from a single piece of wood, with a double handle, neck and lip, and hollow within: only at the bottom a base made from a root is applied. The houses are built of thick round logs and waterproofed with moss or clay, and covered with wood so that you might think yourself in the most primitive of Alpine valleys. Even the field fences are of gigantic treetrunks, on which the people leave only some strong branches on one side; the trunk lies on top, and so trunk after trunk range along the road like monsters with multiple paws. In addition, you must imagine a countryside which a painter could scarcely make more fantastic. Mountain and valley, prairie and field, and the virgin forest which has already been to a considerable extent cleared; in the midst rise up suddenly rocks like ancient fortresses with towers and walls, here as white as snow like an encampment of tents, there lying at length like crouching monsters of stumpy shape. We rode for hours along the heights and descended into the valley where simple sawmills were to be encountered. The water is piped through hollow logs and, to make the troughs higher, a revetment ten metres high is constructed of thick logs.

Quoted from L. Robert, *A Travers l'Asie Mineure* (1980); tr. R. S.

The atmosphere of the Hittite Empire and the chief pre-occupations of its kings are vividly represented in the proclamation of King Telipinus, the last king of the Old Kingdom; by the time of his successor Tudhaliyas II the Empire had been established through the methods Telipinus approved.

Thus speaks King Telipinus, the great king. Formerly Labarnas was the great king. And then his sons, his brothers and his relatives by marriage, the members of his family, and his soldiers were united.

And the land was small; but on whatever campaign he went, by his strength he kept the hostile country in subjection.

And he kept devastating countries, and he made the countries tremble; and he made them boundaries of the sea. But when he returned from the campaign, one of his sons went to each of the countries –

To Hupisnas, Tuwanuwas, Nenassas, Landas, Zallaras, Parsu-hantas, Lusnas. They governed the countries; and the large cities were assigned to them.

Afterwards Hattusilis became king, and then likewise his sons, his brothers, his relatives by marriage, the members of his family, and his soldiers were united. And on whatever campaign he went, he also by his strength kept the hostile country in subjection.

And he kept devastating countries, and he made the countries tremble; and he made them boundaries of the sea. Moreover, when in those days he returned from the campaign, one of his sons went to each of the countries; and the large cities were put into his hands.

But when afterwards the subjects of the princes became rebellious, they began to despoil their holdings, and to shed their blood.

When Mursilis became king in Hattusas, then likewise his sons, his brothers, his relatives-in-law, the members of his family, and the soldiers were united. And by his strength he kept the hostile country in subjection. And he made the countries tremble; and he made them boundaries of the sea.

And he went to Aleppo, and destroyed Aleppo, and brought captives and possessions of Aleppo to Hattusas. Then afterwards he went to Babylon, and destroyed Babylon, and defeated the Hurrians, and carried captives and possessions of Babylon to Hattusas.

. . . .

When I, Telipinus, had seated myself upon the throne of my father, I went to Hassuwas on a campaign, and I destroyed Hassuwas and my infantry was in Zizzilippas. And in Zizzilippas a battle occurred.

When at that time I, the king, came to Lawazzantiyas, Lahhas was hostile to me, and incited Lawazzantiyas to rebellion. And the gods delivered it into my hand.

. . . .

Now bloodshed of the royal family has become common. . . . Now I, Telipinus, have called an assembly at Hattusas. From now on let no one in Hattusas do harm to a son of the royal family, or thrust a dagger into him. . . .

Whoever after me through all the time shall become king, in those days let his brothers, his sons, his relatives-in-law, the members of his family, and his soldiers be united; and you shall come and with your strength hold the hostile country in subjection. But do not speak thus: 'I grant complete pardon', while however, you pardon nothing and actually order his arrest. Do not kill any member of the royal family; it leads to disaster.

from E. H. Sturtevant, A Hittite Chrestomathy<br>(Philadelphia 1935; 1952)

The power of the king is also vividly expressed in the extensive fragments of Hittite Law-codes established by Telipinus and his successors and found in the ruins of Hattusas. (See further O. R. Gurney, *The Hittites*, 1952; 1961.)

The religion of the Hittites revolved around the worship of the Sun, and descriptions of ritual from the same collections of tablets give a lively impression of the splendour and ceremony that must have once brightened the beetling rocks of Yazılıkaya.

## Alaca Hüyük

A third Hittite site is Alaca Hüyük, a little distance to the north of Yazılıkaya. This site was inhabited from the fourth millennium BC, and was the source of a rich hoard of objects in gold, silver and bronze, of about 2000 BC, which is now in the Ankara museum. So another unknown civilisation, even older than the Hittites, glimmers briefly from the earth and is lost to us. The present remains at Alaca Hüyük are Hittite; though Hamilton, its discoverer, had, like Texier, little idea what he had found.

Hafiz Agha reported that he had learned from some peasants, that in the neighbouring village of Euyuk, about two miles off to the S.S.W., there were some curious old stones, in search of which I immediately started. On arriving there I found a Turcoman village, on the southern limits of which was a very curious monument of the oldest times. When I first saw the numerous rude and apparently shapeless stones, forming a kind of avenue, they reminded me of druidical remains, and I thought they might have belonged to the Gallo-Græci, but on further examination they proved to be of a different character. The ruins consist of a large gateway or entrance, facing the south, with part of a massive wall on each side; the two principal stones which form the posts are of gigantic size, being ten or twelve feet high. On the outside of each is sculptured a monstrous figure with a human head, in a very Egyptian style, the body being a grotesque imitation of a bird, the legs of which terminate in lion's claws. The wall, which advances about fourteen feet on each side of the gateway, and then breaks off to the right and left, leaving a paved enclosed space in front of the entrance, has consisted of enormous blocks of Cyclopian character, but is now much ruined; yet on the lower course of stones, which are above three feet high, several figures, nearly of the same height, are rudely sculptured in very flat relief; the first stone towards the west represents children playing upon instruments, but too faint to be distinguished; the second represents three priests clothed in long robes; the third, rams driven to the sacrifice; and the last a bull, very rudely sculptured. Within the gateway, an avenue of large stones leads some distance into the village. A curious feature in this monument is, that on the inside of one of the high door-posts, a double-headed angle has been sculptured, which, however, may have been a more modern addition.

W. J. Hamilton, *Travels and Researches in Asia Minor* (1852)

## Eflatunpınar

Hittite monuments are widely scattered around Central Turkey, and another is found at a place on the eastern shore of Lake Beyşehir with the fascinating name of Eflatunpınar (Plato's Well: on Plato p. 150). Gertrude Bell visited this site in 1907:

Monotonous, colourless, lifeless, unsubdued by a people whose thoughts travel no further than to the next furrow, who live and die and leave no mark upon the great plains and the barren hills – such is central Asia, of which this country is a true part. And that is why the Roman roads make so deep an impression on one's mind. They impressed the country itself, they implied a great domination, they tell of a people that overcame the universal stagnation. It was very hot and still; clouds of butterflies drifted across the path and there was no other living thing except a stork or two in the marshy ground and here and there a herd of buffaloes with a shepherd boy asleep beside them. At the end of the lake a heavy thunderstorm gathered and crept along the low hills to the east and up into the middle of the sky. And so we came to the earliest record of what was probably one of the earliest trade roads in the world and the forerunner of the Roman road; and here the clouds broke upon us in thunder and lightning and hail and rain and I saw the four Hittite kings, carved in massive stone, against a background of all the fury of the storm.

They are seated by the edge of a wide pool, a spring bubbling out of the hillside, from which a swift river flows away to the lake; and above them are figures with uplifted hands, as though they praised the god of Gotat waters.

*Letters*, May 7, 1907

It was a Hittite sculpture that occasioned her first meeting with William Ramsay, the start of a partnership that was to result in their important joint book, *The Thousand and One Churches*.

I was up at 4 to-day and at 5 I rode off to the hills to see one of the great sights of Asia Minor, the Hittite sculptures at Loriz. It was delicious riding at dawn up towards the snow of Taurus and more delicious still when after a couple of hours we entered a wonderful valley with a rushing stream flowing that I did not know, until we came to the village of Loriz at the mouth of a splendid rocky gorge. Above the village the river rushes out from under the rocks, a great stream as clear as crystal and just below its source there is the famous rock on which the sculptures are. Two figures, a god with curly hair and beard and pointed shoes and Phrygian cap adorned with a crown of horns, in his hands the fruits of the earth, corn and bunches of grapes, which he offers to a smaller figure, a king standing before him with hands uplifted in prayer. Behind the two run several lines of that strange script which no one can read, and beneath the rock rushes the clear water of the river. So I sat down under the walnut trees and considered that fine piece of symbolism of 5000 years ago: the river bursting from the mountain side and bearing fruitfulness to all the plain below and the god standing at its source with his trails of grapes and his swathe of corn. And then one came from the village and brought me eggs and milk and honey and the biggest nuts in the world and I feasted by the edge of the river. And if I had known the Hittite language I would have offered up a short thanksgiving in that tongue to the god with the curly hair and the tiara of horns who had brought such good things out of the naked earth. And then I rode back to Eryli – blazing hot it was – and took the train and came back to Konia. The Consul and his wife met me at the station and dined with me at the hotel and I found there besides Professor Ramsay, who knows more about this country than any other man, and we fell into each other's arms and made great friends.

*Letters*, May 16, 1905

## Legends of Central Anatolia

High in the fastnesses of the Anatolian plateau ancient beliefs die slowly, and many writers, both Turkish and foreign, have recorded the tales, customs and superstitions of these people, many of whom have scarcely been touched by Islam or Christianity. There are for example, besides the Yezidis (see chapter 7), the Yürüks with their living legends of the jinns:

'The moon is the devil's agent,' he said. 'She is the weed in the heavenly gardens. She tempts men to sleep under her evil light, and then the devil comes along and takes away the mind.'

But he regarded the *jinns* as more evil, for whereas the moon was predictable, and big enough to be seen anywhere on earth, you never knew where you were with the *jinns*, and one could never be sure what shapes they would take. He called them the 'bad men of the invisible world', and when I asked him about the invisible world he said that this was the twin of our own world, impinging on us everywhere. I thought this was a remarkably sophisticated attitude to take.

The *Yürük* is very afraid of the *jinns*. No *Yürük* will ever cross dirty water without first calling on Allah to protect him, then blowing with his breath three times to scatter the *jinns*. Neither can he throw some unwanted thing – a scrap of paper, the leavings of a meal – out into the night. Night is the realm of the *jinns* and whatever is thrown out might injure one of them. Their revenge will be swift, maybe fatal. A man might break his ankle, his arm, his leg, become paralysed; a fire may burn down his tent, a high wind injure his sheep. And it's too late to say your prayers *after* you have injured a *jinn*. You should have thought of that before, and now you must take what the devil sends. The *shaman* said that Mohammed is supposed to have converted the wickedest of the *jinns* to Islam but there are many others to do damage.

*Jinns* have been known to come up on a man as a faint light, growing larger as the distance decreases. When they are quite close to each other the light grows to monstrous proportions, displaying the head of a toad and the body of a goat with the eerie light outlining the whole apparition in awful brilliance. No man has ever seen this terrible manifestation and escaped unscathed. Some are beaten senseless. Some die at once, the sight too much for them. Others are rendered witless, spending the rest of their days in vacant wandering, feared and shunned by all for the power of the dreadful light is said to be still in their eyes.

There are *jinns* who guard the cemeteries, and often these take the forms of owls or bats. A *Yürük* was found dead the year before last in the cemetery the other side of the mountain. When he was discovered there was a large white owl gliding over him, and the owl attacked the men who were trying to bury their dead comrade.

Sometimes the *jinns* took the form of a beautiful moon maiden, lying in wait for the men coming back from the forest. Usually she became visible to only one of the men, and with beckoning gestures she lured him on, always keeping a little ahead of him, her perfect form showing through the flimsy draperies of her dress. The besotted man would follow her over hill and dale until he reached the place where the *jinns* were waiting to feast on human flesh. The maiden would disappear, then dissolve in the moonlight – some had even been seen flitting up a moonbeam to their home in the sky – and the *jinns* would fall upon the man.

The *shaman* was so sincere in his beliefs, and so persuasive, that for the rest of the time we were in camp I never dared throw anything out of the tent at night. Thus are legends given substance.

Irfan Orga, *The Caravan Moves On* (1958)

Mahmut Makal is the author of one of the most vivid, if not always balanced accounts of Turkish village life. A villager who has been enabled to obtain an education, he is torn between sympathy for his villagers and pity for their lot, and contempt for their, as he sees it, primitive and obstructive superstitions which themselves inhibit progress and the modernisation of Turkey:

### The Hearths of Healing[1]

Don't begin thinking about tiled fire-places! What would contrivances of that sort be doing in a place like this? No; the Hearth is the local solution for all illness. A pain in the knee, or cataract in the eye, a stomach ache – anything under the sun – off you go to the Hearth.

The most favoured Hearth in our village is the Yilancik Centre.[2] Not a day passes but somebody goes there. If people want to be cured, they must pay: if they give little, there's nothing doing. At present they are charging one lira per head. In all these Hearths every illness is attended to; but some of them have specialist branches, as famous doctors do. The blood-letting Hearth is at a place called Kizilgaya, a village quite near our own. Apart from those who come from its own district, someone goes over from our village every day. The Fever Hearth is in the village of Yuva. It is mostly there that they go. People don't go to these Hearths at random. It is decided by

[1] The Turkish word means hearth, or cooking stove of any sort, and is also used in the villages for places where cures are performed by religious or magical means.

[2] *Yilancik*: the word (literally a diminutive of snake) is used for any disease connected with, or thought to be connected with, worms or snakes. Under certain circumstances, people who have recovered from such diseases are thought to have special powers to cure them. (Makal's notes)

divination. A little water is placed in a pot. Needles are then placed in it, each pointing to a village which has a Hearth. The needle which goes rusty first indicates the Hearth which will cure the sickness, and the patient goes off to that Hearth.

Recently, being quite unable to put up with my mother's importunity any longer, when she kept telling me: 'You've got fever,' I paid up like the rest. Apparently the secret is in the hand. A healer who is about to die touches the hand of someone who then becomes a healer. So the Hearths continue – the customers, too.

Mahmut Makal, *A Village in Anatolia* (1954)

# CHAPTER FIVE

# Lycia and the Turkish Riviera

The district between Rhodes on the west and Alanya on the east, now in part given over to the tourist trade encouraged by its fine beaches and mellow climate, was in ancient times the mysterious kingdom of Lycia. The Lycians were an Indo-European people, probably calling themselves Termilae, who despite their essentially Near Eastern culture intensely admired Greek art. In the fourth century they filled the valleys of the kingdom with many series of rock-cut tombs and free-standing monuments to their kings, which were scarcely visited after antiquity until the middle of the nineteenth century. It is the travellers who found these ruins (and in many cases removed them) who provide the most interesting travellers' tales.

But we must begin at the beginning. Lycia was well known to the Greeks even of Homer's period: it was to Lycia that Bellerophon was exiled by King Proetus of Argos when his wife falsely accused the indifferent Bellerophon of attempting to seduce her.

The king, incens'd with her report, resolv'd upon her course,
But doubted how it should be run; he shunn'd his death direct,
(Holding a way so near not safe) and plotted the effect
By sending him with letters seal'd (that, open'd, touch his life)
To Rheuns king of Lycia, and father to his wife.
He went; and happily he went, the Gods walk'd all his way;
And being arriv'd in Lycia, where Xanthus doth display
The silver ensigns of his waves, the king of that broad land
Receiv'd him with a wondrous free and honourable hand.
Nine days he feasted him, and kill'd an ox on ev'ry day,
In thankful sacrifice to heav'n, for his fair guest; whose stay,

With rosy fingers, brought the world, the tenth well-welcom'd
    morn,
And then the king did move to see, the letters he had borne
From his lov'd son-in-law; which seen, he wrought thus their
    contents:
Chimæra, the invincible, he sent him to convince,
Sprung from no man, but mere divine; a lion's shape before,
Behind a dragon's, in the midst a goat's shagg'd form, she bore,
And flames of deadly fervency flew from her breath and eyes;
Yet her he slew; his confidence in sacred prodigies
Render'd him victor. Then he gave his second conquest way
Against the famous Solymi, when (he himself would say,
Reporting it) he enter'd on a passing vig'rous fight.
His third huge labour he approv'd against a woman's spite,
That fill'd a field of Amazons; he overcame them all.
Then set they on him sly Deceit, when Force had such a fall;
An ambush of the strongest men, that spacious Lycia bred,
Was lodg'd for him; whom he lodg'd sure, they never rais'd a head.
His deeds thus showing him deriv'd from some celestial race,
The king detain'd, and made amends, with doing him the grace
Of his fair daughter's princely gift; and with her, for a dow'r,
Gave half his kingdom; and to this, the Lycians on did pour
More than was giv'n to any king; a goodly planted field,
In some parts thick of groves and woods, the rest rich crops did yield.
This field the Lycians futurely (of future wand'rings there
And other errors of their prince, in the unhappy rear
Of his sad life) the Errant call'd.

Homer, Iliad VI; tr. George Chapman

The slaying of the Chimaera was Bellerophon's most
famous deed, and was commemorated for example on the
heroon at Gölbaşı (see below) and also on a tomb at Tlos:

Within the portico is a handsome carved door, or rather imitation
door, with knocker and lock, on each side of which are windows
opening into large tombs. On one side of the portico is carved
a figure, which we may recognise as Bellerophon, mounted on
Pegasus, and galloping up a rocky hill, which may represent Mount
Cragus, to encounter an enormous leopard sculptured over one of
the tomb entrances on the right side of the door. This animal may be
a form of Chimæra, but presents none of the mythological attributes, and is, in all probability, the representation of a 'Caplan,' the
leopard which infests the crags of Cragus at the present day. An
ornamental flourish appears on the door-side near the leopard, and is
repeated on the corresponding panel on the other side; but there is no

animal carved on that panel. On the panels beneath the tomb are carved dogs, and there are also traces of others on the pediment. Pegasus is a Persian horse, having a topknot and knotted tail. A saddle-cloth of ornamental character has been painted on his back. The group of figures appears to have been originally painted. The head-dress of Bellerophon is very peculiar, as also the arrangement of the beard.

T. A. B. Spratt and E. Forbes, *Travels in Lycia* (1847)

According to Servius, the ancient commentator on Virgil (on *Aeneid*, 6.287) the Chimaera was 'in reality a mountain in Cilicia. Even today its summit blazes with fire, and lions dwell nearby; in the middle ranges are pastures where goats abound, and the lower part of the mountain is full of serpents. Here Bellerophon made his home; whence he is said to have slain the Chimaera.'

The explanation of the monster is perhaps too neat to be convincing, though all these creatures (and bears and leopards too) did indeed dwell in Lycia in antiquity; but the fire is authentic. The first modern traveller to notice it was Captain Beaufort (the inventor of the Beaufort Scale) while conducting a hydrographic survey of the Karamanian coast (as it was called) in 1811–12.

We had seen from the ship the preceding night a small but steady light among the hills; on mentioning the circumstance to the inhabitants, we learned that it was a Yanar, or volcanic flame, and they offered to supply us with horses and guides to examine it.

We rode about two miles, through a fertile plain, partly cultivated; and then winding up a rocky and thickly wooded glen, we arrived at the place. In the inner corner of a ruined building the wall is undermined, so as to leave an aperture of about three feet diameter, and shaped like the mouth of an oven: from thence the flame issues, giving out an intense heat, yet producing no smoke on the wall; and though from the neck of the opening we detached some small lumps of caked soot, the walls were hardly discoloured. Trees, brushwood, and weeds, grow close round this little crater; a small stream trickles down the hill hard bye, and the ground does not appear to feel the effect of its heat beyond the distance of a few yards. The hill is composed of the crumbly serpentine already mentioned, with occasional loose blocks of limestone; and no volcanic productions whatever were perceived in the neighbourhood.

At a short distance, lower down the side of the hill, there is another hole, which has apparently been at some time the vent of a similar flame; but our guide declared, that, in the memory of man, there had been but the one, and that it had never changed its present size or appearance. It was never accompanied, he said, by earthquakes or noises; and it ejected neither stones, smoke, or noxious vapours, nothing but a brilliant and perpetual flame, which no quantity of water could quench. The shepherds frequently cooked their victuals there; and he affirmed, with equal composure, that it was notorious that the Yanar would not roast meat which had been stolen.

Captain Beaufort, *Karamania* (1817)

Spratt and Forbes found the fire still in good order in 1842.

We found it as brilliant as when [Captain Beaufort] visited it, and also somewhat increased; for besides the large flame in the corner of the ruins described by him, there were small jets issuing from crevices in the sides of a crater-like cavity, five or six feet deep. At the bottom of this was a shallow puddle of sulphureous and turbid water, regarded by the Turks as a sovereign remedy for all skin diseases. We met here two old Turks attended by two black slaves, who had come from a distance to procure some of the soot deposited from the flames, valued as efficacious in the cure of sore eye-lids, and also as a dye for the eyebrows. They had been enjoying themselves by this ancient fireside for two days, cooking their meals and boiling their coffee on the flames of Chimæra.

T. A. B. Spratt and E. Forbes, *Travels in Lycia* (1847)

A memory of another legend is preserved in the name of the town of Nif, below Cal dağı. It is connected with the Lycian king Hippolochus who fought on Priam's side in the Trojan War.

> Nor did the hapless Trojans leave unwept
> The warrior-king Hippolochus' hero-son,
> But laid, in front of the Dardanian gate,
> Upon the pyre that captain war-renowned.
> But him Apollo's self caught swiftly up
> Out of the blazing fire, and to the winds
> Gave him, to bear away to Lycia-land;
> And fast and far they bare him, 'neath the glens
> Of high Telandrus, to a lovely glade;
> And for a monument above his grave
> Upheaved a granite rock. The Nymphs therefrom
> Made gush the hallowed water of a stream
> For ever flowing, which the tribes of men
> Still call fair-fleeting Glaucus. This the gods
> Wrought for an honour to the Lycian king.

Quintus of Smyrna, *The Fall of Troy*, IV

Louis Robert, the master of all students of Turkish terrain, writes on this place:

No one has investigated the toponym Nif. It is not Turkish nor Arabic nor Persian . . . It is quite simply the Greek Nymph, Nymphai . . . In Greece itself, sanctuaries of the Nymphs have been transmitted to us under the name of Nifi. . . . There is no need to suppose any architectural 'Nymphaeum': such waters attract a cult, a sanctuary of the Nymphs, but they have no need of temple or edifice; a grotto or grove suffices, where one can worship at the spring and thank them for providing the waters which make the country a garden; and so it is with Nif in Lycia.

Louis Robert, *A Travers l'Asie Mineure* (1980); tr. R. S.

## Xanthus

It is Xanthus that exhibited the greatest glory, and that was extensively despoiled by Charles Fellows, who filled with his finds several rooms of the British Museum.

He did not enjoy Turkey, as is clear from his description of Balık near Mt Ida.

I am now writing in a room in Bállook, the most dreary of villages. Tomorrow I shall descend, and expect to find a great difference in the season; a month ago the trees were bursting into leaf in the west country, and above two months since at Syra the corn was beginning to show the ear, whilst here they have only in a few places now begun to plough and sow.

I am at this moment sitting at dinner, stared at by fourteen Turks, all complimentary visitors, who have watched every mouthful I have taken, and are now secretly looking at and talking of me. I was so much annoyed at Altuntash the night before last by this custom of the country, and by the repetition of it by the people again appearing the next morning early with cream and honey as an excuse for remaining to see me dress, that I determined to put a stop to it, at the risk of offending them, rather than have a number of men waiting to see me turn out of my bed; and I gave directions to my servant accordingly. On inquiring afterwards how he had kept them out, I found that he had represented me as unwell, and not able to bear the talking; and thus both I and my servant were left to pursue our occupations undisturbed. These people are so sociable that no one is ever alone, and I believe that I must occasionally represent myself as an invalid, in order to get time for writing and the other occupations of a traveller.

But once at Xanthus life became exciting.

It was noon before we had found the Governor of the tents which form the frontier village of Koonık (Kınık), when taking the riding horses, we started to see the ruins of the city of Xanthus, which lay at about two miles' distance, upon or overhanging the river of that name. The other horses were to wait our return. We had no sooner entered the place of tombs, than objects of such high interest to the antiquarian, sculptor, and artist appeared, that I determined to send for the baggage, and pitch my tent here for the night.

The elegant designs evince that talent of the Greeks, and the highly poetical subjects of the bas-reliefs, the temples, friezes, and tombs, some of them blending in one figure the forms of many, probably to describe its attributes, are also of Greek character. The ruins are wholly of temples, tombs, triumphal arches, walls, and a theatre. The site is extremely romantic, upon beautiful hills; some crowned with rocks, others rising perpendicularly from the river, which is seen winding its way down from the woody uplands, while beyond the extreme distance are the snowy mountains in which it rises. On the west the view is bounded by the picturesquely formed but bare range of Mount Cragus, and on the east by the mountain-chain extending to Patara. A rich plain, with its meandering river, carries the eye to the horizon of the sea toward the south-west.

The city has not the appearance of having been very large, but its remains show that it was highly ornamented, particularly the tombs, two of which I have put in my sketch-book somewhat in detail, as well as some other sculptures. I did not find any well-formed Greek letters; in an inscription over a gateway, and on one or two architectural stones, the Greek alphabet was used, but not the pure letters. There is no trace of the Roman or the Christian age, and yet there are points, such as the costume in the bas-relief, the attitude and appearance of groups of figures, that reminded me of the times of the Crusades and of the Romans.

A year later Fellows was back again, and was eventually able to bring his whole party to the site of their labours.

The party landed consisted of fifteen working men, a boy, the Lieutenant, the Gunner, the Cavasses, a youth, the son of Mr. Wilkinson, our Consul at Rhodes, and myself. Our five tents were soon pitched, fires lighted, and our cutter, galley, and dingy boats secured within the river. High sand-hills arose for miles around us, and no signs of life were visible but the footsteps of the wolves, jackals, and hares. Huge trunks of decayed trees, washed down during past ages, afforded plenty of fuel for our fires, which vied with the full moon in illuminating our encampment, and must have served as a beacon to our ship, which had sailed afar to the northward.

The river Xanthus is one of the most powerful, wild, and unmanageable streams I ever saw: the volume of water is very great, far exceeding that of the Thames at Richmond; the stream rushes probably at the rate of five miles an hour. For the first three miles from its mouth, where it winds through the high range of sand-hills, I had never before seen it, but above this had traced it to its source in the Yeeilassies of the high mountains of the Taurus, probably a course of nearly two hundred miles. Our boats drew two feet and a half of water, and had great difficulty in making head against the heaviest part of the stream, which marked the deepest channel through the bar of sand formed at the entrance to the river. Once within this, to accomplish which cost us much labour and risk, the men having to jump overboard to keep the boats in their course, the waters were deep and comparatively tranquil.

In manning our boats on the morning of the 27th we found that the eight oars in the cutter made no way against the stream; we therefore abandoned them, and set all hands to work in tracking the lightened boats with ropes from the shore, leaving in them only a coxswain and one man, who with a pole had continually to fathom the water ahead. From the gulfy nature of the river the depth often varied, within the length of the boat, from fifteen to two feet, and in the turbid waters these shoals could be avoided only by keeping in the strongest streams; the labour was therefore great; axes and billhooks were in constant use, in cutting away the branches of trees overhanging the river, which interrupted the towing-line. For this labour we soon found our men insufficient to work the two boats; we therefore put all hands to one, and at noon pitched the tents and returned to bring the other boat to our place of halting, which was within the range of sand-hills, and on the plain extending to the ruins of the ancient city of Xanthus. This flat is apparently covered with underwood of myrtle, oleander, storax, and tamarisk, but is occasionally cleared for patches of cultivation. Our encampment soon attracted the attention of the peasants, whose invisible tents and huts were sheltered with their flocks amongst the bushes: their astonishment at everything they saw was evinced by groups collected on every hillock around us; and I soon found that the hospitality and kindness which I had before experienced was with this people a custom: eggs, poultry, fruit, and milk were brought to us, and every attention afforded; they acted as pilots, by wading over the shallows and pointing out our best course for the boats. Four days were we navigating our little stores up the river to the ancient city, a course not exceeding nine miles, and which we afterwards commonly ran down in a boat within three-quarters of an hour.

While they worked hard by day at removing the marbles,

Our evenings were not without amusement; the sailors soon made bats and balls, and cricket was perhaps for the first time played in Lycia; at all events the wonder expressed by the living generation showed that it was not a game known to the present inhabitants. The weather was delightful; the thermometer at night stood at 40°, and in the day 64°. Our nights, which were lighted by a full moon, were often varied by alarm of wild beasts, or rather a hope that we might have some sport; the gunner distributed arms to the men, but the game was too wary for inexperienced sportsmen; when we were still, the wild boars and their young came grunting past our tents, and the wolves and jackals howled around us, but the slightest movement among our men only caused the flight of wild ducks, and all was still again.

Charles Fellows, *Travels and Researches in Asia Minor* (1852)

## Phellus

It was at Phellus that Freya Stark found herself most closely on the track of Alexander the Great, as she sought to trace his route to the south-east and Asia.

We lingered on the way to drink out of a sarcophagus which is the village fountain; and then helped to load a camel which the owner of my horse had left his little boy to deal with. The poor beast, in such small incapable hands, was turning its head with foaming green grimaces that made one notice how much better-looking camels would be if they had better-kept teeth. When we had seen to this, we climbed up in to the morning gold. Step after step, the edge of the world widened with the increase of the light; the pony grew warm beneath his padded collar, and talked with his ears as he snuffed the steep stones before him; in his dim way perhaps he remembered Pedasos, his Cilician forebear, who was put in the side-traces and followed with the immortal horses, for one might remember anything on such a morning; the troubles of the night melted in a happiness suffused with sunlight, luminous and remote.

The people of Phellus must often have felt like this as they looked from their height on to their fields of Chukurbagh and the flat lands of the ridge and the six eastern ranges, pointed or horizontal, that rise to the snows of the Eastern Ak Dagh above Arycanda.

Their town looked down on the two likely routes of Alexander –

the one from Xanthus in the west by Kalkan and Sidek Dagh and Seyret, which is still a road now though unusable by cars at the moment because a bridge is broken, and keeps near the summits above the sharp drop to the sea; and the other from the lower shelves of Massicytus by the Hajioglan valley into the Kassaba depression. It lay spread at our feet, with two passes winding along Susuz Dagh towards Arycanda between the scrubby hills. They looked as un-cultivated and stubbly as the chin of an old Sayyid who shaves himself with scissors; and on our other side, holding all the south, was the sea.

There, round Castellorizo and two little empty islands one fat and one thin, the people of Phellus could see ships as they passed from Syria by Cilicia and Lycia through Rhodes to Alexandria – the trade route of that day. The fashions changed. The quinquereme was invented in Phoenicia or Cyprian waters to supplant the trireme, and cataphracts with rowers enclosed under decks rowed by. Their sides looked straight, from above. All these craft were built to equalize the leverage of a single row of oars, and the curve was built, with wood not too seasoned to bend, under water out of sight. Five men sat to each oar in a quinquereme, so that only one skilled rower in five was needed, even on these coats where the hollow southern seas come with wide spaces between them, and lift the ships' ribs unsupported. The ships grew bigger and bigger through the Hellenistic wars, till the Roman peace came and the pirates stopped, and with smaller shapes returning, the naval speed and skill declined.

From the beautifully cut stone walls of their little city, the people of Phellus looked out through the clean Aegean air; and temples must have shown on their hill-top, for a column half buried was lying at my feet. The hillside was scattered sparsely with tombs, whose doors and windows and rafters were chipped to look like houses, among the giant yellow sage and bright arbutus, and the honeysuckle scent and broom. In the days of the Byzantines, the city's defences had been rearranged with haste and fear before they left it; until raids and wars grew too frequent and the solitude increased.

While the sun climbed like a wet flame, four thousand feet as it seemed below me, I sat for a long time and considered the two roads of Alexander; and felt that there was nothing to choose between them. Perhaps there was a slight tilt in favour of the way we had come, winding through the Chukurbagh gardens in our sight.

. . . .

I wondered idly why I was giving myself so much trouble to discover, in such obscure places, where an army marched so long ago. Not for writing, for I would make these journeys for their own sake alone with equal pleasure. The pure wish to understand, the most disinterested of human desires, was my spur.

Nor does the obscurity of places matter with Alexander, who measured himself by his glory rather than his life and 'wherever I shall fight, shall believe that I am in the theatre of the whole world'. I had come very close, it seemed to me, to the veterans, grizzled and unshaven like the peasants who led my horses, who marched day after day behind the young men who led them, and rested in or by these small walled cities where Greek was spoken, while rumour preceded them and memory followed, and the world's history has rung ever since with their high, hobnailed booted footsteps on the ground.

Freya Stark, Alexander's Path (1958)

Such questions had interested Beaufort too, in his account of Mt Climax, and were of equal interest to Richard Pococke when he sought the Battlefield of Issus (pp. 227–8).


## Myra

Not far from Phellus is Myra where Charles Cockerell (the architect of the Ashmolean and discoverer of the marbles of Aigina and Bassae in Greece) had made more interesting discoveries.

My time would not permit me to examine this great emporium of precious relics; but Mr. Cockerell, a gentleman well known to the literary world by his interesting discoveries in Greece, and who visited Myra the following year [1812], found there the ruins of a considerable city; the theatre was very perfect, and he saw many fragments of sculpture, that were executed in a masterly style.

The inhabitants are chiefly Turks, and he described them as more than ordinarily jealous and ferocious. While examining some statues, one of the mob exclaimed, 'If the infidels are attracted here by these blasphemous figures, the temptation shall soon cease; for when that dog is gone, I will destroy them.' A Mohammedan considers all imitations of the human figure to be impious, and the admiration of them idolatrous. Mr. Cockerell succeeded, however, in making some sketches; and it is to be hoped that the public will be allowed to benefit from his researches there, as well as in other parts of that interesting country.

Captain Beaufort, Karamania (1817)

# Oenoanda

Inland Lycia has its interesting features too. At Oenoanda one Diogenes, a prosperous Roman citizen of the second century AD, caused a building to be erected which was extensively covered by an inscription, the length of a treatise, outlining the principal doctrines of the Epicurean philosophy. It was first discovered in 1884 by two French scholars, Holleaux and Cousin.

Though fragmentary, much of it is still intelligible, particularly the ethical doctrines. (It also contains extensive sections on astronomy and physics). High in this wild country, one man at least tried to live his life by philosophy, and to teach others to do the same.

FRAGMENT 24

Many people pursue philosophy for the sake of (wealth or reputation) as though they will obtain these things from private persons or kings who have come to believe that philosophy is some great and costly possession. But we have not hastened to undertake the same study so that any of the above rewards should come to us also, but so that we may be happy, gaining possession of the end and purpose of life sought by nature. And what this end is, and that neither wealth can provide it, nor political reputation, nor kingship, nor a life of luxury, nor a rich table, nor the pleasures of exquisite love affairs, nor anything else, but only philosophy, (this we will now show, putting before you the whole matter. For this treatise we have prepared not for our own sakes but for yours, fellow citizens, to benefit you and serve as a fitting introduction to the argument here.)

PRINCIPAL DOCTRINE I

The blessed and indestructible being is neither troubled itself nor does it cause trouble to another, and so it is not subject to feelings of anger or partiality; all that belongs to weakness.

PRINCIPAL DOCTRINE 2

Death is nothing to us, for that which has been dissolved into its elements has no sensation and that which has no sensation is nothing to us.

PRINCIPAL DOCTRINE 6

To feel secure against the world the possession of power and kingship is a natural good, so long as that end can be achieved by them.

PRINCIPAL DOCTRINE 8
No pleasure in itself is a bad thing, but the means of producing some pleasures bring annoyances many times greater than the pleasures.

PRINCIPAL DOCTRINE 10
If those things which produce the pleasures of profligates put an end to mental fears about celestial phenomena and about death and pain, and, besides, taught the limits of desire and pain, we should never be able to criticize such men, as they would be sated with pleasures from every source, and know neither mental nor physical pain, which is the evil.

PRINCIPAL DOCTRINE 3
The limit to the intensity of pleasure is the removal of all pain. Whoever enjoys a feeling of pleasure will, as long as it continues, never be annoyed by pain of body or of mind or of both together.

PRINCIPAL DOCTRINE 5
It is not possible to live pleasantly without living sensibly and honourably and justly, nor is it possible to live sensibly and honourably and justly without living pleasantly. Where this is lacking a man cannot live a pleasant life.

from the edition of C. W. Chilton (Oxford 1971)

## Gölbaşı

Besides Oenoanda the most romantic site of inland Lycia is surely the city of Gölbaşı, ancient Trysa, discovered by Augustus Schoenborn in 1842 and explored by Otto Benndorf and Georg Niemann in 1880. The latter pair undertook the huge task of removing the entire frieze from the heroon, many metres long, and transporting it to Vienna where it is now housed in the basement of the Kunsthistorisches Museum. It is a compendium of Greek mythology, with scenes from the Odyssey, the Theban cycle, the Bellerophon saga and much else including depictions of battles and sieges, probably those waged by the king commemorated here; but for Benndorf the pleasures of landscape were at least as great as those of discovery.

Rushing ahead, I worked my way through thick thorny underbrush and shale, arriving breathless at the entrance gate, which opened in the wall an appreciable distance above the precipitous slope. Without waiting at the first structure, the curious nature of which increased my expectation, I climbed excitedly up the masonry of the wall to the lintel of the gate, and found myself suddenly opposite an abundance of sculpture in the interior of the ruin, enchantingly concealed in part by the tall trees nearby and the vegetation that had grown up among them. In the glow of the setting sun the sight was marvellous. I confess that these first moments of contemplation at the long sought and now successfully achieved destination, in the noiseless and solemn silence and desolation of a magnificently expansive Nature, stone desert all around, with a view onto the mountainous landscape deeply gullied and adorned with chains of snow and to the high vaulted and endless sea, count among the deepest impressions of my life.

      O. Benndorf, *Vorläufiger Bericht uber zwei Oesterreichische Archäologische Expeditionen nach Kleinasien* (1883); tr. R. S.

## Antalya

Easternmost of the cities of ancient Lycia is Antalya, ancient Attaleia, named after King Attalus II of Pergamum who founded the harbour city in 158 BC. In AD 1207 it was taken by the Seljuk Turks under Kai Khosrow (Keyhusrev I). It was under Seljuk dominion when the Arab traveller Ibn Battutah visited it.

From 'Aláyá I went to Antáliya, a most beautiful city. It covers an immense area, and though of vast bulk is one of the most attractive towns to be seen anywhere, besides being exceedingly populous and well laid out. Each section of the inhabitants lives in a separate quarter. The Christian merchants live in a quarter of the town known as the Mína [the Port], and are surrounded by a wall, the gates of which are shut upon them from without at night and during the Friday service. The Greeks, who were its former inhabitants, live by themselves in another quarter, the Jews in another, and the king and his court and mamlúks in another, each of these quarters being walled off likewise. The rest of the Muslims live in the main city. Round the whole town and all the quarters mentioned there is another great wall. The town contains many orchards and produces fine fruits, including an admirable kind of apricot, called by them Qamar ad-Dín, which has a sweet almond in its kernel. This fruit is dried and exported to Egypt, where it is regarded as a great luxury.

We stayed here at the college mosque of the town, the principal of which was Shaykh Shiháb ad-Dín al-Hamawí. Now in all the lands inhabited by the Turkmens in Anatolia, in every district, town, and

village, there are to be found members of the organization known as
the *Akhíya* or Young Brotherhood. Nowhere in the world will you
find men so eager to welcome strangers, so prompt to serve food and
to satisfy the wants of others, and so ready to suppress injustice and
to kill [tyrannical] agents of police and the miscreants who join with
them. A Young Brother, or *akhí* in their language, is one who is
chosen by all the members of his trade [guild], or by other young
unmarried men, or those who live in ascetic retreat, to be their
leader. This organization is known also as the *Futúwa*, or Order of
Youth. The leader builds a hospice and furnishes it with rugs, lamps,
and other necessary appliances. The members of his community
work during the day to gain their livelihood, and bring him what
they have earned in the late afternoon. With this they buy fruit, food,
and the other things which the hospice requires for their use. If a
traveller comes to the town that day they lodge him in their hospice;
these provisions serve for his entertainment as their guest, and he
stays with them until he goes away. If there are no travellers they
themselves assemble to partake of the food, and having eaten it they
sing and dance. On the morrow they return to their occupations and
bring their earnings to their leader in the late afternoon. The
members are called *fityán* (youths), and their leader, as we have said,
is the *akhí*.

The day after our arrival at Antáliya one of these youths came to
Shaykh Shiháb ad-Dín al-Hamawí and spoke to him in Turkish,
which I did not understand at that time. He was wearing old clothes
and had a felt bonnet on his head. The shaykh said to me 'Do you
know what he is saying?' 'No' said I 'I do not know.' He answered
'He is inviting you and your company to eat a meal with him.' I was
astonished but I said 'Very well,' and when the man had gone I said
to the shaykh 'He is a poor man, and is not able to entertain us, and
we do not like to be a burden on him.' The shaykh burst out laughing
and said 'He is one of the shaykhs of the Young Brotherhood. He is a
cobbler, and a man of generous disposition. His companions, about
two hundred men belonging to different trades, have made him their
leader and have built a hospice to entertain their guests. All that they
earn by day they spend at night.'

After I had prayed the sunset prayer the same man came back for
us and took us to the hospice. We found [ourselves in] a fine
building, carpeted with beautiful Turkish rugs and lit by a large
number of chandeliers of 'Iráqí glass. A number of young men stood
in rows in the hall, wearing long mantles and boots, and each had a
knife about two cubits long attached to a girdle around his waist. On
their heads were white woollen bonnets, and attached to the peak of
these bonnets was a piece of stuff a cubit long and two fingers in
breadth. When they took their seats, every man removed his bonnet

and set it down in front of him, and kept on his head another
ornamental bonnet of silk or other material. In the centre of their hall
was a sort of platform placed there for visitors. When we took our
places, they served up a great banquet followed by fruits and
sweetmeats, after which they began to sing and to dance. We were
filled with admiration and were greatly astonished at their
openhandedness and generosity. We took leave of them at the close
of the night and left them in their hospice.

Ibn Battutah, Travels 1325–54

# CHAPTER SIX

# Armenia, Pontus and Trebizond

Armenia, the home of one of the oldest continuous civilizations in the world, now straddles Turkey and the Soviet Union. The beginnings of the Armenian people date back to the Bronze Age kingdom of Urartu. The kings of Armenia often came into conflict with Rome, and they loom large in classical sources of the first century AD. Soon thereafter the Armenian nation became Christian, and established the essential forms of a civilization which was only brought to an end by systematic massacres and expulsions by the Turkish government in the 1920s. Despite this the Armenian diaspora retains a lively sense of its historical past, and the shattered remnants of its glory can be seen in many cities of eastern Turkey.

The Christian tradition made Armenia the exact site of the garden of Eden, where both Tigris and Euphrates rise. Satan's visit to that paradise is beautifully imagined by John Milton.

Beneath him with new wonder now he views
To all delight of human sense expos'd
In narrow room Natures whole wealth, yea more,
A Heav'n on Earth, for blissful Paradise
Of God the Garden was, by him in the East
Of *Eden* planted; *Eden* stretched her Line
From *Auran* Eastward to the Royal Towrs
Of great *Seleucia*, built by *Grecian* Kings,
Or where the Sons of *Eden* long before
Dwelt in *Telassar*: in this pleasant soile
His farr more pleasant Garden God ordaind;
Out of the fertil ground he caus'd to grow
All Trees of noblest kind for sight, smell, taste;

And all amid them stood the Tree of Life,
High eminent, blooming Ambrosial Fruit
Of vegetable Gold; and next to Life
Our Death the Tree of knowledge grew fast by,
Knowledge of Good bought dear by knowing ill.
Southward through *Eden* went a River large,
Nor chang'd his course, but through the shaggie hill
Pass'd underneath ingulft, for God had thrown
That Mountain as his Garden mould high rais'd
Upon the rapid current, which through veins
Of porous Earth with kindly thirst up drawn,
Rose a fresh Fountain, and with many a rill
Waterd the Garden; thence united fell
Down the steep glade, and met the neather Flood,
Which from his darksom passage now appeers,
And now divided into four main Streams,
Runs divers, wandring many a famous Realme
And Country whereof here needs no account,
But rather to tell how, if Art could tell,
How from that Saphire Fount the crisped Brooks,
Rowling on Orient Pearl and sands of Gold,
With mazie error under pendant shades
Ran Nectar, visiting each plant, and fed
Flours worthy of Paradise which not nice Art
In Beds and curious Knots, but Nature boon
Powrd forth profuse on Hill and Dale and Plaine,
Both where the morning Sun first warmly smote
The open field, and where the unpierc't shade
Imbround the noontide Bowrs: Thus was this place,
A happy rural seat of various view;
Groves whose rich Trees wept odorous Gumms and Balme,
Others whose fruit burnisht with Golden Rinde
Hung amiable, *Hesperian* Fables true,
If true, here only, and of delicious taste:
Betwixt them Lawns, or level Downs, and Flocks
Grasing the tender herb, were interpos'd,
Or palmie hilloc, or the flourie lap
Of som irriguous Valley spred her store,
Flours of all hue, and without Thorn the Rose:
Another side, unbrageous Grots and Caves
Of coole recess, o're which the mantling vine
Layes forth her purple Grape, and gently creeps
Luxuriant; mean while murmuring waters fall
Down the slope hills, disperst, or in a Lake,
That to the fringed Bank with Myrtle crownd,

Her chrystal mirror holds, unite thir streams.
The Birds thir quire apply; aires, vernal aires,
Breathing the smell of field and grove, attune
The trembling leaves, while Universal *Pan*
Knit with the *Graces* and the *Hours* in dance
Led on th' Eternal Spring.

*Paradise Lost*, IV, 205–67

The tradition is recalled by Robert Curzon who spent a year in Armenia in the 1850s.

Some slight remains of paradise are left, even to our days, in the form of the most lovely flowers, which I gathered on the very hill from whence the three rivers take their departure to their distant seas. Though one of them has a Latin scientific name, no plant of it has ever been in Europe, and by no manner of contrivance could we succeed in carrying one away. This most beautiful production was called in Turkish, Yedi kartash kané (Seven brothers' blood), in Latin, Ravanea, or Philipea coccinea, a parasite on absinthe, or wormwood. This is the most beautiful flower conceivable: it is in the form of a lily, about nine to twelve inches long, including the stalk; the flower and stalk, and all parts of it resembling crimson velvet; it has no leaves; it is found on the sides of the mountains near Erzeroom, often in company with the Morena Orientalis, a remarkable kind of thistle, with flowers all up the stalk, looking and smelling like the honeysuckle. Another beautiful flower found here has not been described. It grows among rocks, and has a tough carroty root, two feet or more in length; the leaves are long grassy filaments, forming a low bush, like a tussock of coarse grass; under the leaves appear the flowers. Each plant has twelve or twenty of them, like large white-heart cherries on a stalk, – in the form of a bunch of grapes, eight or ten inches long; these flowers are merely coloured bladders holding the seed. An iris, of a most brilliant flaming yellow, is found among the rocks, and it, as well as all the more remarkable flowers of this country, blooms in the spring soon after the melting of the snow, that is to say about June.

Robert Curzon, *Armenia* (1854)

When Alexander the Great conquered the Persian Empire, so the legend runs in the Syrian *Romance of Alexander*, he came to this country of the sources of Tigris and Euphrates, and to the land beyond where the people sent three hundred men to meet him and to find out his intentions.

Alexander said to them, 'Who are the nations that live beyond these?' The old men replied, 'Those of Bêth-Âmardâth and the Dog-men;

and beyond the Dog-men is the nation of the Mĕnînê; and beyond the nation of the Mĕnînê there are no human beings but only terrible mountains and hills and valleys and plains and horrible caves, in which are serpents and adders and vipers, so that men cannot go thither without being immediately devoured by the serpents, for the lands are waste, and there is nothing there save desolation. Within all these mountains the Paradise of God appears afar off. Now Paradise is neither near heaven nor earth; like a fair and strong city, so it appears between heaven and earth; and the clouds and darkness which surround it are visible afar off, and the horn of the north wind rests upon it.' And Alexander said to them: 'How do the four rivers go forth?' The old men replied: 'My lord, we will inform thy majesty. God made four rivers to go forth from the Paradise of Eden. Because God knew that men would dare to seize the rivers, and would go by means of them to enter Paradise, He drew the rivers within the earth, and brought them through valleys and mountains and plains, and brought them through a number of mountains, and made them issue forth from the mountains, and there is one which He made to flow from a cave. And He surrounded Paradise with seas and rivers and the Ocean, the fœtid sea; and men are unable to draw near to Paradise, neither can they see where the rivers go forth, but they see that they go forth either from the mountains or from the valleys.'

When Alexander had heard what the old men said, he marvelled greatly at the great sea which surrounded all creation; and Alexander said to his troops, 'Do ye desire that we should do something wonderful in this land?' They said to him, 'As thy majesty commands we will do.' The king said, 'Let us make a gate of brass and close up this breach.' His troops said, 'As thy majesty commands we will do.' And Alexander commanded and fetched three thousand smiths, workers in iron, and three thousand men, workers in brass. And they put down brass and iron, and kneaded it as a man kneads when he works clay. Then they brought it and made a gate, the length of which was twelve cubits and its breath eight cubits. He fixed the gate and the bolts, and he placed nails of iron and beat them down one by the other, so that if the Huns came and dug out the rock which was under the threshold of iron, even if footmen were able to pass through, a horse with its rider would be unable to pass, so long as the gate that was hammered down with bolts stood. And he brought and hammered down a lower threshold and hinge for the gate, and he cast therein bolts of iron, and made it swing round on one side like the gates of Shûshan the fortress. And the men brought and kneaded iron and brass and covered therewith the gate and its posts one by one, like a man when he moulds clay. And he made a bolt of iron in the rocks, and hammered out an iron key twelve cubits

long, and made locks of brass turn therewith. And behold the gate
was hung and stood.

E. A. W. Budge, *The History of Alexander the Great*
(Cambridge, 1889)

This 'gate' is beyond Turkey, and runs from the Castle of
Derbend across the Caucasus to the Caspian Sea, in which
region it is known as the Caspian Gates.

To such fabulous tales did the mysterious regions of
North-east Turkey and the Caucasus lend themselves. Almost
equally astonishing is the legend of the conversion of Armenia
to Christianity, engagingly told by Lord Kinross.

The Emperor Diocletian was in search of a wife, and sent throughout
Rome for portraits of suitable candidates. He fell in love with that of
a young Armenian virgin, in a Roman convent, named Ripsime, and
sent for her. But Ripsime, valuing her chastity and hating the
persecutor of the Christians, refused his advances, and fled with the
Mother Superior and the other nuns in the convent to Armenia. Here
she earned a living, making necklaces of glass beads. Diocletian, on
hearing of her flight, wrote to Tiridates and asked him to put her to
death or to send her back – unless indeed he preferred to keep her for
himself. Tiridates found her, admired her beauty, and proposed to
marry her. His soldiers had to take her by force into his presence.
Tiridates then struggled to overcome her resistance for seven hours,
without success, and had finally to give in from exhaustion. This was
remarkable, in view of his great height and broad shoulders and his
reputation for physical prowess. He could overtake chariots, travelling at full speed, and stop them; he had swum the Euphrates in full
armour, with his war-horse in its trappings; he had defeated a
redoubtable Gothic giant in single combat, and had led him in
triumph to the Emperor. But he could not overcome Ripsime. On
his second attempt 'the inspired Amazon,' writes Lynch, 'was a
second time victorious; she threw the King, destroyed his diadem,
and dismissed him from the chamber, fainting and gathering around
him his tattered robes'. Ripsime, the Mother Superior, and their
fellow nuns were then put brutally to death.

Thereupon Tiridates was transformed, in the proper classical
tradition, into a boar, and his family and attendants into accompany-
ing swine. His sister, inspired by a vision, went to search for
Gregory, whom Tiridates had flung into a deep well for professing
Christianity, fifteen years earlier. To the astonishment of all who
believed him dead, he emerged, coal-black in the face, and was taken

into the presence of the King and his nobles, 'now foaming and devouring their flesh'. Praying to God, he won them back their reason, but not yet their human forms. The martyrs, their bodies still uncorrupted after nine days in the open, were buried, and for two months Gregory prayed and instructed the royal family. Then he had a vision. The heavens opened, and amid rumbles of thunder, in a blaze of light, the Saviour struck the earth with a silver mallet and flattened a space. A complicated edifice then reared itself near the royal palace, crowned by the Cross and the figures of the martyrs. With its golden pedestals, its columns and capitals of cloud and fire, its arches and domes of cloud, it was described by the Saint in some architectural detail, and chapels were built under his direction, so that the martyrs might intercede for the King. Their intercession, and that of St. Gregory, was successful. The horn fell from the royal hands and feet, and the King set to work to dig tombs for the martyrs. Then, having regained his vigour, he climbed to the top of Mount Ararat and returned, carrying on his shoulders eight gigantic blocks of stone, which he placed before Ripsime's chapel. The King and his people were baptized, and a cathedral was erected at Etchmiadzin, now in Soviet Armenia, the site designated in Gregory's vision. It is regarded by Armenians as a foundation of Christ himself, and until the nineteenth century they still placed large blocks of stone in front of it, as offerings.

J. P. D. B. Kinross, *Within the Taurus* (1954)

One of the most powerful legends of the Armenian people is that of the hero Meherr, the heirless and deathless. Though it is clearly influenced by classical legend, it reflects in essence the wild society of early medieval Armenia. Meherr, falsely accused (like Hippolytus) of rape by an aunt whose advances he has spurned, runs away for seven years from his home in Sassoun, to do penance killing demons as well as heathens in Azerbaijan, Aleppo and Baghdad.

When Meherr came back to the castle seven years later he found his mace hanging from the door exactly as he left it. He opened the door and went in. He called out to his wife: 'Gohar, I am back. Where are you, can't you hear me?' He found her seated on their throne, dead, holding a paper in her hand. He took it and read: 'Meherr, when you come back and find me dead please bury me in Sassoun, next to Khandout Khatoun. Do not leave me in this heathen country.'

Meherr took Gohar's body to Sassoun and buried her in the monastery next to his mother's grave on Mount Marouta. He had forty requiem masses sung over his wife and parents, and for all the dead in Sassoun.

Meherr got up and went to his father's grave. He was going to kneel before it and pray when he changed his mind, mounted his horse, and rode off, not knowing where to go, what to do. He had not gone far when he saw that the feet of his horse sank in the earth. He said: 'Hoy-hoy! The earth can no longer support me, as my father predicted. This is the end. The vein was pulled from my loins and I have remained heirless upon this earth, unable to propagate the seed of Sassoun. And I am deathless. I have to wait for Christ's return on judgment day to save my soul.'

He turned back, came and knelt before David's grave, crying out in anguish:

> 'Blessed is our Lord God, great is his mercy.
> Rise up father dear from your dreamless sleep
> I am frozen numb on this wintry peak
> Tell me where to go, O where can I dwell
> On this ancient earth crumbling beneath me
> When I am alone and I have no share
> No part in Sassoun, and without an heir
> Expelled from our House by my own kin
> I wander around with no place to rest
> Longing for your words, your fatherly smell
> Living in exile, homeless everywhere.'

A voice answered him from David's grave:

> 'Son, what can I do, son, what can I do?
> I have lost my strength, my hair and my sight
> Serpents and scorpions have made me their nest
> I am powerless now to help you find rest.
> Stop roaming around, your journey's at end
> You are immortal, deathless on this earth
> There is no freedom from all your torment
> Save in Raven's Rock. Go to Raven's Rock
> That's the door to knock. Wait till judgment day
> The end of this world. It will be destroyed
> And a new world built to support the feet
> Of your fiery horse. When that happens, son
> And you ride again, the whole world is yours.'

Meherr turned to his mother's grave:

> 'Rise up mother dear, rise up from your sleep
> The child of your bosom, your own son Meherr
> Is back at your tomb, cast off from Sassoun.
> I went everywhere and I never found

A mother like you, to you I am bound
With my heart and soul, I never did meet
A mother so good, so patient and sweet.
Tell me what to do, I have lost my way.'

A voice answered him from the tomb of the lady Khandout:

'Son, what can I do, son, what can I do?
I have lost my looks, my hair and my sight
Serpents and scorpions have made me their nest
I am powerless now to help you find rest.
We live in this world and then pass away
That's the end for all, but you are without
This one last comfort of mortality
And you do not have an heir of your own.
Stop wandering around and go there, go there
Where your bread is baked and your meal is cooked
And you never need fear of going hungry
In the Rock of Van, Raven's Rock, Meherr.'

The voice stopped speaking. Meherr rose sobbing to his feet,
mounted his horse, and rode off to find the Rock, praying on his
way:

'O merciful God
Take pity on me
Let me get to Van
And to Raven's Rock.'

He did not know where it was. He was starved, had nothing to eat.
He rode in the mountains of Akhlat and went up to the summit of
Mount Sipan, looking for Raven's Rock. He wandered around Lake
Van. In the great gorge of Vostan a prince caught him and his horse
and tied them up. Meherr remembered his prayer: 'Bread and wine,
the living God, Marouta's High Mother of God, the Victory Cross
on my right arm.' He drew his sword and cut the chains, the iron and
gold, and freed himself and his horse from the clutches of this prince.

The earth shook and gave way under the feet of his horse. The
Colt Jalali sank deeper in the crumbling sod. It came up to his knees.
Meherr urged him on, and on, and reached the plain of Van. 'Keep
me or fight me,' he said to God in his despair. God sent seven
mounted angels to fight him. The Lightning Sword had no effect on
the angels. They tortured him. He fought, in vain, from noon to
sundown. Then as he looked up he saw a talking raven of fiery colour
flying over the plain. He took aim with his bow and shot an arrow
that struck the raven, and the wounded bird flew off and disappeared

in a cave, pursued by Meherr. He halted before the Rock, on Tospa's hill. Swinging his mace he said with tears in his eyes: 'If I can split this rock open, I am not guilty. If I cannot, I am guilty.'

He struck, and split the Rock wide open. God took him in. He rode into the cave and dismounted on firm ground. As the two halves of the Rock came together and it closed over him Meherr heard a voice say: 'You shall stay in this Rock until a grain of wheat is as big as the berry of sweet-briar, and a grain of barley grows to the size of a hazel-nut. When that day comes, you will be allowed to go out.'

L. Surmelian, Daredevils of Sassoun (1966)

The individuality of Armenian culture did not fit well with the Ottoman Empire; and the travellers of the nineteenth and early twentieth centuries who found much to admire in the civility of the Turk (as well as his usefulness as an ally against Russia) would share his contempt for the Armenian:

However, during my subsequent travels in Armenia , the impression gradually dawned upon my mind that the Turks were, first of all, very wise not to wish to receive the Armenians into their houses; and, secondly, if they had been good-natured enough to do so, to destroy the mattresses after the departure of their guests. The Armenians in their habits of body are filthy to the last degree. Their houses and clothes are infested with vermin. The Turks, on the contrary, are much cleaner, and are most particular about the use of the bath. An Englishman would not be pleased if his house became filled with what it is not here necessary to mention. If he did under such circumstances admit strangers, he would probably destroy their bedding the moment that they departed.

F. J. Burnaby, Through Asia Minor on Horseback (1898)

Enthusiasm for the Turk led men like Aubrey Herbert (the 'Man who was Greenmantle') to minimise or even discount tales of the massacres of the 1920s. Talaat Pasha was both a friend and a gentleman: could he then be responsible for such barbarity? (He was, as documents later proved.) Herbert's friend Mark Sykes, (1879–1919) who left University to travel in the Near East, and later became a government adviser on Near Eastern policy, made equally light of the massacres and even contrived to suggest they were all the Armenians' fault.

When one first hears the tale of the Malatia massacre, one says, now indeed there was no excuse for the Turks; this was a brutal, organised attempt to destroy a harmless population; but on inquiry it is the same foolish, hopeless tale, the usual boastful Armenian threats, the inevitable noisy talk of freedom and liberty; the cry that the Turks were on the verge of collapse! the arms collected! the usual pointless intrigue and the inevitable betrayals by each other; the final provocation given and the natural outbreak of the Moslems, resulting in a massacre. The Armenians had intended to fight; had prepared for a revolution; had collected weapons from all parts; but as usual, on the very first onslaught they were hopeless and panic-stricken, and what they intended to have been a battle ended in a pitiful slaughter.

The only few who maintained anything like a bold front were those who took possession of the Armenian Church and held it against the mob; but my admiration for them was lost when I learned that these miserable hounds when they saw the Franciscan monks escaping from their convent fired on them at two hundred yards in hopes of killing a European, and so forcing the hand of the Powers. This ruse I have alluded to before, and it seems to be a favourite stratagem, exhibiting the Armenian nature in its most unpleasant light.

How massacres could well have been avoided is hard to imagine. The Armenians insisted on threatening revolution; only boasted that the Powers would help them; silently intrigued against the Government; silently betrayed one another's intrigues; collected arms and gave offence to the Moslems, and yet possessed no more cohesive fighting power or military capacity than rabbits. On the other hand, their enemies the Turks and Kurds, the bravest and boldest of men, were so ignorant that they believed the Armenians would be assisted by the Christian Powers. Hearing vague rumours and anxious to defend their faith, anxious to loot the bazaars, moved in fact by the feelings of the Crusaders (this is said in no irreverent sense), with a nature no more savage than the troops of the Powers at Pekin, they eventually broke out in irresistible fury, the weaker, intellectually superior to the stronger, constantly pressing against the stronger, constantly taunting the stronger, constantly writing silly poems about the stronger, until one day the stronger rose in his strength, delivered himself over to blind rage for twenty-four hours, and the mission-bred revolutionaries and their hopes of an Armenian republic were dashed to hopeless ruin. What, indeed, was the Turkish Government to do? Weak, badgered by the diplomatists, seeing a rebellion brewing, unable to imprison the guilty, obliged to release the revolutionaries, their only hope that the revolution might be averted was that the Moslems should be first in the field.

Mark Sykes, *Dar-ul-Islam* (1904)

Luckily, perhaps, such controversies need no longer spoil the travellers' pleasure in landscape, church and ruin. The great Armenian cities have sunk into history, dead but still fascinating. It requires an effort to realise their vigorous past.

## Erzurum

After Tournefort, it is Robert Curzon who gives the most vivid picture of the beauty, the climate and the barbarism of Erzurum.

This town is the thoroughfare and resting place for all the merchandises of the Indies, especially when the Arabs are upon the watch round Aleppo and Bagdad. These merchandises, the chief whereof are the silk of Persia, cotton, drugs, painted cloths, only pass through this country; very few of them are sold here by retail, and they would let a sick man die for want of a dram of rhubarb, though there were ever so many entire bales of it. They sell nothing but the caviar, which is a most odious dish. 'Tis a common proverb here, that if a breakfast were to be presented to the devil, he should be treated with coffee without sugar, caviar and tobacco; I should add a glass or two of Erzeron wine to the bill of fare. Caviar is only the spawn of sturgeon salted, which is prepared about the Caspian Sea. This meat burns the mouth with its high seasoning, and poisons the nose with its nasty smell. The other merchandises before mentioned are carried to Trebisond, where they are shipped for Constantinople. We were surprised to see arrive at Erzeron so great a quantity of madder, which they call Boia: it comes from Persia, and is used in the dying of cloth and leather. Rhubarb is brought hither from Usbeq in Tartary. The worm-seed comes from Mogul. There are some caravan-masters, that from father to son meddle with nothing but carrying of drugs, and that would think they degenerated from their ancestors, if they troubled their heads about other goods.

J. P. de Tournefort, *Voyage into the Levant* (1741); tr. J. Ozell

In the neighbourhood of the consulate . . . there were several large heaps and mounds of earth, and it was difficult to the uninitiated to discriminate correctly as to which was a house and which was a heap of soil or stones. Streets, glass windows, green doors with brass knockers, areas, and chimney-pots, were things only known from the accounts of travellers from the distant regions where such things are used. Very few people were about, the bulk of the population hybernating at this time of year in their strange holes and burrows. The bright colours of the Oriental dresses looked to my

eye strangely out of place in the cold dirty snow; scarlet robes,
jackets embroidered with gold, brilliant green and white costumes,
were associated in my mind with a hot sun, a dry climate, and fine
weather. A bright sky there was, with the sun shining away as if it
was all right, but his rays gave out no heat, and only put your eyes
out with its glare upon the snow. . . . Another inconvenience has an
absurd effect: the breath, out of doors, congeals upon the mustaches
and beard, and speedily produces icicles, which prevent the possibility of opening the mouth. My mustaches were converted each day
into two sharp icicles, and if anything came against them it hurt
horribly; and those who wore long beards were often obliged to
commence the series of Turkish civilities in dumb show; their faces
being fixtures for the time, they were not able to speak till their
beards thawed.

Robert Curzon, Armenir (1854)

Curzon's recollections encompass, besides such humorous
details, and the architectural splendours of the city, the harsher
aspects of Turkish justice. Here he is in conversation with
Kiamili Pasha, the Governor and Viceroy of Erzurum.

'The other day you hung a Koord opposite my windows; he was a
murderer, and you did right: it is by acts like these that a country
such as this can be kept in order, and that protection is assured to
those who do well.'

'I am sorry,' said the Pasha, 'that they hung the Koord before your
windows. I told them not to hang him before the house of the Persian
Plenipotentiary, where there is a gibbet; but to take him to any place
where the Koords resorted, and as there are many coffee-houses near
you, that is the reason probably why they hung him there. His story
is a curious one: I have been looking after him for the last three years;
he has robbed and murdered many people, though he was so young a
man, but he had always escaped my agents. At last, a few days ago,
he stole a horse, in a valley near here, from a man who was travelling,
and whom he beat about the head and left for dead. He brought the
horse to Erzeroom and offered it for sale, when the owner, who had
recovered, saw him selling the horse, and gave him up to the guard.
He was brought up for judgment before me, when I said to him,
Who are you? After a silence, the man said, "There is fate in this, it
cannot be denied. I am ★ ★ ★ ★ whom you have been searching for
these three years. My fate brought me to Erzeroom, and now I am
taken up for stealing one poor horse. I felt when I took that horse that
I was fated to die for it. My time is come. It is fate." And he went to
be hung without any complaint.'

I said he deserved it, and hoped others would take warning by his
death.

. . . .

The Koord above mentioned was hanged in so original a manner that
I must shortly describe it, as it took place immediately under my
window. What we called at school a cat-gallows was erected close to
a bridge over the little stream which ran down the horse-market,
between my house and the bottom of the hill of the citadel. The
culprit stood under this; the cross-beam was not two feet above his
head; a kawass, having tied a rope to one end of the beam, passed a
slip-knot round the neck of the Koord, a young and very handsome
man, with long black hair; he then drew the rope over the other end
of the beam, and pulled away till the poor man's feet were just off the
ground, when he tied the rope in a knot, leaving the dead body
hanging, supported by two ropes in the form of the letter V. Hardly
any one was looking on, and in the afternoon the body was taken
down and buried.

                                        Robert Curzon, *Armenia* (1854)

Evliya's tales of Erzurum in the seventeenth century were even
more tremendous.

### Description of Mount Egerlí

This is a high mountain, at half an hour's distance on the south side of
Erzerúm, its name is derived from its form, which is like a saddle
(Eger); its top is bifurcated, it abounds in medical herbs, particularly
in the Tútia flower, the scent of which perfumes the air. Oculists
come here to collect the plant Tútia, and with it cure people who
have been diseased for forty years. The odour of aromatic plants and
scented flowers fills the atmosphere.

I once played Jeríd at the foot of this mountain, when I fell from
the horse, and in falling said to myself, 'Where art thou now,
saddle-mountain (Egerlítág)?' Having recovered my senses I
mounted another horse, and galloping full speed towards the mountain, I ascended it. I saw on the top a large tomb, on which I first said
a fátihah, and having measured it by my steps, I found it eighty paces
in length, with two columns, which marked the situation of the head
and the feet. I was looking on the tomb, when a bad smell arose, very
disagreeable both to me and my servants, who held the horses; I
looked on the grave, and saw that the earth within it, being black and
greasy, was boiling like gruel in a pan. I then returned, and having
related my adventure in the Páshá's company in the evening, Ja'afer
Efendi of Erzerúm, a learned and elegant writer, warned me not to
visit this place any more, because it was the grave of Balaam, the son
of Baúr, who had died an Infidel by the curse of Moses, and whose
grave was now boiling, both in winter and summer, by subter-
raneous fire. At the foot of the same mountain, Abd-ur-rahman

Ghází, the standard-bearer of the prophet, lies buried. One day I ascended from the south side of the convent about two thousand paces, when I saw on the second top of this bifurcate mountain a tremendous dragon turned into black stone. It measured seven hundred and seventy paces from the head to the tail, the head looks to the field of Erzerúm, the tail to the castle of Meláz Kerd. If snow falls on the mountains, the figure of this black dragon is easily distinguished from the windows of the Páshá's palace; the circumference of its body is two hundred paces, each of its four feet is as large as ten men put together, and its tail is raised like a minareh. It remained whole until the reign of Selím I when it was broken by an earthquake, so that its fragments now lay scattered about. The head was then split asunder, and one of the eye-balls rolled down on the south side towards Melázguerd, where it lies on the plain like a cupola; the left eye-ball of the same size, yet remains in the petrified head, and is seen very distinctly with its ears, tongue, nose, and mouth every time it snows, because no snow will remain on this black stone, but melts away, and renders more prominent the black colour of it. In winter the stone becomes hot, and emits vapour; in summer it is cold, and exhales a pleasant odour. The legend reports that this most tremendous dragon was changed into stone by the Prophet's standard-bearer, when it came to swallow up the inhabitants of Erzerúm as food for its young, who were shut up in a cave of Mount Siján, on the borders of the lake Ván.

Evliya Celebi*

## Mt Ararat and the Yezidis

And there beside is another hill that men clepe Ararat (but the Jews clepe it Taneez) where Noah's ship rested, and yet is upon that mountain and men may see it afar in clear weather. And that mountain is well a seven mile high. And some men say that they have seen and touched the ship and put their fingers in the parts where the fiend went out when that Noah said *Benedicite*. But they that say such words say their will. For a man may not go up the mountain for great plenty of snow that is always on that mountain, neither summer nor winter, so that no man may go up there; nor never man did sith the time of Noah save a monk that by the grace of God brought one of the planks down, that yet is in the minster at the foot of the mountain.

Mandeville's Travels

Marco Polo adds the information that Mt Ararat is shaped like a cube and that it takes two days to travel around it. The tradition that it was the place where the Ark came to rest seems to be immemorial, and from time to time reports still occur of travellers who have sighted timbers of a ship on its summit.

It was in this region that the Yezidis dwelt, who were reputed to be devil-worshippers. Both Burnaby and Gertrude Bell give interesting accounts of them.

We turned our backs upon Mount Ararat, and, ascending a low range of hills covered with loose rocks and boulders, arrived at a Yezeed (devil-worshippers) village.

The houses were built in the sides of a hill. Cone-shaped huts made of tezek, and filled with that fuel, showed that the inhabitants had no objection to heat in this world, however hot they might expect to be in the next.

An old man, considerably above the middle stature, approached our party. Addressing the Usebashe, he invited us to dismount. It was about luncheon-time. I determined to avail myself of the opportunity afforded me to learn a little about the ways and habits of these strange people.

'Here we are, sir, with the worshippers of Old Scratch!' observed Radford, as he was preparing the mid-day meal, which consisted of a freshly-killed hen, boiled with some rice. 'Mohammed has just been telling me something about them. All I know is that Old Nick has not much to complain of so far as his flock is concerned. They have been at our sugar already, and would have carried off Mohammed's tobacco if he had not been on the look out. I suppose they think it right to steal, so as to keep on good terms with their master.'

The Yezeeds' religion, if such it may be called, is based upon the following dogma: that there are two spirits – a spirit of good and a spirit of evil. Allah, the spirit of good, can do no harm to any one, and is a friend to the human race. The spirit of evil can do a great deal of harm, and he is the cause of all our woes. From this starting-point the Yezeeds have been brought to believe that it is a waste of time to worship the spirit of good, who will not hurt them, and that the proper course to pursue is to try and propitiate the spirit of evil, who can be very disagreeable if he chooses. To do so they never venture to make use of the name of the devil, as this they believe would be an act of disrespect to their infernal master.

They are visited twice a year by different high priests, when certain rites are performed. These rites are kept a great secret. The Turks who gave me some information about the Yezeeds were unable to give me any details about the nature of the ceremonies. I was informed that the Yezeeds are divided into two sects; that the one looks upon the devil as the Grand Vizier of Allah, and the other regards him as the private secretary of the good spirit. It was said that the two sects hated each other to such an extent that, if a man belonging to the one which looks upon the devil as being the Grand Vizier of Allah were to enter a village belonging to members of the rival faith, the new arrival would have a great chance of losing his life.

.    .    .    .

'Do you look upon the devil as the Grand Vizier of Allah?' I now inquired.

If a bombshell had exploded in the room where I was sitting, there could not have been greater consternation than that which was evinced by the members of my host's family. Springing to their feet, they fled from the building – an old woman very nearly upsetting Radford's cooking-pot in her haste to escape into the open air. The captain looked at me, and then indulged in a sort of suppressed laugh.

'What has frightened them?' I inquired.

'Effendi,' he replied, 'you mentioned the word "Shaitan" (devil). It is very lucky for you,' continued the old man, 'that there are five of us, and we are all well armed; for, if not, the Yezeeds would have attacked our party for a certainty. Any disaster which may happen in this village during the next twelve months will be put down to you. If a man's cow or camel dies, the fellow will say that it is all your fault; the sooner we continue our march the better.'

F. J. Burnaby, *Through Asia Minor on Horseback* (1898)

I began delicately as we sat in the doorway of the little church at Kefr Lāb by asking whether the Yezīdis possessed mosque or church.

'No,' replied Mūsa. 'We worship under the open sky. Every day at dawn we worship the sun.'

'Have you,' said I, 'an imām who leads the prayer?'

'On feast days,' said he, 'the sheikh leads the prayer, but on other days every man worships for himself. We count some days lucky and some unlucky. Wednesday, Friday and Sunday are our lucky days, but Thursday is unlucky.'

'Why is that?' said I.

'I do not know,' said Mūsa. 'It is so.'

'Are you,' I asked, 'friends with the Mohammadans or are you foes?'

He answered: 'Here in the country round Aleppo, where we are few, they do not fear us, and we live at peace with them; but every year there comes to us from Mosul a very learned sheikh who collects tribute among us, and he wonders to see us like brothers with the Muslimīn, for in Mosul, where the Yezīdis are many, there is bitter feud. In Mosul our people will not serve in the army, but here we serve like any other – I myself have been a soldier.'

'Have you holy books?' said I.

'Without doubt,' said he, 'and I will tell you what our books teach us. When the end of the world is near Hadūdmadūd will appear on earth. And before his time the race of men will have shrunk in stature so that they are smaller than a blade of grass, – but Hadūdmadūd is a mighty giant. And in seven days, or seven months, or seven years, he will drink all the seas and all the rivers, and the earth will be drained dry.'

'And then,' said the partner, who had followed Mūsa's explanation eagerly, 'out of the dust will spring a great worm, and he will devour Hadūdmadūd.'

'And when he has eaten him,' continued Mūsa, 'there will be a flood which will last seven days, or seven months, or seven years.'

'And the earth will be washed clean,' chimed in the partner.

'And then will come the Mahdi,' said Mūsa, 'and he will summon the four sects, Yezīdis, Christians, Moslems and Jews, and he will appoint the prophet of each sect to collect his followers together. And Yezīd will assemble the Yezīdis, and Jesus the Christians, and Muḥammad the Moslems, and Moses the Jews. But those that while they lived changed from one faith to another, they shall be tried by fire, to see what creed they profess in their hearts. So shall each prophet know his own. This is the end of the world.'

'Do you,' said, I, 'consider all the four faiths to be equal?'

Mūsa replied (diplomatically perhaps): 'The Christians and the Jews we think equal to us.'

'And the Moslems?' I inquired.

'We think them to be swine,' said Mūsa.

Gertrude Bell, The Desert and the Sown (1907)

## Van

In the farther reaches of Turkish Armenia lies Van, a city reputedly founded by Queen Semiramis of Babylon. She fell in love with the beautiful King Ara of Armenia: when he refused her, she declared war on him, and he was defeated and slain in the plain of Ararat. She set up his son, also named Ara, as king in his stead. Here let the Armenian historian Moses of Chorene take up the tale.

And after these things Semiramis, having remained in the plain called Aïrarat after Ara, went into the hill country towards the south. For it was summer time and she wished to disport herself in the valleys and the flowery plains. And seeing the beauty of the land and

the purity of the air, the clearness of the fountains and the murmuring of the gliding rivers, she said, 'It is needful that we build for
ourselves a city and palaces in this balmy clime and beautiful
country, by the side of these pure waters; so that we may spend the
fourth part of the year, which is the summer season, with enjoyment
in the land of Armenia; and the three cool seasons of the year we will
spend in Nineveh.'

And passing over many places she came to the eastern shore of the
salt lake. And on the shore of the lake she saw a long hill lying
towards the setting sun. And south of the hill was a wide valley like
unto a plain, which came down from the eastern flank of the hill unto
the shore of the lake, spacious and of goodly shape. And the rills of
sweet water descending from the mountains ran down the ravines,
and meeting around the spurs of the hills they hastened to join the
river. And there were not a few buildings erected in the valley on the
right and left banks of the waters. And she selected a small hill on the
eastern side.

After gazing thence for a while that evil and hard-hearted woman
Semiramis commanded that twelve thousand unskilled workmen
and six thousand of her chosen men skilled in all manner of wood,
stone, copper, and iron work should be brought from Assyria and all
other lands to the desired place. And it was done according to her
command. And immediately a great multitude of diverse workmen
were brought, and of wise and gifted workers in all the arts. And she
commanded first to make the dyke of the river, of boulders and great
rocks cemented together with clay, of great width and height; the
which it is said remains firm until this day, so that in the clefts of
these dykes pirates and exiles do fortify themselves as in the caves of
the mountains, none being able to wrench even one stone from the
dyke. And when one looked upon the cement it appeared like a
torrent of fat. Thus having taken the dyke round over much ground
she brought it unto the intended site of the city. There she commanded the multitude of the workers to be divided into diverse sections,
placing over each section a chosen master of the arts. And under such
oppression did she keep them that after a few years the wondrous
rampart with its gates of wrought copper was completed. And she
made beautiful buildings in the city, and palaces of different stones
decorated with colours, two stories and three stories high. For each
one she did build summer-houses, separating the various quarters of
the town from each other by beautiful streets. She built also wondrous baths in the midst of the city for the use of the people, and
divided the water passing through the town into two parts, one for
watering the fragrant orchards and flower-gardens, and the other for
the drinking water of the city and its surroundings. On the east,
north, and south of the city she built pleasure houses, and planted

orchards with leafy trees that bore diverse kinds of fruit and foliage; she also planted many vines. The whole city she surrounded with stately ramparts, and caused great multitudes to dwell therein.

But concerning the far end of the city, and the miraculous works that were done there, it surpasseth the power of a man to tell, neither can they be understood by man. For there, surrounded by fortifications, she did construct the Royal Palace, in great mystery. For the entrances were hard, and the passages leading out of it like those of hell. Concerning the manner of its making we have never read a true description, neither do we propose to weave it into our history; but we only say that of all royal works it is, as we have heard, esteemed the first and greatest. And on the west side of the rock – whereon no man can now make any impression, even with iron – in this adamantine substance she constructed many temples, bed-chambers, and treasure-houses; and great trenches, so that none knoweth for what manner of things she made these marvellous preparations. And smoothing the face of the rock as one would smooth wax with a pen, she wrote many inscriptions thereon; so that even to look at it causeth a man to be amazed.

Moses of Chorene; tr. Z. Boyajian*

At Van, Burnaby found accommodation as disagreeable as any he had known, which led him to a diatribe on the uncleanliness of Armenian habits. But his description of Van is very thorough.

Van is surrounded on three sides by a chain of hills, which are at a distance of from three to seven miles from the town. On the fourth side it is bounded by the lake which bears its name. There is a swamp towards the west, and close to the houses. This makes the place very unhealthy in the summer months – typhus and other fevers are prevalent in the district.

.   .   .   .   .

I now learnt that the lake contains natron. The townspeople have a very simple manner of obtaining this substance. In the summer months they pour water from the lake into large shallow basins; the heat of the sun evaporates the water, and carbonate of soda is deposited at the bottom of the vessels. It is afterwards sent to Erzeroum and Stamboul. The inhabitants of Van use this substance for washing purposes as a substitute for soap.

The road wound round the height on which the citadel stands. After about a fifteen minutes' climb our horses reached the summit. Here there were several very old guns, some dating back more than 250 years. Large piles of stone balls lay behind many of the pieces; the commander, pointing at them, remarked that now-a-days they

would not be of any use, although in the last century they had struck terror into the midst of a Persian host. The modern citadel, if it may be termed by that name, is merely a block-house, with accommodation for about 100 soldiers
. . . .

There is a well of naphtha about fifty yards from the blockhouse. The commandant, going with me to the spot, made a soldier draw out some of the contents. The well was very deep, and the inhabitants of Van had used the naphtha from time immemorial. The doctor was doubtful as to whether it was a natural well, or merely a large cistern which had been filled many years ago with this liquid, possibly for the use of the garrison.
. . . .

We came to a place in the rock where it descends abruptly for several hundred feet. 'An Englishman was let down from here by a cord some years ago,' observed the doctor. 'About 200 feet below this spot there is an inscription cut on the stone. The inscription is about Semiramis. Formerly we all wished to know what was the meaning of the writing; but, no one in Van was bold enough to descend the rock, or, even if some Armenian or Turk had dared to make the attempt, he would have been unable to decipher the characters. Well,' continued the speaker, 'an Englishman came here and was lowered by cords over the precipice. If he had fallen even from the spot where the inscription is cut, he must have been dashed to pieces, as it is a long way above the rocks. However, your countryman succeeded in taking an impression of the characters, and I believe a translation of them is in the British Museum. You can see the inscription from the town itself,' he added. 'The letters are very large, they occupy a place about twelve feet long by eight wide.'

F. J. Burnaby, *Through Asia Minor on Horseback* (1898)

Burnaby seems to have been incorrectly informed. The student of the Urartian cuneiform inscription was Fr Edward Schultz of Giessen, who was indeed lowered on a rope to study it in 1827. Two years later he was murdered by Kurds, and the inscription was not published until 1840. It was however not until 1882 that it was deciphered by A. H. Sayce, thus putting the study of second millennium BC Armenia on a scholarly footing.

## Ani

Ani, which now lies on the Russian border, is a young town in Armenian terms. Its history begins at the end of the tenth century BC, and in about the sixth BC it became the capital of the Armenian kingdom. Disputing through the eleventh and twelfth centuries AD the title of capital with Kars, it was, under the feudal Armenian lords of the Mongol kingdom, adorned with a large number of fine churches. Soon after this it ceased altogether to be inhabited, its lovely structures and its paintings mouldering through six centuries. Its desolation was the subject of lament already six centuries ago when Aristakes of Lastivert wrote:

Where are the thrones of our kings? They are seen nowhere. Where are the legions of soldiers that massed before them like dense cloud formations, colourful as the flowers of spring, and resplendent in their uniforms? They are nowhere to be seen. Where is our great and marvellous pontifical throne? Today it is vacant, deprived of its occupant, denuded of its ornaments, filled with dust and spiderwebs, and the heir to the throne removed to a foreign land as a captive and a prisoner. The voices and the sermons of the priests are silent now. The chandeliers are extinguished now and the lamps dimmed, the sweet fragrance of incense is gone, the altar of Our Lord is covered with dust and ashes . . . Now if all that we have related has befallen us because of our wickedness, then tell heaven and all that abide in it, tell the mountains and the hills, the trees of the dense woodlands, that they too may weep over our destruction.

quoted from John Freely, *Companion Guide to Turkey*

A more recent traveller has responded evocatively to the ruins:

As I advanced up the nave towards the wrecked high altar, mounting the sanctuary steps through the dust of centuries at my feet, the music of the spheres sounded from the walls and a great echo of chanting filled the cathedral, now resplendent with vestments and paintings. The candles guttered from every alcove and the sound of warrior voices mingled with the intonings of the monks as the patriarch, high at the apex of the ceremony, lifted the jewelled crown to the head of the young King Gagik. A great shout went up and the trumpets sounded. But it was not the shout of thanksgiving, nor the trumpets of triumph. The splendour faded, the painted cathedral darkened, and from the city walls came the mingled battle sounds of Byzantine and Arab, of Georgians and Mongols. The turrets stood out against the flames and armed men streamed into the city. Then the cannon were silent and a strange stillness settled over the cathedral, the silence of utter abandonment. The candles went out one by one, the few priests crept cowering from the sanctuary. There was a rumbling and a trembling and the whole edifice shook, as outside terrified screams sounded through the near-deserted city. The sun darkened and, to the music of the tempest that rose, the dome of the cathedral of Ani crashed to the ground, the dust of many ikons rising suffocatingly to the night sky that peered, inquisitively, through the gaping roof. There was a sound of terror-crazed wailing in the city, as the ghosts of the Zacharides, Artsrunis, Bagratids, Mamikonians, Pahlavides, Artaxiads and Arsacids fled before the dawn of barbarism and the mourners went about the streets.

I looked around from the sanctuary steps. There was no one there; just the pigeons flitting about the pillars up near the roof. It had stopped raining and I went outside. The Turkish guard was waiting for me, smiling, and we went together across to join the others.

John Marriner, *Trebizond and Beyond* (1969)


## The Pontic Alps

North of the Armenian tableland the Pontic Alps slope, steep and dense with coniferous forests, down to the Black Sea. It is a 'sea of trees' (ağaç denizi) with the highest rainfall in Anatolia and with a culture, like that of the Lebanese coastline or the southern shore of the Caspian, quite distinct from that of the interior.

It was through this inhospitable country, probably near Mt Gumuşhane, that Xenophon's Ten Thousand, the romantic heroes of every Victorian schoolboy, brought their long march to an end with a first sight of the sea that to the Greeks meant safety.

On the fifth day they reached the mountain, the name of which was Theches. No sooner had the men in front ascended it and caught sight of the sea than a great cry arose, and Xenophon, with the rearguard, catching the sound of it, conjectured that another set of enemies must surely be attacking in front; for they were followed by the inhabitants of the country, which was all aflame; indeed the rearguard had killed some and captured others alive by laying an ambuscade; they had taken also about twenty wicker shields, covered with the raw hides of shaggy oxen.

But as the shout became louder and nearer, and those who from time to time came up, began racing at the top of their speed towards the shouters, and the shouting continually recommenced with yet greater volume as the numbers increased, Xenophon settled in his mind that something extraordinary must have happened, so he mounted his horse, and taking with him Lycius and the cavalry, he galloped to the rescue. Presently they could hear the soldiers shouting and passing on the joyful word, *The sea! the sea!*

Thereupon they began running, rearguard and all, and the baggage animals and horses came galloping up. But when they had reached the summit, then indeed they fell to embracing one another – generals and officers and all – and the tears trickled down their cheeks. And on a sudden, some one, whoever it was, having passed down the order, the soldiers began bringing stones and erecting a great cairn, whereon they dedicated a host of untanned skins, and staves, and captured wicker shields, and with his own hand the guide hacked the shields to pieces, inviting the rest to follow his example. After this the Hellenes dismissed the guide with a present raised from the common store, to wit, a horse, a silver bowl, a Persian dress, and ten darics; but what he most begged to have were their rings, and of these he got several from the soldiers. So, after pointing out to them a village where they would find quarters, and the road by which they would proceed towards the land of the Macrones, as evening fell, he turned his back upon them in the night and was gone.

After some battles with the inhabitants, the Greeks were victorious, and found quarters in numerous villages which contained supplies in abundance. Here, generally speaking, there was nothing to excite their wonderment, but the numbers of beehives were indeed astonishing, and so were certain properties of the honey. The effect upon the soldiers who tasted the combs was, that they all went for the nonce quite off their heads, and suffered from vomiting and diarrhoea, with a total inability to stand steady on their legs. A small dose produced a condition not unlike violent drunkenness, a large one an attack very like a fit of madness, and some dropped down, apparently at death's door. So they lay, hundreds of them, as if there had been a great defeat, a prey to the cruellest despondency. But the next day, none had died; and almost at the same hour of the day at which they had eaten they recovered their senses, and on the third or fourth day got on their legs again like convalescents after a severe course of medical treatment.

Xenophon, Anabasis, IV. 8.

The honey of Trebizond still retains the intoxicating qualities which Xenophon and Strabo attributed to it in their accounts of its effects upon the Greeks in their retreat, and upon the soldiers of Pompey. I even found that all the honey here had a very bitter flavour, although it is chiefly the wild honey which possesses such deleterious qualities. It is said to be produced by the bees feeding on the flower of the Azalea Pontica, which grows in great luxuriance on the hills above the town. Pliny says that the honey was extracted from the flower of the Rhododendron, which is also very abundant on the hills; but in this he may have been mistaken, for the flower of the Rhododendron has no smell, whilst that of the Azalea is very powerful and delicious, and therefore more likely to attract the bees. It grows, as I had afterwards an opportunity of ascertaining, all along the coast, and I heard in other places of the noxious qualities of the honey.

W. J. Hamilton*

This country is the scene of action of the Book of Dede Korkut, the compilation of the heroic tales of the pre-Ottoman Turks. The hero Kan Turali braved its perils when he undertook an adventure that seems closely to parallel the story of Princess Turandot.

Now the infidel King of Trebizond had a mightily beautiful and beloved daughter. She used to draw two bows at once, to her right and to her left. The arrow she shot never fell to earth. That girl had three beasts waiting with her dowry. Her father had promised, 'Whoever subdues those three beasts, conquers and kills them, to him shall I give my daughter.' But if anyone failed to kill them, he would cut off his head. Thus the heads of thirty-two sons of infidel princes had been cut off and hung on the battlements. One of those three beasts was a raging lion, one a black bull and one a black camel-stallion. Every one of the three was a monster. Those thirty-two heads which hung on the battlements had never so much as seen the faces of the raging lion and the black camel; all they had done was to perish on the horns of the bull. Kanli Koja saw these heads and these beasts, and the lice on his head were heaped up round his feet. He said, 'I'll go straight to my son and tell him that if he's clever enough he can come and take her; otherwise let him be satisfied with the girls at home.'

The horse's hoof is fleet as the wind; the minstrel's tongue is swift as a bird. Kanli Koja made his way back and went up to the Oghuz land. News was brought to Kan Turali that his father had come, and he went with his forty young men to meet him. He kissed his hand and said, 'Dear father, have you found a suitable girl for me?' 'I have, my son,' said he, 'if you are clever enough.' Kan Turali replied, 'Does it need gold and silver, or mules and camels?' 'Son, it is cleverness that's wanted, cleverness.' 'Father,' said Kan Turali, 'I shall saddle my black-maned Kazilik horse, I shall raid the bloody infidels' land, I shall cut off heads and spill blood, I shall make the infidel vomit blood, I shall bring back slaves and slave-girls; I shall show my cleverness.' 'O my dear son,' said Kanli Koja, 'that is not what I mean by cleverness. They keep three beasts for that girl. They will give her to whoever subdues those three beasts. If he does not subdue them and kill them, they will cut off his head and hang it on a turret.' 'Father,' said Kan Turali, 'you shouldn't have told me this. Now you have told me, I really must go, lest I bring disgrace on my head and shame on my face. Lady mother, lord father, farewell!' Kanli Koja said, 'Do you see what I have brought on myself? I must tell the boy dread tales, so that he will not go.' Thereupon Kanli Koja declaimed; let us see, my Khan, what he declaimed.

> 'Son, in the place where you would go,
> Twisted and tortuous will the roads be;
> Swamps there will be, where the horseman will sink and never
> emerge;
> Forests there will be, where the red serpent can find no path;
> Fortresses there will be, that rub shoulders with the sky;
> A beautiful one there will be, who puts out eyes and snatches
> souls;
> An executioner there will be, whisking heads off in an instant;
> A soldier there will be, with shield dancing on his back.
> To a terrible place have you set your foot; stay!
> Bring not tears to your white-bearded father, your aged mother!'
> *The Book of Dede Korkut*

Needless to say the young man surmounts the trials set him, successfully wrestles the bull and the lion, and wins the hand of the king's daughter.

There is perhaps an echo of this legend, or another like it, in the tale recounted by Johan Schiltberger (1381–1440?), who joined the army of King Sigismund of Hungary against the Turks in 1394, and after being captured successively by the Emperor Bayezid I and by Tamburlaine, travelled through most of Asia Minor and parts of Russia.

There is on a mountain a castle, called that of the sparrow-hawk. Within, is a beautiful virgin, and a sparrow-hawk on a perch. Whoever goes there and does not sleep but watches for three days and three nights, whatever he asks of the virgin, that is chaste, that she will grant to him. And when he finishes the watch, he goes into the castle and comes to a fine palace, where he sees a sparrow-hawk standing on a perch; and when the sparrow-hawk sees the man, he screams, and the virgin comes out of her chamber, welcomes him and says: 'Thou hast served me and watched for three days and three nights, and whatever thou now askest of me that is pure, that will I grant unto thee.' And she does so. But if anybody asks for something that exhibits pride, impudence, or avarice, she curses him and his offspring, so that he can no longer attain an honourable position.

. . . . .

During the time that I and my companions were there, we asked a
man to take us to the castle, and gave him money; and when we got
to the place, one of my companions wanted to remain and keep
watch. He who brought us advised him against it, and said that if he
did not carry out the watch, he would be lost, and nobody would
know where he went; the castle is also hidden by trees, so that
nobody knows the way to it. It is also forbidden by the Greek priests,
and they say that the devil has to do with it, and not God.

*The Bondage and Travels of Johan Schiltberger 1896–1427* (1879)


## Samsun

It was in the Pontic Alps between Samsun and Trabzon, on the
banks of the river Iris (now Yeşilirmak) that St Basil the Great
made his mountain dwelling, which he described in a letter to a
friend (no. 14).

'It is a lofty mountain, clothed with a dense forest, and irrigated on
its northern face with cool transparent streams. At the foot of this lies
outspread a level plain, ever enriched by the waters that descend
from the mountain. Round this plain grows a natural grove, composed of a variety of trees of all kinds, which serves almost as a fence
to it, so that in comparison of it, even Calypso's isle would be
insignificant, which Homer seems to have admired above all others
for its beauty. For it is not far removed from being an island, because
it is inclosed by boundaries all round. On two sides of it lie deep
abrupt gorges, and the river, which skirts it in a precipitous course,
itself forms a continuous and impracticable wall; and as the mountain
extends opposite to this, and makes curved bends where it joins the
gorges, it cuts off the accessible parts of the lower slopes. To these
there is a single access, of which I have the command. Then after the
dwelling-house comes another neck of land, which throws up a lofty
ridge at the summit, in such a way that this level lies extended to the
view, and it is possible from that elevation even to see the river
flowing round it.' He then goes on to praise the clearness and rapidity
of the stream, the profusion of flowers and number of singing-birds,
and above all the tranquillity which such a retreat afforded him.
Notwithstanding this highly coloured description, neither the rug-
gedness of the spot nor the severity of the life seems to have been
agreeable to Gregory, to judge from two letters which he addressed
to his entertainer after his return from a visit to this retreat. They are
couched in a tone of banter, and in a third letter the writer half
apologises by laying stress on the delights of the spiritual exercises
they there enjoyed; but there is sufficient evidence in them that the

hardships had made a strong impression on his mind. But anyhow there was a great difference in this matter between Pontus and Cappadocia; for the latter country was not only bare of trees while Pontus was wooded, but it was also, as Strabo remarks, the colder of the two, notwithstanding its lying further to the south. Basil had good reason to know it, for at the commencement of his episcopate, writing from Caesareia to Eusebius, to apologise for a long silence, he tells him that he had been unable to send a letter on account of the severity of the weather, which had such an effect on his people that they would hardly put their heads outside their doors; and he adds that the snowfall had been so great, that for two months they had been covered by it, houses and all, and seemed to be lurking in dens. Now this valley is 1,000 feet higher than Kaiserieh, being not less than 5,000 feet above the sea. When we add to this the rudeness of the dwellings and the difficulty of obtaining fuel, we may easily judge that a spirit of self-mortification was required to induce men to dwell here. It was a very different thing from a life, however ascetic, in the genial climate of the Thebaid in Egypt.

H. F. Tozer, *Turkish Armenia and Eastern Asia Minor* (1881)


## Trabzon (Trebizond)

The capital of this region, and almost the only good harbour on the south coast of the Black Sea, is Trabzon – drab metamorphosis of medieval Trebizond, the ancient Greek Trapezous (Table-land).

It would be hard to match Robert Curzon's pithy synopsis of Trapezuntine history.

For more than a thousand years the history of Trebizond remains enveloped in the mists of obscurity and insignificance; various dukes, princes, and counts, succeeded each other in a long line of inglorious pride.

In the thirteenth century the chivalrous house of Courtenai, by the assistance of the heroes of the Crusades, mounted the throne of Constantinople, and the ancestors of the Earl of Devon produced three emperors, who reigned in succession over the Oriental portion of the Roman empire. The ancient dynasty of the Comneni, being expelled from the dominions over which they had presided for centuries, fled for refuge into various lands. Alexius, the son of Manuel and grandson of Andronicus Comnenus, obtained the government of the duchy of Trebizond, which extended from the unfortunate Sinope to the borders of Circassia. He seems to have reigned in peace. The acts of his son, who succeeded him, are as unknown as his name, which has not even descended to posterity. The grandson of Alexius was David Comnenus, who, with an assurance and presumption which is almost ludicrous, took upon himself the style and title of Emperor of Trebizond. Puffed up with vanity and self-conceit, this feeble prince enjoyed for a short period the imperial dignity which he possessed only in name. The erection of this quaint and ridiculous Christian empire appears to have made a great sensation among the knights and troubadours of the fifteenth century. The geographical knowledge of those days was confined to few, and the empire of Trebizond, like that of Prester John, whose extent and situation were equally apocryphal, formed the theme of many a fabulous adventure and many a romance, which served to beguile the evening hours by the firesides of the castles and convents of England and France. Fairies and wizards, ogres and giants, peopled the realms of fancy in this distant empire. Lovely princesses were rescued from the thraldom of paynim castellans, and followers of Mahound and Termagaunt, by valiant Christian knights armed with cross-hilted swords, and lutes, and talismans, the gift of benignant fairies, whose existence was only to be found in the imaginations of the unknown but delightful authors of the romances of chivalry, and the poems and ballads of the trouveurs and troubadours.

. . . .

David Comnenus descended from his golden throne in the year 1461, and with his family was sent, apparently as a prisoner, to a distant castle, where, being accused of corresponding with the King of Persia, he and his whole race were massacred by the orders of his furious conqueror. With him ended the illustrious dynasty of the Comneni, and the history of the independent state of Trebizond, which has since those times remained a remote, and till lately an almost unexplored province of the Turkish empire.

Robert Curzon, *Armenia* (1854)

The fall of Trebizond to Mehmed II was a brief affair, but it rapidly became clothed in legends nearly as colourful as those of the fall of Constantinople.

The Turks of Trebizond preserved a legend that the citizens, expecting relief before dawn, agreed to surrender at cock-crow; but on that fatal occasion the cocks crowed in the early hours of the night, whereupon the Turks kept the besieged to their word. Another Turkish tradition described how a girl, dressed in black, held out in the tower of the palace, consequently called in Turkish 'the Black Girl's palace' (*Kara kezoun serai*), and, when all was lost, threw herself down from it. A ballad seems to show that the mountain region of Matzouka (which remained purely Greek by race and religion) and Chaldia retained independence for several decades. Other poems sing of the fall of Kordyle, defended by a Greek Joan of Arc against the janissaries until she, too, threw herself from a window, still extant up to the Crimean War.

William Miller, *Trebizond*

The magnificence of Imperial Trebizond is the theme of one of the longest extant descriptions of a medieval Greek city, the Encomium of Trebizond by George Bessarion, the Cardinal and humanist who was born there and who departed to Italy on the fall of the little Empire.

In such a land, in such a country, surrounded by mountains, hills, plains, and the sea of all seas the most gentle and friendly to men, our forefathers chose the most beautiful and secure spot to erect their city. It is a hill rising not very high above the land, cleft on either side with deep ravines and surrounded also as it were with ditches, far above the average of ditches. Through these, perpetual rivers run to the sea, fuller than usual in winter but not drying up in spring or even in summer, so that within there is not only perfect security by sufficient water for refreshment and for washing. Refuse and sewage can all be easily and lightly removed with their help, for the river runs so to speak past every front door. And this hill, which rises gently and unforested from the sea, climbs more steeply to the heights, is closed off on either side by ravines and hemmed in by cliffs, forming at the top a high and level place suitable for dwellings and for the enjoyment of the different seasons. On this place, now an acropolis, they built, trusting in their own valour more than in the site and their works; and yet they encircled it with strong walls, towers, battlements, fortifications and so on, second to none.

.   .   .   .   .

The number and beauty of the houses is a result of the skill of the architects, who uniquely deserve the poet's phrase, 'the skilful craftsman', and the traffic from the hills which provide plenty of timber of varied kinds, and better than elsewhere. . . . The buildings of the palace are situated on the acropolis itself, and this acropolis is superior to any in the strength of its wall, the brilliance of its adornment, and the size and beauty of all its features. The wall toward the west, which divides the acropolis and the public offices, serves the same purposes for both of them, rising to the second storey of the acropolis and the palace, and the wall above the public offices rises as much above that of the acropolis, as the latter does above the earth. The wall on either side, excellent in its workmanship, height and thickness . . . alone suffices to withstand any approaching enemy and to protect those inside; having a double gate and a single doorway, it is built with entire security. On either side one area is set aside for the halls and the king's servants; in the centre is the palace, with its entrance raised up high and reached by a staircase. As you enter you are greeted by anterooms and vestibules, supreme in size and beauty, and wind vanes surround the building, facing in every direction to catch every breeze. On the other side is a long building of great beauty, its foundation being all of white stone, and its roof decorated with gold and other colours, painted flowers and stars, emitting beams of light as if it were the heaven itself, remarkable for artistry and sumptuousness. All around the walls are painted the series of the kings, both of our own day and the days of our forefathers, and there are paintings of the dangers that our threatened city has overcome and of those who were worsted by our countrymen. Above it is the king's balcony, with a pyramidal roof, supported by pillars in the form of monsters, and surrounded likewise by white stone lattices which reach up to the roof to keep the subjects from the kings. Here the king appears to give instructions to the authorities, to speak with ambassadors, and to give audiences. Further on is another royal balcony, much greater in breadth and height, roofed and colonnaded. . . . where the king is wont to hold banquets for the authorities and the rest of his staff. Then on the left are a large number of rooms, one in particular with four walls and rectangular in shape, which contains images of the creation of the universe, of the origins of man and of his first societies. On the right are rooms and anterooms, wind-towers, bedrooms and chambers, divided by porticoes, each ending at an angle, impossible to exceed, of different sizes, all of indescribable beauty and decorated with fitting taste. And there is a holy church, brilliant with paintings and dedications of marvellous beauty.

G. Bessarion, *Praise of Trebizond*; tr. R. S.

The most colourful early description of Trebizond comes from the Ottoman period, and is by Evliya Celebi the topographer.

Outside of the courtyard of the mosque of the middle castle is the college of Mohammed II, with a great number of cells and students. There is a general lecture (Dersí-a'ám), the lecturer holds the degree of a Molla; it is a mine of poets, and meeting-place of wits. The college of Katúnieh is adorned with cells on four sides; the students receive fixed quantities of meat and wax for their subsistence. The college of Iskender Páshá on the north side of the mosque, that bears the same name, is richly endowed with stipends for the students. The reading-houses of Trebisonde are those of the middle castle, at the

mosque of Mohammed II, where reading after the manner of Ibn
Kether is introduced; that of Khatúnieh, where works on the Korán
are read after the seven established methods of Jeserí and Shátebieh;
and that of Iskender Páshá close to its mosque. The abecedarian
schools for boys are that of Mohammed II in the middle castle; the
school of the new mosque, a school so blessed, that a boy who has
been taught here to read the Bismillah (in God's name!) cannot fail to
be a learned man; the elegant school of Khatúnieh on the west side of
the mosque is built of stone, with a cupola, where orphans are
supplied with mental and bodily food, with dresses on great festivals
and presents besides; and the schools of Iskender Páshá; these are the
most celebrated.

. . . .

The fish which are worthy of mention are Lorek-bálighí, Kefál-
bálighí (Cephalus), the Kalkán-balighí (Rhombus), which if eaten by
women renders them prolific; the fish called Kiziljeh-tekerbálik,
with a red head and delicious to taste; the gold fish, the Sgombro
which is taken in the season Erbain (forty days). But the most
precious of all, which frequently causes bloody strifes and quarrels in
the Market-place, is the Khamsí-bálighí taken in the season of
Khamsan, (the fifty days when southerly winds blow); these fish
were formerly thrown on the shore at Trebisonde by virtue of a
talisman erected, as is said, by Alexander, before the gate of the
town, representing a fish of this kind in brass on a column of stone;
but on the birth-night of the prophet, when all talismans lost their
power, the same happened to this at Trebisonde; thus the fish are no
longer thrown on the shore, but the sea abounds with them during
the said fifty days. At this season boats loaded with these fish arrive
in the harbour, and the dealers in fish cry them in a peculiar manner,
at the same time sounding a kind of horn or trumpet; as soon as this
sound is heard, the whole town is in an uproar, and people who hear
it, even when at prayer, instantly cease, and run like madmen after it.
It is a shining white fish of a span's length, and is an aphrodisiac
of extraordinary potency; strengthening and easy of digestion, does
not smell like fish, creates no fever in those who eat it, and also cures
sore mouths. If the head of this fish, Khamsí-bálighí, pronounced
Khápsi-bálighí, is burnt, serpents and other venomous reptiles are
killed by the smoke. The people use it during forty days in all their
dishes, to which it gives a peculiar flavour, it is thus used with
yakhní, roasts, pies, and baklava (mixed pies), a dish called pílegí is
made of it in the following manner, the fish is first cleaned, then cut
into slices on which is laid parsley and celery, then another layer of
fish, the best oil is then poured on it, and it is cooked over the fire for
one hour, it thus becomes quite a luminous dish, which may be said
to illuminate those who eat it. But however this fish may be dressed

and eaten, it is extremely useful to the stomach and the eyes, and is a dish of friendship and love.

Evliya Celebi, *Travels**

By the time Robert Curzon was in Armenia, Trebizond had degenerated into a sleepy pashalik.

What the Pasha looked like, and what manner of man he was, it was not easy to make out, seeing that to the outward eye he presented the appearance of a large green bundle, with a red fez at the top, for he was enveloped in a great furred cloak; he seemed to have dark eyes, like everybody else in this country, and a long nose and a black beard, whereof the confines or limits were not to be ascertained, as I could not readily distinguish what was beard and what was fur. Every now and then his Excellency snuffled, as if he had got a cold, but I think it was only a trick; however, when he lifted up his voice to speak, the depth and hollow sound was very remarkable. I have heard several Turks speak in this way, which I believe they consider dignified, and imagine that it is done in imitation of Sultan Mahmoud, who, whether it was his natural voice or not, always spoke as if his voice came out of his stomach instead of his mouth. Abdallah Pasha paid us his compliments in this awful tone, and, till I got a little used to it, I wondered out of what particular part of the heap of fur, cloth, &c., this thorough-bass proceeded. I found, to my great admiration, that the Pasha knew my name, and almost as much of my own history as I did myself; where he had gained his very important information I know not, but an interest so unusual in anything relating to another person induced me to make inquiries about him, and I found he was not only a man of the highest dignity and wealth, possessing villages, square miles and acres innumerable, but he was a philosopher; if not a writer, he was a reader of books, particularly works on medicine. This was his great hobby. In the way of government he seemed to be a most patriarchal sort of king: he had no army or soldiers whatever; fifteen or sixteen cawasses were all the guards that he supported. He smoked the pipe of tranquillity on the carpet of prudence, and the pashalic of Trebizond slumbered on in the sun; the houses tumbled down occasionally, and people repaired them never; the secretary of state wrote to the Porte two or three times a year, to say that nothing particular had happened. The only thing I wondered at was, how the tribute was exacted, for transmitted it must be regularly to Constantinople. Rayahs must be squeezed: they were created, like oranges, for that purpose; but, somehow or other, Abdallah Pasha seems to have carried on the process quietly, and the multitudes under his rule dozed on from year to year. That was all very well for those at a distance, but his immediate attendants suffered occasionally from the philosophical inquiries of their master. He thought of nothing but physic, and whenever he could catch a Piedmontese doctor he would buy any quantity of medicine from him, and talk learnedly on medical subjects as long as the doctor could stand it. As nobody ever tells the truth in these parts, the Pasha never believed what the doctor told him, and usually satisfied his mind by experiments *in corpore vili*, many of which, when the accounts were related to me, made me cry with laughter. They were mostly too medical to be narrated in any unmedical assembly.

Robert Curzon, Armenia (1854)

All that is left in the drab and mercantile town is scope for such fantasy and imagination as Rose Macaulay is supreme mistress of.

After I had fished in the morning I would lunch on sandwiches and raki, and spend the afternoon exploring, and sketching, often up in the citadel. There was much less left of this and of the Byzantine palace than there had been at the end of the last century, when Lynch was there and drew the plan that Charles had copied. The outer walls then seem to have been almost complete, and set with massive towers; houses were built inside and against them, but now they were jumbled ruins whose stones had been used to build a labyrinth of cottages and small houses in a wilderness of gardens, so that the plan was lost and overgrown in roofs and trees and shrubs. But one could make out, with the plan, how it had been, and where the different fortresses and gates had stood, and there was the palace banqueting hall, roofless now, and grown with long grass and fig trees, and eight pointed windows with slim dividing columns. It was in the banqueting hall that I spent most time, painting, and looking out through the Byzantine windows at the mountains behind, and down the steep ravine to the sea in front, and imagining the painted walls and the marble floors and the gold-starred roof, and the Comnenus emperors sitting on their golden thrones, and the Byzantine courtiers and clergymen talking to one another, intriguing, arranging murders, discussing the Trinity, in which they took such immense interest, talking of the barbarians who were threatening the Empire and later, after Constantinople had fallen, and Trebizond was the Empire, debating how to hold it, how much tribute could be paid to the Turks, how best to form an anti-Turkish union, whose eyes should be put out, what envoys should be sent to Rome. All the centuries of lively Byzantine chatter, they had left whispering echoes in that place where the hot sun beat down on the fig trees and the small wind and small animals stirred in the long grass. The Byzantines had been active in mind and tongue, not lethargic like the Turks; they had had no dull moments, they had babbled and built and painted and quarrelled and murdered and tortured and prayed and formed heresies and doctrines and creeds and sacramentaries, they had argued and disputed and made factions and rebellions and palace revolutions, and to and fro their feet seemed to pass among the grasses that had been marble floors, and the last Greek empire brooded like a ghost in that forlorn fag end of time to which I too had come, lost and looking for I did not know what, while my camel munched the leaves of the carob tree outside the ruined wall.

Churches had once stood all about this place; St. Eugenios, on a hill below the palace, and the Cathedral of the Gold-headed Virgin, now both mosques, could be seen from the windows; once, it was said, there had been a thousand churches in Trebizond. Most were destroyed, many were now mosques, many used for dwellings or store-houses.

. . . .

When the Turks went on repeating that the Comnenus palace and the citadel were Turkceji, I got annoyed, and as they would not accept 'Ellenceji,' I said 'Inglizce,' because I thought we had as much claim to have built the palace and citadel as Turks had. They looked at me suspiciously when I said this, as if they thought I was saying that the English were planning to capture and occupy Trabzon, and I wished we could do this, except that we spoil anywhere we occupy, like Cyprus and Gibraltar, with barracks and dull villas and pre-fabs. Actually, if we took Trebizond, we should probably clear away the Turkish houses and gardens and alleys from the citadel and cut away the trees and shrubs and leave it all stark and bare like a historical monument, and we should build a large harbour and fill it with cargo ships, and a few battleships, and there would be a golf club and a yacht club and a bathing beach and several smart hotels and a casino and a cinema and a dance hall and a new brothel, and several policemen, and a hospital, and a colony of villas, and soldiers and sailors would crowd about the streets and call it Trab, and large steamers would ply every day to and from Istanbul bringing tourists, and the place would prosper once more, not as it used to in its great days when the trade from Persia and Arabia flowed into it by sea and caravan, and gold and jewels glittered like the sun and moon and stars within the palace, for no place any more can prosper like that, but it would be prosperous, it would have trade, it would have communications, inventions, luxury, it would have great warehouses on the quays and a great coming and going. The Greek enchanters would dive further underground, Christian churches would spring up, Anglican, Roman Catholic, Dissenting, where the

British colony would pray, and there would be a Y.M.C.A. and a Y.W.C.A., where billiards and boxing would be played, and English women would drive about the streets and sit and drink coffee and tea in the gardens, and Turkish women would become like the women of Istanbul and Ankara and Izmir, walking the streets with naked faces unashamed. And that would be the end of the Trebizond of legend and romance, and of the Byzantine empire fallen under the heavy feet of Turks but still a lovely, haunting, corrupt and assassinating ghost, whispering of intrigue and palace revolutions and heresies in the brambled banqueting hall among the prowling cats beneath the eight Byzantine windows.

Rose Macaulay, *The Towers of Trebizond* (1956)

# CHAPTER SEVEN

# Cilicia and The Syrian Marches

East of Antalya (p. 183) the Mediterranean coastline of Turkey continues through a series of green and mountainous undulations, scented with thyme, marjoram and wild flowers, until a steep curve southwards announces imminent arrival at Iskenderun, the ancient port of Alexandria or, in medieval times, Scanderoon. This is the beginning of Crusader country, and every town of any size boasts its castle perched on the precipitous cliffs. The one at Alanya, the Red Tower, is not of the Crusaders but of the Seljuk Sultan Alaeddin Keykubad who conquered the city of Coracesium in 1221; and the one at Anamur dates from the medieval kingdom of Lesser Armenia which finally fell to the Ottomans in the fourteenth century. But at Silifke, the ancient Seleuceia, a fortress of the Byzantine period was taken by the Crusaders in 1098. Changing hands repeatedly over the next four centuries between Armenians, Byzantines, Seljuks, Crusaders and Karamanids, it finally fell to Ottoman dominion in 1471. The existing structure is essentially Crusader workmanship, and in its heyday may have been as magnificent a creation as Krak des Chevaliers in Syria. Through Silifke runs the Göksu river, the ancient Calycadnus, in which the Emperor Frederick Barbarossa was drowned at the head of his army in 1190.

## Korykos

North-west of Silifke on the coast lies the ancient city of Korykos. Spectacular chasms here bear the names of Paradise and Hell; and here too is the Corycian Cave, the bed of the monster Typhon of Greek mythology. From the sea the extensive and shining white ruins of Korykos give the impression of a splendid and populous city, as was remarked by Captain Beaufort in 1811. The archaeologist Austen Henry Layard, later to achieve fame as the excavator of Nineveh, travelled this way in 1839 and made a careful and evocative description of the ruins.

A vast mass of ruins occupies the ancient town of Corycus of Cilicia Tracheia, the name of which is still retained in Korgos. Near it was the Corycian cavern, better known as the Cilician cave of Pindar and Æschylus and the bed of the giant Typhon. Around are, on all sides, ancient tombs cut in the rock, sarcophagi and monuments to the dead. Sometimes the rock itself has been fashioned into a sarcophagus, the pent roof lid of which has been removed by those who in former times rifled it of its contents. Many of these resting-places of the dead had inscriptions, some Pagan, some Christian, but they had all been obliterated more or less by time or man.

It would be impossible to describe all the ruins and tombs we saw during our day's ride. Some of the mausolea, or small sepulchral temples of white marble, were of singular beauty, ornamented with exquisitely chiselled architectural devices, and marvellously well preserved. This fact I attributed to the absence of a population which would have used the materials of these ancient buildings to construct their own habitations. It is probable that, when the cities which existed on this rocky coast had fallen and been deserted, and the aqueduct ceased to supply them with water, no attempt was made to form fresh settlements upon their sites.

The mausolea, which usually stood on an eminence or on a rock hanging over the sea, consisted generally of two vaulted chambers, the outer of which was completely open by a wide arched entrance to the air. It communicated by an arched doorway with an inner chamber, in which stood a sarcophagus. Access was also had to this inner room by a small square doorway at the back of the monument. They had pent roofs of square slabs of stone and pediments supported by pilasters of the Corinthian order.

A. H. Layard, Autobiography (1903)

## Tarsus

The next major city along this route to the east takes us back to a completely different period of history: Tarsus, famous above all as the city of St Paul, had established its fame as an intellectual centre by the beginning of the Christian era. The geographer Strabo, who wrote in the reign of Augustus (31 BC–AD 14), described it thus:

The people at Tarsus have devoted themselves so eagerly, not only to philosophy, but also to the whole round of education in general, that they have surpassed Athens, Alexandria, or any other place that can be named where there have been schools and lectures of philosophers. But it is so different from other cities that there the men who are fond of learning are all natives, and foreigners are not inclined to sojourn there; neither do these natives stay there, but they complete their education abroad; and when they have completed it they are pleased to live abroad, and but few go back home. But the opposite is the case with the other cities which I have just mentioned except Alexandria; for many resort to them and pass time there with pleasure, but you would not see many of the natives either resorting to places outside their country through love of learning or eager about pursuing learning at home. With the Alexandrians, however, both things take place, for they admit many foreigners and also send not a few of their own citizens abroad. Further, the city of Tarsus has all kinds of schools of rhetoric; and in general it not only has a flourishing population but also is most powerful, thus keeping up the reputation of the mother-city.

Strabo, *Geography*, 14.5.13

But its history went back many centuries before this, even to Assyrian times. Sir William Ramsay, who made the study of the churches and the Christian traditions of Asia Minor his lifetime's work, reported in his *Cities of St Paul* the legend that it had been founded by Sennacherib.

About the Assyrian Tarsus we have no information except in the form of foundation legends. Alexander Polyhistor says that Sennacherib, king of Nineveh (705–681 BC), was the founder. A more Hellenised form of the legend, related by Strabo and many others, makes Sardanapalus the founder of Tarsus, and tells how he recorded on his tomb at Anchiale, fourteen miles south-west from Tarsus, that he had built those two cities in one day. The story ran that on this tomb was a statue representing Sardanapalus snapping his fingers, with an inscription in Assyrian letters: 'Sardanapalus, son of Anakyndaraxes, built Anchiale and Tarsus in one day. Eat, drink, and play, for everything else is not worth this (action of the fingers).' The poet Choirilos versified the sentiment, and Aristotle quoted it, remarking that it was more worthy to be written on the grave of an ox than on the tomb of a king.

W. M. Ramsay, *Cities of St Paul* (1907)

Tarsus provided, too, the scene for the famous meeting of Antony and Cleopatra immortalised in one of Shakespeare's most famous descriptions.

*Maecenas, Enobarbus, Agrippa*

*Maec.* She's a most triumphant lady, if report be square to her.
*Eno.* When she first met Mark Antony, she pursed up his heart, upon the river of Cydnus.
*Agr.* There she appeared indeed; or my reporter devised well for her.
*Eno.* I will tell you:
> The barge she sat in, like a burnish'd throne,
> Burnt on the water: the poop was beaten gold;
> Purple the sails, and so perfumed that
> The winds were love-sick: with them the oars were silver
> Which to the tune of flutes kept stroke, and made
> The water, which they beat, to follow faster,
> As amorous of their strokes. For her own person,
> It beggar'd all description: she did lie
> In her pavilion, (cloth of gold, of tissue,)
> O'er-picturing that Venus, where we see
> The fancy outwork nature: on each side her
> Stood pretty dimpled boys, like smiling Cupids,
> With divers colour'd fans, whose wind did seem
> To glow the delicate cheeks which they did cool,
> And what they undid, did.
*Agr.*                 O, rare for Antony!
*Eno.* Her gentlewomen, like the Nereides,
> So many mermaids, tended her i' the eyes,
> And made their bends adornings: at the helm
> A seeming mermaid steers; the silken tackle
> Swell with the touches of those flower-soft hands,
> That yarely frame the office. From the barge
> A strange invisible perfume hits the sense
> Of the adjacent wharfs. The city cast
> Her people out upon her; and Antony,
> Enthron'd in the market place, did sit alone,
> Whistling to the air; which, but for vacancy,
> Had gone to gaze on Cleopatra too,
> And made a gap in nature.
*Agr.* Rare Egyptian!
William Shakespeare, Antony and Cleopatra, II. ii.

Layard writes evocatively of the setting of this ancient city, even as he continues eastwards towards Karataş.

As we continued along the coast we passed many ruins, some apparently of small temples, others of tombs and the remains of buildings. During the day we had seen in the distance to the east the mountains of Syria rising majestically from the sea. As we forced our way through myrtle and olive bushes and marshy ground, game of many descriptions rose in all directions – francolins (the black partridge), partridges, quails, snipe, ducks, widgeon, and various kinds of water-fowl. The sun went down in all its glory, lighting up this beautiful coast and the distant mountains of Taurus and Syria, and turning the blue Mediterranean into a sheet of purple and gold. In the distance, close to the coast, rose the picturesque castle of Korgos, built upon a small island. I never saw anything more lovely, nor had I ever enjoyed so many delightful sensations as our day's ride afforded me. I have never forgotten it. The beauty of the distant mountains, the richness of the vegetation, the utter loneliness and desolation of the country, the wonderful remains of ancient civilisation, the graceful elegance of the monuments, the picturesque aspect of the ruins, the blue motionless sea reflecting every object, with here and there a white sail, all combined to form a scene which it would be difficult to equal and impossible to surpass.

A. H. Layard, *Autobiography* (1903)

## Çukurova

The landscape of this south-eastern corner of Turkey has surely never been better described than by Yashar Kemal, Turkey's foremost living novelist: it is the setting for his novels *Memed My Hawk* and *They Burn the Thistles*, which centre around the life of the still prevalent bandits of the hinterland.

The slopes of the Taurus Mountains rise from the shores of the Eastern Mediterranean, on the southern coast of Turkey, in a steady ascent from the white, foam-fringed rocks to the peaks. They then spread inland, at a tangent to the curve of the coast. Clouds in white masses always float over the sea. The coastal plains between the mountains and the shore are of clay, quite smooth, as if polished. Here the soil is rich. For miles inland the plain holds the tang of the sea, its air still salt and sharp. Beyond this smooth ploughed land the scrub of the Chukurova begins. Thickly covered with a tangle of brushwood, reeds, blackberry brambles, wild vines and rushes, its deep green expanse seems boundless, wilder and darker than a forest.

A little farther inland, beyond Anavarza on one side and Osmaniya on the other, on the way towards Islahiye, begin the broad marshes. In the summer months they bubble with the heat. Filthy, unapproachable because of their stench, they reek of rotting reeds and rushes, rotting grass and timber, rotting earth. The surface of the water is then hidden by the decomposing vegetation. In winter the whole area is covered by the sheen of stagnant flood-water, unrolling like a carpet. Beyond the marshes there are more ploughed fields. The earth is oily, shining, warm and soft, ready to repay forty-fold, fifty-fold, the seed that it receives.

Only beyond the low hill-tops crowned with heavy-scented myrtle do the rocks suddenly begin to appear, and with them the pine trees. The crystal-bright drops of resin ooze from the trunks and trickle down to the ground. Beyond the pines are plateaux where the soil is grey and arid. From here it looks as if the snow-capped peaks of the Taurus are very close, almost within arm's reach.

. . . .

Old men used to talk of the old-time Chukurova. In the days of Memed's brigandage, Big Ismail, then more than ninety years old, spoke repeatedly of those times. He had moss-green eyes, a sparse beard and a pointed chin, like all the Turcomans. His broad shoulders were still as strong as in his youth, his eyes as sharp as a hawk's. He had not yet given up hunting and would sing sad Turcoman songs too, or tell about tribal feuds. At the end of every tale he would proudly show the wounds he himself had earned in such feuds.

The sedentary life of the village often weighed on him unbearably, seeming too restricted. He still wanted to live the old Turcoman way of life and preserve every detail of it intact.

Some days he would be brimful with memories of it and become like a drunken man. Mounting the wild red foal he had reared with his own hand, he would gallop off to the mountains, to their scents of pine, thyme and marjoram.

Like a wind blowing from the homeland of the old Turcomans, Big Ismail would tell of migrations, exile, and the long struggle against the Ottomans; of the fine old rifles decorated with little mirrors, the beating of the huge wooden mortars in the tents, all the tents replendent with green and red, a wondrous sight as the tribe moved slowly from the mountains to the Chukurova plain.

'Up to fifty years ago,' Big Ismail would begin – and once he had begun he never stopped, as if he were reciting a love story or a song – 'the Chukurova was nothing but swamps and bullrush beds with only a few tiny fields at the foot of the hills, not a soul living in the whole wide plain except the nomads. When the bare trees and the earth would deck themselves out for the spring, the Turcoman migration would begin in all its majesty, a riot of red and green. We would set forth over the mountains and pitch our tents for the summer on the highlands of Binbogha. When winter set in we would come down again to the Chukurova plain. In those days the plain was so thick with reeds and brush that a tiger could not penetrate it; throughout all twelve months of the year, the grass was knee-deep in the flat fields. Herds of bright-eyed, timid gazelles grazed there. We rode valiant and swift horses to hunt them, the quality of a steed being proven in this hunt. The reeds and bulrushes used to grow as tall as poplars in the Chukurova, along the shores of the lakes. From end to end the Chukurova was covered with narcissus in spring. Day and night the winds were laden with the scent of the flowers as the silvery sea-waves beat upon the Chukurova's far shores, foaming white. The tribes would pitch their tents all over the plain, the smoke of their settlements curling up to the sky.'

Yashar Kemal, *Memed My Hawk* (1961)

## Issus

At the deepest point of the Bay of Iskenderun, near Dörtyol, is the presumed site of the Battle of Issus where Alexander the Great defeated the Persian army in 333 BC, and opened the way to Asia and the beginnings of world empire.

Needless to say, the attempt to define the exact spot at which the battle took place proved a tough chestnut for the topographically minded travellers of modern times. Richard Pococke convinced himself that he had found it, though it seems pretty certain that the monument he describes is of at least Roman date: later the Armenians had their customs post here.

To the north of Baias is the famous pass into Asia Minor. The plain in which Baias stands is about two miles long; at the south end of it there is a rising ground or low hill, over which there is a road for about a mile that leads into a plain three-quarters of a mile wide, and about a mile and a half long, having the mountains to the east, and the sea to the west; at the south end of it are some low hills, which extend four miles to the south, almost as far as Scanderoon. The reason why I am thus particular, is, because I take this to be the very plain in which Alexander vanquished Darius. . . . At the south east corner of the plain there is a small single hill, the foot of which joins to the hills that are to the south: from this there has been a trench cut to the sea, and Alexander's army being encamped on those hills to the south, over which the road crosses from Scanderoon, a fitter place could not be found for the tent of Alexander, nor a more proper situation to receive the unfortunate family of Darius. . . . But what seems to determine that famous action to this place, is a very curious piece of antiquity, which no body has taken any notice of as such: on the hills to the south, in the face of the plain, and rather inclining down to the sea, there is a ruin that appears like two pillars, which are commonly called Jonas' pillars, on some tradition not well grounded, that the whale threw up that prophet somewhere about this place. It was with the utmost difficulty that I got to this ruin, by reason that it is in the middle of a thick wood; when I came to it, I found it to be the remains of a very fine triumphal arch of grey polished marble. . . . what remains of the architecture has in it so much beauty that one may judge it was built when that art flourished, and might be erected in honour of Alexander by one of the kings of Syria.

Richard Pococke, *Description of the East* (1743–5)

## Antakya (Antioch)

Antioch was founded by King Seleucus I in 300 BC after his defeat of Alexander's successor king Antigonus the One-Eyed at the Battle of Ipsus. It became the capital of his Syrian kingdom under his son and successor Antiochus I. From capital of the Seleucid Empire it became in 64 BC capital of the Roman province of Syria, and in the next centuries became the most magnificent city in the world, Rome and Alexandria only excepted. C. P. Cavafy imagined the elegant life of the city in the later days of the Roman Empire, when Julian the Philosopher, who restored the now Christian Empire briefly to paganism, was reigning.

### Julian and the Citizens of Antioch

'The letter CHI, they say, had never done their city any harm, nor had the letter KAPPA. . . . And we having found some to explain . . . were given to understand that these were the initial letters of two names, and stood the one for Christ, and the other for Konstantios.'

Julian's *Misopôgôn*

Was it possible that they should ever deny
Their comely way of living; the variety
Of their daily recreations; their splendid
Theatre where they found a union of Art
With the erotic propensities of the flesh!

Immoral to a certain, probably to a considerable extent,
They were. But they had the satisfaction that their life
Was the much talked of life of Antioch,
The delightful life, in absolutely good taste.

Were they to deny all this, for to give their minds after all to what?

To his airy chatter about the false gods,
To his annoying chatter about himself;

To his childish fear of the theatre;
His graceless prudery; his ridiculous beard.

Most certainly they preferred the letter CHI,
Most certainly they preferred the KAPPA – a hundred times.
C. P. Cavafy; tr. John Mavrogordato

Antioch, like Constantinople, attracted curious legends around the history of its foundation and the monuments of the city.

It is plain that the men of Antioch live in the country of the Giants, because, two miles from Antioch, there is a place where human bodies are found. By the anger of God these were turned into stones, which to this day are known as Giants. And they say that a certain Pagras, a Giant, who lived here, was consumed by fire.

.   .   .   .   .

Apollonius of Tyana was visiting the city of Antioch in the company of its leading men, to observe its situation, when he came upon a column of porphyry, placed in the middle of the city. Seeing that nothing was mounted on it, but that the column had been touched by volcanic fires, he asked what it was. They replied 'A certain Debborius, a philosopher and enchanter, erected this column here after the city had been shaken by earthquake in the time of Gaius Caesar, and had placed a marble statue upon it. On the breast of the image was written "Unmoved, Unshaken". He did this to protect the city, to prevent it being ruined by earthquarkes. But when the first of lightning fell on it, the image on the column was seized by the thunderbolt and fell to the ground; and now we fear for our city, lest it suffer the same fate. Therefore we beg you to deign to prepare an enchantment to keep our city unshaken for the future.'

Apollonius groaned, and hesitantly deferred a reply about making such a spell. And when they saw him sigh, they became even more insistent. So he accepted the tablets and wrote as follows: 'Thou, wretched Antioch, shall be twice unhappy! Again a time will come when thou shalt be grievously shaken by earthquake. Twice indeed, if no more than twice, thou shalt be burnt as far as the banks of the

Orontes.' Then Apollonius gave the tablets to the leading men of the
city. He then left Antioch, and went to Seleucia, and to Egypt.

John Malalas (491–578), *Chronography*, VIII, 258, 344

In AD 1098 Antioch was the scene of one of the most
prolonged sieges of the Crusades, under the leadership of
Bohemund, after which it became the capital of the Frankish
principality of Antioch. An exceedingly long poem by
Richard the Pilgrim, a French writer who was present at the
siege, describes it in all its barbarity and agony.

Great was the famine the Christians underwent to save their cause.
Anyone who could find a small piece of bread would willingly give
two golden bezants for it. The tail of a donkey, raw, was sold for a
hundred sous; five sous was the price of a pear when one could be
found; two beans for a denier were much sought after. Many would
scarcely refuse to eat a boot or sandal, or even leather overshoes,
unsalted, so unwilling were they to collapse from hunger.

I wish to tell you of our Christian forces abroad in the east . . . they
had no victuals, they were driven to distraction. Then Peter the
Hermit sat down before his troops, the Tafur kings came to him and
many of his barons, more than thousand of them, racked with
hunger.

'Sire, advise us, for the love of charity, for we are going to die of
hunger and weakness.'

And Peter replied, 'That is the result of your idleness. Go, take
those dead Turks whose dead bodies have been thrown there; they
will be good to eat if cooked and salted.'

And the Tafur kings said, 'You are right'.

Peter turned from the army, he had given his orders. There were
more than ten thousand of his officers gathered there. They grilled
the Turks and removed their entrails, and cooked the flesh by boiling
or roasting it. They had enough to eat, but not a taste of bread. The
Pagans were horrified; they came right up to the walls attracted by
the odour of meat, and watched the while by twenty thousand
pagans. Not a single Turk but bewailed them with his eyes:

'Ah! Mohammed! lord, what great cruelty! Take vengeance on
these who have contemned you. Inasmuch as they eat our men, they
have ceased to be human, they are not Franks, they are mere
cannibals. Mohammed, curse them and their Christianity, for by
what they are doing we are all shamed.'

Richard the Pilgrim, *Chanson d'Antioche*; tr. R. S.

Despite the Turks' justifiable outrage, the stratagem kept the army
alive until it was able to overcome the city, after a siege of several
months.

Eight and a half centuries later, Antioch had been made the pleasant home of the scholar of William Burkhardt Barker, the godson of the explorer Lewis Burkhardt. Layard visited him in his old age.

Mr Barker was an old resident in the East and of what is called a 'Levantine' family, well known in Syria, and especially at Aleppo, where it had been connected in trade with the Levant Company, and where he himself had been for some years Consul. He had been officially employed in various parts of Syria during the critical period of Napoleon's wars, when the influence and interests of Great Britain were seriously menaced in the East. He had been able, through his knowledge of the country, his influence and experience, to render signal services to the British Government, and had been rewarded by the appointment of Consul-General in Egypt, from which he had recently retired. His habits and his connections – his wife was, I believe, a native Christian lady of Aleppo – and his repugnance to a northern climate, had induced him to establish himself at Suedia. He could not have chosen a more delightful spot to close his days. This plain was a little paradise, and would have been in every way perfect had it not been for the prevalence, during certain months of the year, of intermittent fever – that curse of all parts of the Turkish dominions, which, however, here showed itself in its lightest form. The climate throughout the year was delightful. In the summer the air was refreshed by the cool breeze from the Mediterranean. In winter the little plain was protected by the mountains and high land, by which it was surrounded, from the cold winds, and seemed to enjoy a perpetual spring.

. . . .

We visited with him two of his gardens and summer residences high up on the mountain sides. Their sites were chosen with admirable taste. Each commanded the loveliest of prospects over land and sea. One was built near a small Armenian village called Huder (? Hyder) Beg, with a copious spring of the finest water gushing out of a rock, and celebrated throughout the district. The other was at a considerable elevation upon the range of Mount Rhossus. It took us about two hours and a half on horseback to reach it. His cottage was near the little hamlet of Bitias. It would be difficult to describe the beauty of the spot, and of the varied views which it commanded. A bright mountain stream had been led through the grounds, falling in cascades, and feeding graceful fountains. Near the house were the ruins of a Greek temple, which at one time had been converted into a Christian church. The ruins of other edifices were strewed around, and where the rain had washed away the soil were the remains of Roman mosaics. Above the spring, which, issuing from the rock, formed the stream that watered the gardens, was an arch of Greek masonry. The ancients had not overlooked the surpassing loveliness of the place.

A. H. Layard, *Autobiography* (1903)

W. B. Barker's book on Cilicia is a mine of fascinating and diverse information on ancient lore and religion, natural history, topography, history and contemporary affairs. One might single out, but for its length, his account of the brigand chief Kutchuk Ali, who had flourished about 1800 near the town of Bayas. His power was such that he could even imprison the Dutch consul with impunity.

When the news spread abroad that Kutchuk Ali had entrapped an European, the mountaineers descended in crowds to see how much humanity the tyrant exhibited; and Mr. Masseyk used to relate that being one day engaged in writing, a man who had thrust his head through the bars of his prison-window, after contemplating his person and occupation for some time, exclaimed with reproachful indignation, 'What, is it possible the wretch is so lost to all sense of shame as to hold an *effendi* (a clerk) in captivity?' referring evidently to the well-known rights and *immunities* enjoyed by the learned, as well in this barbarous region as in Europe. This picture indeed resembles more the state of society in the twelfth and thirteenth centuries than that of the nineteenth; and to those who are unacquainted with Oriental ideas and customs, which have undergone so few changes for centuries past, might appear unfaithful to nature, were it not for what history has related to those dark ages.

It is worth noting that the practice of brigandage differs in its essentials not at all from that described in the present day novels of Yashar Kemal.

Most travellers today would surely share the excitement of Gertrude Bell on arriving at this city famed in history:

It was with some excitement that I gazed on the city of Antioch, which was for so many centuries a cradle of the arts and the seat of one of the most gorgeous civilisations that the world has known. Modern Antioch is like the pantaloon whose clothes are far too wide for his lean shanks; the castle walls go climbing over rock and hill, enclosing an area from which the town has shrunk away. But it is still one of the loveliest of places, with its great ragged hill behind it, crowned with walls, and its clustered red roofs stretching down to the wide and fertile valley of the Orontes. Earthquakes and the changing floods of the stream have overturned and covered with silt the palaces of the Greek and of the Roman city, yet as I stood at sunset on the sloping sward of the Noṣairiyyeh graveyard below Mount Silpius, where my camp was pitched, and saw the red roofs under a crescent moon, I recognised that beauty is the inalienable heritage of Antioch.

. . . . .

Forty years ago the walls and towers of the Acropolis were still almost perfect; they are now almost destroyed. The inhabitants of Antioch declare that the city is rocked to its foundations every half-century, and they are in instant expectation of another upheaval, the last having occurred in 1862; but it is prosperity not earthquake that has wrought the havoc in the fortress. The town is admirably situated in its rich valley, and connected with the port of Alexandretta by a fairly good road; it might easily become a great commercial centre, and even under Turkish rule it has grown considerably in the past fifty years, and grown at the expense of the Acropolis. To spare himself the trouble of quarrying, the Oriental will be deterred by no difficulty, and in spite of the labour of transporting the dressed stones of the fortress to the foot of the exceedingly steep hill on which it stands, all the modern houses have been built out of materials taken from it. The work of destruction continues; the stone facing is quickly disappearing from the walls, leaving only a core of a rubble and mortar which succumbs in a short time to the action of the weather. I made the whole circuit of the fortress one morning, and it took me three hours. To the west of the summit of Mount Silpius a rocky cleft seamed the hillside. It was full of rock-cut tombs, and just above my camp an ancient aqueduct spanned it. On the left hand of the cleft the line of wall dropped by precipitous rocks to the valley. Where large fragments remained it was evident that the stone facing had alternated with bands of brick, and that sometimes the stone itself had been varied by courses of smaller and larger blocks. The fortifications embraced a wide area, the upper part leading by gentle slopes, covered with brushwood and ruined foundations, to the top of the hill. In the west wall there was a narrow massive stone door, with a lintel of jointed blocks and a relieving arch above it. The south wall was broken by towers; the main citadel was at the south-east corner. From here the walls dropped down again steeply to the city and passed some distance to the east of it. They can be traced, I believe, to the Orontes. I did not follow their course, but climbed down from the citadel by a stony path into a deep gorge that cuts through the eastern end of the hill. The entrance to this gorge is guarded by a strong wall of brick and stone, which is called the Gate of Iron, and beyond it the fortifications climb the opposite side of the ravine and are continued along the hill top. I do not know how far they extend; the ground was so rough and so much overgrown with bushes that I lost heart and turned back. There was a profusion of flowers among the rocks, marigold, asphodel, cyclamen and iris.

Gertrude Bell, *The Desert and the Sown* (1907)

## Commagene: Nemrut Dağı

North-east of Antioch lay the ancient kingdom of Commagene, ruled by a series of kings named Antiochus. The First of the name, Antiochus the Great (first century BC), was responsible for the extraordinary monument at Nemrut Dağí, where vast and trunkless heads of stone gaze out over the mountains; a visit to this spectacular sanctuary at dawn makes an unforgettable experience. The monument lay forgotten for centuries, forgotten as Ozymandias, until its rediscovery in 1839 by the Prussian officer Hermann von Moltke. Forty-four years later Moltke sponsored two successive expeditions to the site by the archaeologists Otto Puchstein and (on the second occasion) Carl Humann, fresh from his discoveries at Pergamum (p. 102). It was in April 1883 that Humann and Puchstein ascended together to the site, as Humann described in his published account.

We left the horses at our camp ground and climbed further until we reached at another 247 m the peak of Nemrud Dagh and thereon the tumulus of King Antiochus. The first impression was truly overwhelming. Like one mountain upon another, the grave mound rose up on the highest peak, soaring to 40 m above the terrace to which we had climbed. The gigantic images of five divinities sat on a rocky ridge with their back to the mound; only one of them was entirely undamaged.

After the first look at the nearer scene our gaze swept involuntarily to the distance. If the sea swept by a hurricane were suddenly to solidify, while a counter wind piled up the bristling mountain waves to dizzy heights and hurled them down again in crazy heaps, that would give no impression of the view that met us to east, north and west as far as our gaze could reach, and also for some miles to the south. The white foam crests of the waves are here the snow-glittering ridges of the Taurus. Perhaps the valleys and ravines organised themselves into continuous, if damaged, lines, but to us it all seemed wild confusion, out of which, as a resting point for the eye, a massive peak occasionally rose up. To the south a sea of rock fell away; from time to time the mirror of Euphrates flashed and disappeared beyond the horizon in impenetrable distance, deep into Mesopotamia.

We hardly knew what to look at first, the nearby or the distant scene. Before us lay the tumbled heads of statues, each one larger than the height of a man; a mountain of blocks of stone; slabs with relief sculptures before low walls with holes on the top in which the slabs had once stood. The whole place was a terrace retrieved from the rock. We went round the tumulus; the stones cut sharply into our shoe leather; for the whole hill is covered with regular, artificially cut pieces of limestone just like our street cobbles, except where the slope was too steep to retain them. On the other side of the hill we reached, on the west, another terrace, significantly lower than the first. Here the statues are quite destroyed, the individual blocks on which they stood lie in heaps, and the heads have rolled far away down the hill. A vast quantity of relief slabs opposite the statues attracted our eyes; to the north another type of relief slab formed a continuation of the row of five divine statues, which formerly had lain on their faces and been only partly visible, from underneath, by Puchstein in 1882. Now they had been stood upright by Hamdy Bey [the head of Turkey's archaeological service from 1882 to 1910] and leant against the rubble. At last we went further north round the monument, climbed over a third terrace where there were no statues, and climbed down again to the camp site.
(The next day was devoted to the making of photographs and casts, before the expedition continued eastwards).

Carl Humann, *Reisen in Kleinassen und Nordsyrien* (1890); tr. R. S.

## St George of Cappadocia

A surprising link with England is provided by our last topic in south-eastern Turkey. The patron saint of England, that louche usurper of beatitude, has long been regarded as a singularly improbable subject of canonisation, and with only the remotest connection with England. He was in fact a native of Cilicia, where he shared a number of characteristics with a local Turkish hero called Chederle, of whom Ogier de Busbecq recounts that he rescued a maiden from a dragon, and even accompanied Alexander the Great in his search for the water of immortality.

Gibbon's irony finds full scope on the historical George.

George, from his parents or his education surnamed the Cappadocian, was born at Epiphania in Cilicia, in a fuller's shop. From this obscure and servile origin he raised himself by the talents of a parasite: and the patrons, whom he assiduously flattered, procured for their worthless dependant a lucrative commission, or contract, to supply the army with bacon. His employment was mean; he rendered it infamous. He accumulated wealth by the basest arts of fraud and corruption; but his malversations were so notorious that George was compelled to escape from the pursuits of justice. After this disgrace, in which he appears to have saved his fortune at the expense of his honour, he embraced, with real or affected zeal, the profession of Arianism. From the love, or the ostentation, of learning, he collected a valuable library of history, rhetoric, philosophy, and theology; and the choice of the prevailing faction promoted George of Cappadocia to the throne of Athanasius. The entrance of the new archbishop was that of a Barbarian conqueror; and each moment of his reign was polluted by cruelty and avarice. The Catholics of Alexandria and Egypt were abandoned to a tyrant, qualified, by nature and education, to exercise the office of persecution; but he oppressed with an impartial hand the various inhabitants of his extensive diocese. The primate of Egypt assumed the pomp and insolence of his lofty station; but he still betrayed the vices of his base and servile extraction. The merchants of Alexandria were impoverished by the unjust, and almost universal, monopoly, which he acquired, of nitre, salt, paper, funerals, &c.; and the spiritual father of a great people condescended to practise the vile and pernicious arts of an informer. The Alexandrians could never forget nor forgive the tax which he suggested on all the houses of the city; under an obsolete claim that the royal founder had conveyed to his successors, the Ptolemies and the Cæsars, the perpetual property of the soil. The Pagans, who had been flattered with the hopes of freedom and toleration, excited his devout avarice; and the rich temples of Alexandria were either pillaged or insulted by the haughty prelate, who exclaimed, in a loud and threatening tone, 'How long will these sepulchres be permitted to stand?' Under the reign of Constantius, he was expelled by the fury, or rather by the justice, of the people; and it was not without a violent struggle that the civil and military powers of the state could restore his authority and gratify his revenge. The messenger who proclaimed at Alexandria the accession of Julian announced the downfall of the archbishop. George, with two of his obsequious ministers, count Diodorus, and Dracontius, master of the mint, were ignominiously dragged in chains to the public prison. At the end of twenty-four days, the prison was forced open by the rage of a superstitious multitude, impatient of the tedious forms of judicial proceedings. The enemies of gods and men expired under their cruel insults; the lifeless bodies of the archbishop and his associates were carried in triumph through the streets on the back of a camel; and the inactivity of the Athanasian party was esteemed a shining example of evangelican patience. The remains of these guilty wretches were thrown into the sea; and the popular leaders of the tumult declared their resolution to disappoint the devotion of the Christians, and to intercept the future honours of these *martyrs*, who had been punished, like their predecessors, by the enemies of their religion. The fears of the Pagans were just, and their precautions ineffectual. The meritorious death of the archbishop obliterated the memory of his life. The rival of Athanasius was dear and sacred to the Arians, and the seeming conversion of those sectaries introduced his worship into the bosom of the Catholic church. The odious stranger, disguising every circumstance of time and place, assumed the mask of a martyr, a saint, and a Christian hero; and the infamous George of Cappadocia has been transformed into the renowned St. George of England, the patron of arms, of chivalry, and of the garter.

Edward Gibbon, *Decline and Fall of The Roman Empire*, ch. 23

To save a maid, St George the Dragon slew,
A pretty tale, if all is told be true.
Most say, there are no Dragons; and 'tis said,
There was no George; 'pray God there was a Maid.

Quoted by John Aubrey, *Remaines of Gentilisme and Judaisme*

# Bibliography and Guide to Further Reading

1. FREQUENTLY QUOTED WORKS

Some of the most frequently quoted accounts are given only brief details in the text: full citations are given here. These references are indicated in the text by an asterisk. (Throughout this bibliography, place of publication is London unless otherwise indicated).

Zabelle C. Boyajian, *Armenian Legends and Poems* (1916)
Frederick J. Burnaby, *Through Asia Minor on Horseback* (1898; reprinted 1985)
E. D. Clarke, *Travels in Various Countries* (London 1810–1823)
Thomas Coryate, *Travels to, and Observations in Constantinople and other Places*; in Purchas his Pilgrimes, Hakluyt society publications, extra ser. (1905), vol. 10, 389ff
Richard Davey, *The Sultan and his Subjects* (1897)
Evliya Celebi, *Travels in Europe Asia and Africa*, translated by J. von Hammer (1834–50)
W. J. Hamilton, *Researches in Asia Minor* (1852)
William Lithgow, *The Rare Adventures and Painefull Peregrinations* (1632; last reprinted 1906)
*Parastaseis Syntomoi Chronikai*, in A. Cameron and J. Herrin, *Constantinople in the Eighth Century* (Leiden 1984)

2. OTHER WORKS OF PARTICULAR INTEREST, INCLUDING MODERN ACCOUNTS AND GUIDEBOOKS

Basic resources are the guidebooks of John Freely: *The Blue Guide to Istanbul* (1983), which supersedes his *Strolling through Istanbul*, written jointly with Hilary Sumner-Boyd (Istanbul: Redhouse 1972, 1983), and *Companion Guide to Turkey* (1979).

On archaeological matters one must consult the four books of George Bean: *Aegean Turkey* (1966), *Lycian Turkey* (1978), *Turkey Beyond the Maeander* (1971) and *Turkey's Southern Shore* (1968). Also indispensable is Ekrem Akurgal, *Ancient Civilizations and Ruins of Turkey* (fifth edition, Istanbul: Haşet 1983).

A valuable bibliography is Meral Güclü, *Turkey: A Bibliography* (Oxford: Clio 1981)

There is particularly good and informative reading in the following:
O. G. de Busbecq, *Turkish Letters* (originally published in 1633; translated by E. S. Forster, Oxford 1927)
Robert Curzon, *Armenia: a year at Erzurum* (1854)
Daniel Farson, *A Traveller in Turkey* (1985)
J. P. Grelot, *A Late Voyage to Constantinople* (translated by J. Philips from the French edition of 1680: 1683)
Philip Glazebrook, *Journey to Kars* (1984)
Sibylle Haynes, *Land of the Chimaera* (1974)
J. P. D. B. Kinross, *Within the Taurus: a journey in Asiatic Turkey* (1954), and *Europa Minor* (1956)
John Marriner, *Trebizond and Beyond* (1969)
Irfan Orga, *The Young Traveller in Turkey* (1957; a fictionalised travel account)
Michael Pereira, *Mountains and a shore: a journey through southern Turkey* (1966)
Tim Severin, *The Jason Voyage* (1985)
Freya Stark, *Ionia: A Quest* (1955); *The Lycian Shore* (1956); *Alexander's Path* (1958)
Joseph Pitton de Tournefort, *Voyage into the Levant*, translated by John Ozell (1718)
Gwyn Williams, *Turkey: A Traveller's Guide and History* (1967)

## 3. TURKISH HISTORY

Some readable and useful works on the history of Turkey, both ancient, medieval and Ottoman (excluding Istanbul: see below).

Ernle Bradford, *The Sultan's Admiral: the life of Barbarossa* (New York 1968)
Ernle Bradford, *The Great Betrayal: Constantinople 1204* (1967)
Averil Cameron, *Procopius* (1985); a scholarly account of Justinian's official historian
R. H. Davison, *Turkey: A Short History* (1968)
F. W. Hasluck, *Christianity and Islam under the Sultans* (two volumes Oxford University Press 1929); a mine of curious lore and legend
H. Inalcik, *The Ottoman Empire* (1973)

J. P. D. B. Kinross, *Ataturk: The Rebirth of a Nation* (1964)

Harold Lamb, *Suleiman the Magnificent: Sultan of the East* (New York 1951)

A. Maalouf, *The Crusades through Arab Eyes* (1984)

Stanley Mayes, *An Organ for the Sultan* (1956); marvellous evocation of seventeenth-century conditions in the Ottoman Empire, especially Constantinople

William Miller, *Trebizond: the last Greek Empire* (1926)

C. P. Rouillard, *The Turk in French History, thought and literature (1520–1660)* (Paris 1941; New York 1973)

Steven Runciman, *The Crusades* (Cambridge 1951)

E. K. Shaw, *English and Continental views of the Ottoman Empire 1500–1800* (Berkeley: University of California Press 1972)

E. K. Shaw, *History of the Ottoman Empire and Modern Turkey* (Cambridge 1976)

Freya Stark, *Turkey: A Sketch of Turkish history* (1971)

Richard Stoneman, *Land of Lost Gods: The Search for Classical Greece* (1987)

Tamara Talbot Rice, *The Seljuks in Asia Minor* (1961)

F. Yeats-Brown, *Golden Horn* (1932); an exciting tale of the author's adventures in Turkey during the First World War.

### 4. BOOKS ABOUT ISTANBUL

J. A. Cuddon, *The Owl's Watchsong* (1960; reprinted 1986)

G. Dagron, *Constantinople Imaginaire* (1984); about the legends of medieval Constantinople

John Freely, *Stamboul Sketches* (Istanbul: Redhouse 1973); Istanbul's answer to Norman Douglas

Robert Liddell, *Byzantium and Istanbul* (1956)

Alexander van Millingen, *Byzantine Constantinople* (1899) and *Byzantine Churches in Constantinople* (1912)

Michael Pereira, *Aspects of a City* (1968)

Steven Runciman, *The Fall of Constantinople* (Cambridge 1969)

Philip Sherrard, *Constantinople: Iconography of a Sacred City* (Oxford 1965)

### 5. BIOGRAPHIES

Several Turkey travellers have been interesting enough to merit biographies of their own. Here is a selection.

Lesley Blanch, *Pierre Loti* (1983)

Margaret Fitzherbert, *The Man who was Greenmantle: a Biography of Aubrey Herbert* (1983)

Aubrey Herbert, *Ben Kendim: a record of Eastern Travel* (1932)

Robin Lane Fox, *Alexander the Great* (1973)

Stanley Lane-Poole, *Life of the Rt Hon. Stratford Canning, Viscount Stratford de Redcliffe* (two volumes 1888); still the most detailed biography, though two or three more have been published since

Caroline Moorehead, *Freya Stark* (1985)

H. V. F. Winstone, *Gertrude Bell* (1978)

## 6. FICTION

Turkey, and especially Istanbul, seems to stir the imagination to creations even more delightful than its extraordinary subject. Most people will find at least one novel to enjoy among the following.

John Buchan, *Greenmantle* (1916); espionage in Eastern Turkey

Lawrence Durrell, *Tunc* (1968); secret societies in Istanbul and elsewhere

Yashar Kemal, *Memed my Hawk* (1958; English translation 1961); a novel on a heroic scale about banditry and poverty in south-eastern Turkey. Several of Kemal's other novels, such as *They Burn the Thistles*, are concerned with the same subject matter.

Yashar Kemal, *The Sea-crossed Fisherman* (1985); an epic novel set in Istanbul and its vicinity by Turkey's greatest modern writer

Pierre Loti, *Aziyadé* (1879); a love story of rather dated sentimentality, but still evocative of Constantinople

Rose Macaulay, *The Towers of Trebizond* (1956); a group of wonderfully absurd and comic travellers in Turkey

Robert Graves, *Count Belisarius* (1938); historical novel about the sixth century

Walter Scott, *Count Robert of Paris* (1827); historical novel about the twelfth century

Barry Unsworth, *The Rage of the Vulture* (1982); historical novel about the last days of Abdul Hamid II before the First World War

Turkey's finest poet is Nazim Hikmet, whose works are unobtainable in the UK but in print in the USA, published by Persea Books, New York: see especially *Human Landscapes* (1982) and *The Epic of Sheik Bedreddin* (1977)

On a more popular level, the art of the Karagöz theatre is interestingly surveyed by Metin And, *Karagöz: Turkish Shadow Theatre* (Istanbul: Dost Yayınları 1975; 1979)

A convenient anthology of poetry is *The Penguin Book of Turkish Verse*, edited by Nermin Menemencioglu (1978)

Dedicated researchers may profit from the following:

Lawrence S. Thompson, 'Libraries of Turkey' (*Library Quarterly* 22.3 (1952), 270–84), and 'The availability of research materials in the libraries of Istanbul' (*Libri* 2.4 (1953), 297–319).

# Index